Advance Praise for
The Silk Finisher

"In this meticulously researched memoir, Dan Melchior digs into so much that our country continues to wrestle with—blue collar men breaking apart, homophobia, racism, doctors dealing drugs, and gun violence. The story, set in Evansville, Indiana, relives decades of challenges that continue to haunt America today. Fortunately, there's hope in the shape of people like the author's mother Dolores—loving, hardworking "in the margins," and accepting of others. *The Silk Finisher* introduces readers to this quietly remarkable woman who witnessed it all."

—Mary Collins, author of *At the Broken Places:
A Mother and Trans Son Pick Up the Pieces*

"Time and again, Daniel Melchior dares to take us past the forgotten headlines, deeper into the shadows of the past. In doing so, he gives us a heartfelt story about family, loss, and, ultimately, the true measure of perseverance."

—Tim Wendel, author of *Rebel Falls*

THE

SILK
FINISHER

BIGOTRY, MURDER, AND SACRIFICE
IN THE CROSSROADS OF AMERICA

A TRUE CRIME MEMOIR

DANIEL MELCHIOR

Post Hill
PRESS

A POST HILL PRESS BOOK
ISBN: 979-8-88845-623-1
ISBN (eBook): 979-8-88845-624-8

The Silk Finisher:
Bigotry, Murder, and Sacrifice in the Crossroads
of America
© 2024 by 3 White Binders, LLC
All Rights Reserved

Cover design by Cody Corcoran

Post Hill Press
New York • Nashville
posthillpress.com

Published in the United States of America
1 2 3 4 5 6 7 8 9 10

To Mom.

There are simply no words, but then again there was quite simply no other.
That's why this page is yours and yours alone.
Sorry I took so long, but I know you won't mind because you saw me trying.

TABLE OF CONTENTS

PART III

PROLOGUE

● ● ●

Rudy Ziemer blinked to the sound of the turn signal. The green glow of the speedometer faded in and out like a firefly. Sitting in the middle of the bench seat, he purposely spread his legs like hedge clippers so that they would touch the legs of the soldiers who sat next to him. The paratrooper on Rudy's left steered with his right hand, while his left hand flapped in the late winter nearly spring breeze. The paratrooper to his right fiddled with the radio, finding more static than music. Rudy let out a long moist sigh, sounding like a whale surfacing after a too-long dive.

Neither man spoke to Rudy, nor amongst themselves, but their breath, a meld of beer, wine, and perhaps a burger or two, whispered a secret. They were drunk too. Rudy enjoyed the middle seat of his own car, although tonight was his first time there. His eyes, open for a second or two longer than the last blink, absorbed the green needle of the speedometer falling toward zero like a felled tree. The sound of loose gravel under slow rolling tires crunched in his ears and masked the sound of the blinker.

Crisp air caressed Rudy's right cheek as the soldier rolled down the passenger window. The gentle wind caused Rudy's eyes to close. He didn't bother opening them and instead let the breeze chill the boozy fever coursing his veins. The gravelly chorus returned as another car slowed and stopped next to Rudy's 1962 station wagon. A girlish voice rode the gentle wind.

"Where're we going?"

"I don't know," said the soldier to Rudy's right. "I don't live here. Where the hell are we?"

"Riverside Drive."

"We're gonna roll him," the soldier said.

Without an objection uttered, the two cars resumed their slow wander through the south side of Evansville, Indiana. Near Holy Spirit Catholic Church, the soldier driving Rudy's car steered toward the Colonial Apartments, where Great-Uncle Bud slumbered. As the trio passed my sleeping relative's window, Rudy Ziemer reached his right arm toward the driving soldier, grabbed him around the chest, and licked and kissed his right cheek. The soldier instinctively pulled away, jerked his right hand from the steering wheel, and karate chopped Rudy across the nose. Rudy's browline glasses snapped as blood gushed from his nose. The soldier to his right battered Rudy with his fists. Rudy groaned and yelled for help, but no one heard his cries. The breeze no longer cooled Rudy nor covered the stench of the soldiers' breath.

"Fucking faggot."

"Take his wallet."

"Give me that."

"Fuck."

Rudy heard car doors slam and tires screech from a car he couldn't see, his head too heavy to lift. Blood from his lips, nose, and teeth stained the driver's seat as his pounding head rested near the steering wheel. His consciousness faded in and out like the turn signal that had echoed in his ears moments before. The low rumble of the idling engine gently rocked and vibrated him into a peaceful but painful sleep. He'd been here before, almost ten years ago, when two men he had invited to his riverfront home decided to beat him senseless and steal his beloved Cadillac. As blackness enveloped his body and head, Rudy thought of that beating and the taunts that accompanied it like a fine orchestra. Fists played the drums while voices played the horns and strings. The symphony throbbed in his head.

"Faggot."

"Queer."

"Bitch."

Da-dum-da-dum. Da-dum-da-dum.

"Faggot."

"Queer."

"Bitch."

Da-dum-da-dum. Da-dum-da-dum.

Rudy's swollen eyes opened slightly revealing the bottom curve of the steering wheel. He grabbed the wheel and pulled himself toward the open driver's-side door. He needed air.

He pulled himself far enough to allow his head to hang toward the road like a dying dandelion reaching through a crack in the sidewalk. He gasped the crisp air as if he'd surfaced from a long dive like the ocean mammal he'd mimicked with his moist sigh. His breaths gargled with the blood in his nostrils, sinuses, and throat. His chest heaved, his diaphragm labored, his heart pounded. He closed his eyes.

Rudy heard a rumble. Headlights penetrated the darkness behind his eyelids. A tire barely screeched, like a worn-out crow or a young Cooper's hawk. His neck, shoulders, and back were too tired to lift his head, so blood continued rushing to his brain and out of his mouth and nose. He tried to open his eyes but couldn't muster the will. He needed rest.

He felt the warmth of a hand cradling his bloody and swollen head. Another hand grabbed his left shoulder. The warmth disappeared. Suddenly he was upright, behind the wheel as a driver should be. And then, just like that, he lay on his right shoulder, as if we were taking a nap. A slamming door shook the white station wagon. Rudy groaned and rested as best he could.

The sound of gravel echoed once more in his head.

"Follow me," someone yelled.

Rudy's ear, pressed against the bloody vinyl seat, took in the bumps, cracks, and rocks along the road. The car stopped, turned, slowed, and sped up over and over. Rudy couldn't open his eyes. He tried to sit up, but his nerves and muscles wilted like cooked spaghetti. The stopping, turning, slowing, and speeding continued. The click-clack of the blinker returned before the road sounds faded.

"Where the hell are you going?" a girlish voice yelled from outside of the car.

"I don't know. I told you I don't live here," the soldier yelled back.

"Goddammit," Rudy thought he heard. The voices began to sound like a shorted-out speaker. He tried again to sit up. He couldn't move. His head throbbed as he coughed up the blood in his throat. Something hard, perhaps the back of a hand, struck his nose. More blood gushed onto the seat. This is different; this is long, drawn out, he thought. The stench of his blood and snot mixed with the whisky and beer. Death has a taste, a smell, a sound—a feel but no sight. Only blackness, pupil black. Rudy knew death and knew it well.

Someone's voice garbled in his ear. More garbling. Argument garbling. Rudy's ears gave up as the garbling grew fainter and the black grew blacker. He felt vibrations and shaking. He felt the gravel he could no longer hear: deafness, not even a ringing in his ears. He felt his body gently rocking to and fro. Helpless as a baby in a cradle or perhaps a hatchling in a nest but actually a drunken, beaten man riding shotgun in his own car with another man he'd just met.

Rudy felt his body roll hard against the back of the seat. Seconds later he slammed into the dashboard and glove box. The car skidded to a halt. Rudy crumpled like a pile of dirty clothes between the seat and the dashboard, his clothes, bloody and wrinkled.

He felt a chilly breeze against his face; his hands ached. He groaned and breathed as deep as lethargy allowed. The garbling returned; the volume grew. His ears listened again.

"Help me wipe this off," a man said.

"Let's leave, goddammit."

"Get down here. Wipe this shit off."

"Come on, let's go."

"Wipe the steering wheel."

"Fuckin' faggot."

Rudy felt another hand grab his arm. Sitting up again, his chin grazed his tie. The hand moved from his arm to his chin. His head snapped back. He felt a pull on his tie—the tie he had just purchased days before. The pull became a tug, a wrench, a garrote. Blood gathered in his throat. His head pulled to the left. He inhaled through the pooling blood and garroted necktie.

"Fuckin' faggot."

And with that, the hands shoved Rudy back into his car and slammed the door. Rudy fell over onto the passenger seat. He heard the door open again. He felt someone sit down on the seat. The vibration returned and then stopped. Rudy heard water lapping with the tempo of the turn signal.

"Goddammit," Rudy heard.

The vibrations stopped. A new sensation, a new movement, a new motion, like that of a floating boat, rocked Rudy. The boozy fever simmered within him like warming water. His breaths shallowed. His head, perfectly still, rested on the vinyl seat. Sound faded. He needed rest.

His crossed feet lay near the accelerator and brake pedals. They jerked when water creeping over the door and into the window hit his once-polished shoes. Water flowed up Rudy's ankle, his shin, his knee, his thigh, and finally his groin. Rudy's feet and legs numbed. And then, it stopped. The water stopped.

Two men stood on top of a levee and watched as another man, standing waist deep, turned around and exited the Ohio River floodwaters. Rudy's white station wagon, half in the water, resembled a marshmallow melting in a cup of hot chocolate. Inside, Rudy rested.

On top of the levee, the two men walked toward an idling car. The third man, standing on the shore, brushed at his wet pants with his hands. He shook water from his shoes. He walked slowly and deliberately up the earthen levee. The other men yelled at him to hurry. Standing by the idling car, the trio argued. Red taillights bobbed. Clouds covered the moon as Rudy rested.

Floodwaters streamed into the windows like a waterfall. The car lurched forward and groaned. The third man turned around and watched the red taillights disappear. Water cocooned Rudy's body and head. He drank until it filled his stomach, throat, and mouth. Searching for air, Rudy Ziemer gulped. Ohio River floodwater filled his lungs. His car gently rocked forward. The roof faded into the chocolate-colored water. Rudy Ziemer had taken his last breath.

—

Eight days later, as mourners departed Rudy's funeral service to go home or back to work, in the Vanderburgh County jail sat three active-duty paratroopers. Authorities had arrested the three men five days earlier and preliminarily charged them with murder in Rudy's death. Residents of Evansville wondered how three clean-cut all-American United States Army paratroopers, in town for a night of drinking and dating, wound up getting involved with Rudy Ziemer, a notorious man about town, known by some as the queer undertaker.

—

Evansville, Indiana, at the very bottom of the Crossroads of America state, is a grayscale town that Madonna, in town filming *A League of Their Own*, compared to Prague before Prague became hip. Buildings are often white and gray, occasionally red brick but mostly monotone. The once-tallest building, recently imploded, sat eighteen stories high and, like the diminutive remaining others, often blurred and blended with the clouds, especially in winter. Inside these bland structures, Tri-

Staters seek mostly innocent but sometimes guilty pleasures: sins, some believe.

Resting at a low point in the Ohio River Valley, the city of almost one hundred twenty thousand slopes into the water at Dress Plaza, where the Ohio River bends like a horseshoe. Two hundred ninety miles south of Chicago, rolling hills succumb to a valley that captures heat and humidity in the summer. The heavy air, laced with the aroma of plastic manufacturing and coal plant energy, hangs like musty drapes in the seedy motels that dot Fares Avenue near Highway 41.

Highway 41, the north-south corridor that divides the east-side "Cake Eaters" from "West Siders" as fiercely as the Mason-Dixon, also gives Evansville the nickname Stoplight City. On a map, Evansville resembles a crucifix, with Highway 41 serving as the stipes and Lloyd Expressway the crossbar. A slightly tilted crucifix would put Reitz Memorial Catholic High School and Mater Dei Catholic High School about a wingspan apart. Memorial educates the Cake Eaters, while Mater Dei serves the offspring and descendants of calloused-handed farmers, miners, and workers and turns out a nationally recognized wrestling program every year. The schools are bitter rivals on the gridiron and wrestling mats. If a divide ever did occur, the West Siders would devour the Cake Eaters.

One thing the rivals do agree on is their dislike for the trashy "Southsiders," a mix of hillbillies, minorities, immigrants, and down-on-their-luck white folk. The south side is where one can find rusting appliances on the crumbling porches of dilapidated homes.

The south side is where I spent my childhood. In one of the places we stayed, Mom and Dad had a box. A handy department-store gift box big enough to hold a dozen donuts, twelve marigold seedlings, or perhaps a pair of trousers. I write the word *trousers* because that's the term used in the dry-cleaning industry, Mom's workplace for forty years and the nexus of the tales told here.

The box sat on the shelf of the hall closet near my sister Amy's room. A white, wooden door with a glass knob concealed musty, staticky air. We couldn't afford a humidifier, so Dad used to put a bucket of water near the furnace. He claimed that it worked, but all winter, I could stick a balloon to any wall in the house after rubbing it against my fiery orange Bobby Brady-style hair. In the closet hung Dad's army jacket, the olive-green type with MELCHIOR spelled out in block letters. An old pair of weathered, tan, steel-toed work boots with hooked eyelets from toe to tongue rested on the floor. Those boots contributed to the malodorous nature of the closet that housed our loosely boxed memories.

We sat around the kitchen table and passed pictures as we looked at relatives and friends named Great-Uncle Bud, Forrest, or Uncle John. We saw a boat, a dam on the Ohio River, Lincoln's boyhood home, and army hats. We saw Dad in a flashy red-and-white sport coat, his thick black mustache making him look like a white Richard Pryor. We heard explanations about the pictures like:

"Because your dad was drafted into the army."

"Your Great-Uncle Bud was in the army when his fiancée died."

"Rainbow Cleaners never made any money."

"I quit high school after my sophomore year. Daddy made me."

"Your Uncle Bill got hit by a coal truck."

We also heard stories without pictures. Stories that everyone knew, or at least thought they knew.

"Rudy started Ziemer funeral home, and your dad went to school with his nephews. He had a river camp next to your grandpa's partner's camp, and he was a customer at Rainbow Cleaners. I think everyone knew he was gay. Uncle John was gay. Did you know that? I'm not sure why those army paratroopers killed Rudy, maybe because he was gay. Who knows?" We passed the pictures like playing cards before tossing them back into Mom and Dad's box, the one big enough to hold a pair of trousers.

Mom, Aunt Mary, Uncle Bill, Grandpa Al, or Grandma Bessie of the Evans clan or Dad, Great-Uncle Bud, Grandma Mil, Grandpa George, Aunt Kate, or Uncle Dave, all of the Melchior family, told me about the stories in this book. I listened as they each told them in their own way, adding their own flavor. Not only did I listen, but I also conducted my own research, more than a decade's worth. Thousands of miles driven in search of court and real estate records, newspaper articles, interviews, birth, death, and marriage records, and court recordings. What I discovered is there is truth in every story, but also exaggerations and, in some cases, lies or avoidance of the truth by saying nothing.

Rather than focusing too much on my family's versions and their accuracy, I ask you to look for threads; threads that bind three lives born over the span of sixty years; threads that compelled me to research a man I never met and stories I never knew and to tell stories I've never told; threads that connect plutonium, murder, blindness, tragedy, triumph, yesteryear and yesterday; threads that bind encephalitis to COVID, bennies to opioids, and bigotry and hatred to tolerance, forgiveness, and love; threads that weave through the crossroads, known today as "flyover country"; threads that twist and turn like fate that I don't believe in; threads like the millions, billions, and trillions that Mom pressed during her life as a silk finisher.

> 'silk 'fin-ish-er - 1: a skilled presser of garments, one who removes the most difficult wrinkles from the most delicate weaves 2: a master at pressing all types of garments with speed, skill, and dexterity, also a laborer in the dry-cleaning industry

I hear her voice now, as I begin to pick up the threads. "Don't tarry, son…don't tarry."

PART I

NATIVE HOOSIERS

● ● ● ● ●

On May 16, 1906, as one thousand spectators arrived at the Evansville fairgrounds on South Kentucky Avenue to watch famed American race car driver Barney Oldfield in his Green Dragon and German racer Paul Albert in his White Streak push the limits of speed, Anna Ziemer looked forward to giving birth to her soon-to-be sixth child.

Oldfield, wearing a green arriving coat, had entered the track first and chewed on a cigar stump as he waited for Albert, who came wearing a long brown ulster. Organizers scheduled the pair to compete in three separate races that afternoon, the first automobile races ever witnessed in these parts. The drivers prepared, and the crowd waited as a band of horses grazed in the infield of the half-mile dirt track. The first heat, a five-lapper, introduced the public to Oldfield's technique of sliding the turns versus braking to allow the custom-made elongated Green Dragon to maintain speed throughout the corners. The method created so much dust on the dirt track that spectators strained to see the racers while the drivers could see only a few feet in front of their cars. In that first heat, Albert used the sliding technique to best Oldfield by inches.

During the third heat, the drivers, now accustomed to the track, sped faster as dust swirled and twisted about the oval. A sudden blast of dirty wind blew open one of the infield gates, and three of the grazing horses ambled onto the track. The crowd gasped in horror, according to the following day's headlines, as Oldfield's and Albert's cars, barely visible in the plumes of dust, blindly sped toward the horses. The wide-eyed creatures turned and galloped furiously, trying to stay ahead of the mechanical beasts.

Terrified organizers watched with the crowd as the desperate horses lost ground to the unaware racers. Both drivers finally spotted the horses along the inside lane, and both knew that a collision would end in almost certain death to the drivers and absolute death to the horses and spectators who lined that part of the track. Too close to brake, their only chance to avoid disaster was greater speed and the ability to swerve to the outside of the oval. Oldfield and Albert accelerated, and like schools of catfish in the nearby Ohio River, the cars swerved in unison, barely missing the trio. As the two racers sped alongside them, the horses conceded the chase and dropped back, slowing to a canter, and living to graze another day. The crowd exhaled, and local fascination with automobile racing was born.

The next day in the *Evansville Courier*, a cartoon depicting the race appeared on the front page.

The following day, the *Courier*'s daily cartoon depicted a sharply dressed woman wearing a hat, gazing at another hat in a millinery. "Well now, isn't that a beauty," she comments in the caption. In the distance, a fight breaks out as she admires the hat. A second caption in the cartoon reads, "If We Had Women Police in Evansville."

Sometime in the twenty-four hours between those two cartoons, one depicting a near disaster involving three animals and two cars and the other an attempted sexist glimpse into the future, Anna Ziemer gave birth to child number six, Rudolph Severin Ziemer.

Ted and Anna Ziemer raised their family in a cozy home on First Avenue, nearer to the West Siders than the Cake Eaters. Ted made a living as a superintendent of woodworkers in one of Evansville's many furniture factories. The Ziemers led a quiet life, their name appearing in the paper only once when Anna served as an attendant at a wedding between a soldier on leave and his promised bride. Almost three years to the day that Rudy was born, Anna welcomed her seventh child, Ted Jr., and seven years later, at the age of forty-eight, her final one, Agnes Mary. The Ziemers, with their big family and work ethic, typified Evansville's conservative, churchgoing population.

In 1918, when Rudy was twelve, Evansville native Fred Gresser, twenty-six, endured a bout with the Spanish flu. An army recruit, Gresser contracted the disease at

Camp Custer, Michigan, named for Lieutenant Colonel George Armstrong Custer, who was killed in action at Little Big Horn.

"For two days, I wanted to sleep and not wake up...I guess that means I wished I was dead," Gresser recalled many years later.

One in five men who contracted the flu at the Michigan camp died, including Fred's Evansville buddy, Frank, who had a head so large the army had to search for a cap to fit him. During the peak of the flu, almost one of every hundred men in the seventy-seven-thousand-strong camp died within a twenty-four-hour period. The flu killed 548,000 people in the United States and 20 million around the world.

"I remembered there was a shortage of doctors and nurses and food for the sick, and one morning when I was able to sit up, a nurse came by with maybe fifteen or sixteen halves of oranges on a tray. Is this my breakfast? I asked her, and she said, 'Yes, but you can have more than one.'"

"I took all of them. And ate them too," Fred recalled to an Evansville Press reporter.

Fred Gresser survived that bout with Spanish flu and returned to Evansville after serving in the army. My family didn't know Mr. Gresser, but eventually would for an unimaginable reason.

In 1923, Ted Ziemer, age fifty-eight, succumbed to hypertrophic cirrhosis of the liver. His funeral took place at the family home on First Avenue. Rudy, seventeen and lost, dropped out of high school for a year or so. Where Rudy went or what he did during this time is uncertain, but when he came back to school, he told classmates he wanted to be an undertaker. They hoped he was kidding.

Rudy graduated high school in 1926 at the age of twenty. He had not been kidding. Immediately after graduation, he enrolled at the C. G. Askin College of Embalming in Indianapolis, an affiliate of the Indiana University School of Medicine. A year later, upon graduation, he returned to Evansville to open a funeral parlor less than a mile from the family home. An undertaker at twenty-one, Rudy had arrived.

By 1933, the year Mom was born, Rudy hatched plans to expand his business. As he did so in 1934, Dad arrived as the first child of Grandpa George and Grandma Mil. While Mom and Dad crawled around the floors of different houses not that far away from Ziemer Funeral Home, Rudy acted on his plans to expand by partnering with his youngest brother Ted Jr., who also had graduated from the C. G. Askin College of Embalming.

In 1935, Rudy and Ted Jr. advertised, via a full-page spread in the *Evansville Press*, the opening of their beautiful new Ziemer Funeral Home. The brothers had purchased and renovated the three-story house of former Evansville mayor Benjamin Bosse and turned it into one of the finest and most modern funeral parlors in the state of Indiana. The renovated house stood at the corner of First Avenue and Delaware, mere blocks from the previous site of the original Ziemer Funeral Home. On Saturday and Sunday of that week, curious residents toured the grand facility. In the main hall, visitors admired the original inlaid hardwood floors and expensive oriental rugs, light fixtures, and cheery furnishings that emphasized the beauty of the surroundings. An eight-car garage allowed for loading the casket and family funeral cars under cover. The entire structure was air-conditioned and heated year-round, which was quite unusual at that time. The basement housed a modern operating room with tile walls and floors and the latest equipment, including a hydraulic enamel operating table. The configuration of the main salon accommodated two simultaneous funerals. Not yet thirty, Rudy's career as an undertaker soared.

While Rudy and Ted basked in the glow of their grand funeral home and business success, another Evansville resident plotted and strived to make something of himself. Charles E. Moehlenkamp personified the typical ambitious graduates of Evansville's Catholic schools. Like Rudy, Moehlenkamp graduated from Reitz Memorial High School, attended Evansville College (now the University of Evansville), and then enrolled in the Indiana University School of Medicine. My family would come to know Dr. Moehlenkamp for the same unimaginable reason they would learn the name Fred Gresser.

In 1935, as Charles Moehlenkamp prepared to graduate, Grandma Bessie and Grandpa Al reluctantly carried another mouth to feed, and a sickly one at that, over the threshold of their shotgun-style house on Harriet Street, joining Mom and her four-year-old brother, Charlie. Already struggling to make ends meet during the Great Depression, they had contemplated abortion, but Grandpa Al, born into Catholicism, and Grandma Bessie, a convert, decided against it after talking to a priest.

Little Bill, sometimes called Billy Joe, suffered from eczema so bad that he would writhe, squirm, and scratch himself bloody. Grandpa Al and Grandma Bessie solved the daytime scratching by securing a pair of small mittens to his hands. At night, to avoid bloody sheets, they tied Uncle Bill's hands to the crib. Mom wept every time she pictured her little brother tossing and writhing, trying to soothe his itching and searching for a way to sleep with his tiny hands tied to the crib. Not only was Uncle Bill another mouth to feed, but he also required more attention than most, which must have deepened convert Grandma Bessie's regret in choosing to have him.

A few days after Uncle Bill's second birthday, Franklin Delano Roosevelt delivered his second-term inaugural speech, promising to fight social injustice. A crowd between 150,000 and 200,000, down from the nearly 300,000 who witnessed his 1932 inauguration, shivered in the cold and wet conditions.

"I see one-third of a nation ill-housed, ill-clad, ill-nourished. It is not in despair that I paint you that picture. I paint it for you in hope—because the nation, seeing and understanding the injustice in it, proposes to paint it out.

"The test of our progress is not whether we add more to the abundance of those who have much. It is whether we provide enough for those who have too little,"

Forty miles north of Evansville, as Roosevelt spoke in the nation's capital, the White River in Hazelton, Indiana, foreshadowed an inevitable flood in Evansville. From Pittsburgh, Pennsylvania, to Cairo, Illinois, water flowed unimpeded into towns, businesses, homes, and schools. A week later, the Ohio River crested at over fifty-three feet.

Flooding cut off Highway 41 to the south toward the river. Rising waters forced hundreds of people to abandon their homes, and many others became marooned. Indiana's governor declared martial law for twenty-six southern Indiana counties. President Roosevelt met with five agencies to discuss relief plans for flood victims. More than 350,000 people across ten states became homeless. Amazingly, in Indiana, The Crossroads of America state, no one perished in the floodwaters. Fortunately, neither the Evans nor Melchior families suffered any damage in the disastrous flooding.

Grandpa Al's normally surly mood brightened in early 1939 when he secured a steady job working as a heat tester at the Sunbeam factory that churned out locomotive headlights, generators, and other electrical items. Pregnant again, this time with a bit more money in her pocketbook, Grandma Bessie gave birth to Mary Alice in April 1939, on a day when spring temperatures topped eighty degrees. With Grandpa Al earning a regular and robust Sunbeam paycheck, Mary Alice became the center of attention, not another mouth to feed, while Uncle Bill and Mom faded into the background. Grandma Bessie didn't believe in equally distributing gifts to her four children, so on Christmas Eve, Mom's birthday, Charlie and Mary received the bulk of the gifts. Mom got a few, but never a separate birthday gift or even a birthday card, and "Poor Bill" got nothing but lumps of coal, not as a playful tease to be replaced later with candy or gifts but as a message: "We don't like you." Watching her brother get coal every year stole the joy Mom's birthday held.

Mom and Uncle Bill faded from the picture so much that a few of Grandma Bessie's friends and co-workers did not know she had four children. They only heard her speak of Charlie and Mary Alice. What almost no one knew was that she actually had five.

The Muscatatuck State School, originally the Indiana Farm Colony for Feeble Minds, had more than eighteen hundred acres of rolling land near family farms and natural woodlands. It was sixty miles north of Louisville, Kentucky, and home to thirteen thousand residents in the 1920s, including John Jenne Jr., who joined the community near the end of the decade.

Grandma Bessie, then Bessie Wilkerson, is believed to have married John Jenne, a blacksmith, at age seventeen. When or if they married is not clear, but they did have a son, John Jenne Jr., three days before Grandma Bessie's eighteenth birthday. Their relationship didn't last but a few years, as John Jenne Sr. married another in November 1927. Whether unwilling or unable to care for their developmentally challenged son, Grandma Bessie and John Sr. put John Jr. in the Muscatatuck State School. Grandma Bessie returned to Evansville and married Alvin Andrew Evans: my Grandpa Al. John Jr. remained at the Muscatatuck State School.

Due to the flood, in 1939, the Army Corps of Engineers began construction on a levee system that would protect Evansville from floodwater levels up to fifty-seven feet. As engineers worked on the levee and Adolf Hitler prepared to invade Poland, Evansville celebrated late summer with the annual Junior Chamber of Commerce River Regatta co-sponsored by Ziemer Funeral Home. Organizers planned twelve speed events in both inboard and outboard motorboats. Enjoying his wealth and status as a prominent businessman, Rudy partied with friends the day before the event. His Saturday night out extended into early Sunday morning. On Riverside Drive, around 4:00 a.m., Rudy's car, carrying six passengers and traveling at a high rate of speed, approached a fast-moving car carrying three and traveling in the opposite direction. The two cars collided head-on, awakening residents on Evansville's southeast side. A startled woman called police and reported the crash. Three ambulances raced to the scene. Rumors swirled that six people had died. Ambulances did transport six people to the hospital, but despite both cars being totaled, all suffered relatively minor cuts, scrapes, and lacerations. Rudy's injuries, considered the most severe, included a concussion and a broken arm. While Rudy rested and recovered at St. Mary's Hospital, forty-five thousand spectators lined the Ohio River to watch William "Wild Bill" Cantrell set an unofficial world record for Class 725 inboard hydroplanes in his craft named *Why Worry.*

The next day, the top headline read: "WORLD RECORD SET AT REGATTA HERE." Beneath that, another headline involving speed:

August 7, 1939

**Nine Suffer
Minor Hurts In
Bad Crash**

-

**Head-On Collision at Dawn
on Riverside Drive
Demolishes Cars**

Nine persons in two
automobiles...

Ziemer Worst Hurt

By the following day, police had confirmed that Rudy had been behind the wheel of his car during the crash and not a twenty-one-year-old male friend as originally reported. Within weeks, passengers in the other car filed lawsuits against Rudy. One man sought $10,000 in damages for permanent wounds that required 133 stitches. Two other passengers sought damages totaling $5,500.

Two months later, attorney O. H. Roberts Sr. filed a libel suit on behalf of Rudy against two attorneys. Rudy's suit claimed the attorneys "wickedly and maliciously with intent to injure, vex, harass, oppress and discredit him, had caused to be filed the suits of" the passengers in Rudy's car. Rudy sought $20,000 in damages from each attorney.

After Rudy shared the front page with the regatta that day in 1939, for the most part, the Ziemer name faded to its proper place in the death notices.

In October 1942, as WWII raged in Europe, Great-Uncle Bud enlisted in the army, but not before proposing to Lorraine Denison, nine years his elder. Lorraine worked in the children's department at Strouse & Bros. alongside Great-Uncle Bud, who had started there as an elevator operator at age eighteen. Five months after enlisting, he completed Radio Operators and Mechanics training at the Army Air Forces Technical School in Sioux Falls, South Dakota.

While Great-Uncle Bud served as a radar mechanic and radio operator supporting air combat missions over Normandy, Ardennes, and Rhineland, Grandpa Al refused to drive Grandma Bessie to see young John. Grandma Bessie often referred to Grandpa Al as her "second fiddle" to John Sr. Perhaps that's the reason he refused to drive her. After nineteen years, four months, and twenty-eight days of life, mostly spent at the Muscatatuck State School, John Jenne Jr. died of acute cardiac dilation of the heart. On his death certificate, "Bessie Evans" is listed as his mother, a mom he never knew. It's not clear whether he knew or remembered his dad, who had died when John Jr. was only eight. (Given John Jr.'s plight, it's no wonder I only learned of his story while researching this book. We are, after all, a private bunch.)

While John Jenne Jr. rested in his plot at the Odd Fellows Cemetery in Princeton, Indiana, as the end of WWII in Europe crept closer and closer, Great-Uncle Bud, an "odd fellow" himself, departed Europe for the United States. He landed a few days later at Scott Field in Illinois. Just over a month later, while Great-Uncle Bud finished out his duties, his fiancée fell ill. Grandma Mil got word to her brother that doctors had admitted Lorraine to the hospital, but because she was only his fiancée and not his wife, the army did not allow Great-Uncle Bud to travel to Indiana to see her. While he finished serving his country, just 150 miles away, Lorraine Denison died of shock due to a bowel obstruction. Great-Uncle Bud never got to say goodbye and was not allowed to leave the base to attend her funeral. One of Rudy Ziemer's competing funeral homes handled the arrangements and burial.

Strouse & Bros. placed a commemoration in the *Evansville Courier*.

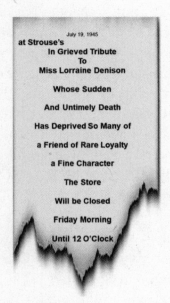

July 19, 1945
at Strouse's
In Grieved Tribute
To
Miss Lorraine Denison

Whose Sudden

And Untimely Death

Has Deprived So Many of

a Friend of Rare Loyalty

a Fine Character

The Store

Will be Closed

Friday Morning

Until 12 O'Clock

While Great-Uncle Bud mourned, Rudy enjoyed great business success despite the nearly catastrophic car crash. He sold the family home on First Avenue in 1946 as the area turned commercial except for several nearby older homes, like Grandpa Al's on Harriet Street. Rudy purchased a brand new three-thousand-square-foot home resting on a half-acre lot. The house at 3201 Lincoln Avenue epitomized those on Evansville's growing and thriving east side, where many residents paid to have their lush lawns maintained. Rudy lived in the house with his mother, Anna, sisters Elizabeth and Agnes Mary, and brother George, a priest. Rudy also rented a home on Roth Road overlooking the Ohio River.

While the new house surely provided more comforts for the four adult children living with their mother, neighbors found the family dynamic strange. Early in that year, the Ziemer name began, once again, to appear in the section of the newspaper where neighbors often look to find someone they know or maybe the new residents on a fancy block.

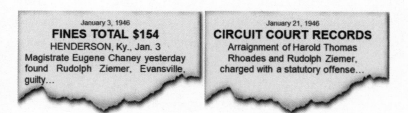

January 3, 1946
FINES TOTAL $154
HENDERSON, Ky., Jan. 3
Magistrate Eugene Chaney yesterday found Rudolph Ziemer, Evansville, guilty...

January 21, 1946
CIRCUIT COURT RECORDS
Arraignment of Harold Thomas Rhoades and Rudolph Ziemer, charged with a statutory offense...

Officials eventually dismissed the statutory charge involving sodomy. In exchange for the dismissal, the now thirty-nine-year-old Rudy had accepted the judge's order to spend at least one year in a St. Louis institution to deal with his affliction.

As Evansville residents began to see Rudy Ziemer's name in the paper for something other than funeral notices, they also learned a newly minted doctor had come back to town. After serving as a physician in the armed forces during WWII, Dr. Charles Moehlenkamp opened a practice on the west side of town, and because he often did not charge for services, including delivering babies, he quickly became known as "the poor man's doctor." Dr. Moehlenkamp and Rudy Ziemer, both graduates of Reitz Memorial Catholic High School, earned their living and reputations on opposite ends of life's spectrum.

Two years after Lorraine's death, Great-Uncle Bud, age thirty-five, married Doris Mae Ellerbush, daughter of Walter Ellerbush, a co-worker of his at Strouse's. Doris, age nineteen and a Strouse's employee, wore a dark blue gaberdine suit with blue accessories and a white orchid corsage. They married at St. Paul's Lutheran church. Grandma Mil, wearing a dark green suit with brown accessories and a lavender orchid, served as an attendant, as did Grandpa George. Their roles caused quite a ruckus among their Catholic friends, as the Catholic Church forbade members from participating in non-Catholic ceremonies and services. Grandma Mil, a convert, certainly didn't care, and because she didn't, Grandpa George didn't either.

Rudy's name again appeared in the local papers, detailing the first time police arrested him for driving while intoxicated. He pleaded guilty to reckless driving and paid a ten-dollar fine.

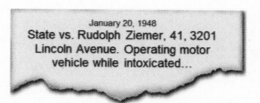

January 20, 1948
State vs. Rudolph Ziemer, 41, 3201
Lincoln Avenue. Operating motor
vehicle while intoxicated...

Nearly seven months later and thirteen years after the new Ziemer Funeral Home announcement, Rudy finally got the type of press he craved when he appeared in the Society section wearing a shirt and tie while driving his beloved sixteen-foot Truscotteer speedboat. His mother sat next to him, wearing her Sunday best. As much as anyone, Rudy loved the Ohio River and especially showing off his slick craft at Dress Plaza, where the regatta was held in 1939.

The shine of that headline dimmed twenty-three days later.

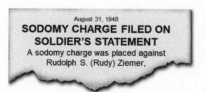

August 31, 1948
**SODOMY CHARGE FILED ON
SOLDIER'S STATEMENT**
A sodomy charge was placed against
Rudolph S. (Rudy) Ziemer,

A soldier, who had been arrested for the theft of four cars, testified Rudy committed an act of sodomy on or about December 1, 1947. Officials postponed his arraignment. His brother, Ted Jr., paid Rudy's bond of $2,000.

RAINBOW CLEANERS

● ● ● ● ● ●

Dry cleaning is neither dry nor clean.
I often watched Dad and Grandpa dip their thick rubber-gloved hands and forearms into a washer, dryer, or spinner to remove clothes that smelled, to me, like turpentine or gasoline or spray paint or something I could not quite identify. The type that makes your head feel like a helium balloon. At age five or six, I remember thinking this didn't seem like a fun job, and I didn't even understand what it meant to have a job.

If I ever do need a job and must work here, I want the job of opening the firebox door to check the fire, I thought. Inside Rainbow Cleaners, a coal-fired boiler stood tall and round, like a silo, near the back. A red brick smokestack extended out of the building like a sacred statue, or so it seemed to a kid. A silo and a holy figure came to mind because farms and churches dot the landscape in Evansville, like bars and beer halls. Silos, churches, bars, and beer halls summed it up.

"That's my grandpa's cleaners," I announced when riding by in a car and pointing out the smokestack to friends or family.

The boiler stood behind two commercial dryers, so the adults had to crouch down between the round dryers, which together resembled a giant pair of binoculars. At five, even I had to bend down a bit to get back there, but it was worth the effort to get one look into that firebox, especially on a cold winter day.

As the first year of Rainbow ended, Grandma Mil, when not working at the cleaners, which she did six days a week, would have been baking Christmas cookies. Grandma Mil, from whom I got my auburn hair, loved Christmas more than any other holiday and cherished spending that time of the year with Dad and Aunt Kate, who were fourteen and eleven.

Inside a wood-frame, two-bedroom bungalow with a half-finished attic that served as Dad's bedroom, Grandma Mil decorated the Christmas tree with C5 multi-colored lights and silver tinsel. A balsa-wood nativity set with ceramic figures, including the three wise men, Melchior being one, rested on a white bedsheet laid out to resemble rolling hills covered in fresh snow. The living room, where the tree stood front and center, smelled like tobacco candles, real tobacco, freshly baked cookies and pine needles.

Because Grandma baked cookies weeks in advance and stored them in everything from decorative tins to actual cookie jars, the house smelled like Christmas for all of December. Too much temptation for Dad, Aunt

Kate, and even Grandma and Grandpa, many of the cookies disappeared before Christmas Eve.

All celebrations in my family involved booze more than coffee, so Christmas Eve became the time to celebrate and open presents, not Christmas morning. In 1947, Christmas Eve fell on a Wednesday, so Grandpa George closed Rainbow Cleaners early and probably headed to Roy's Tavern for a beer or two before heading home. Just over a mile away, between morning and afternoon, Ziemer Funeral Home conducted four funerals. Earlier in the week, they had buried an infant. Death rarely takes a holiday.

As Grandpa George and Grandma Mil sipped beers later that evening at home while smoking cigarettes and cooking food for the Christmas Eve celebration, the phone rang. Mr. Flowers, a black man and friend of the family who lived behind the cleaners, called to let Grandpa George know the burglar alarm, which sounded just like a school bell reminding children recess had ended, was repeatedly ringing on what should have been a peaceful evening. Grandpa George thanked Mr. Flowers, took a swig of beer, and promised his family, "I'll be back in a jiff." Dad wanted to go with him, but Grandpa George knew better than to take his son to a possible burglary in progress.

The alarm often went off in windy and wet weather or for some other innocent reason, but not this time. Upon arrival, Grandpa George discovered someone had broken into the front door. He went inside, called the police, and then looked around to see if the burglars had stolen anything. Luckily, they hadn't. However, the broken door and feeling of vulnerability fouled his mood as he drove back home to resume the celebration.

Much of Grandpa George's insecure nature stemmed from him being passed among relatives after his dad died of brain cancer at thirty-eight. His mom had to make a living as a housekeeper and often traveled to clean houses, sometimes staying for days or weeks. She didn't need a little one holding her back and couldn't find or afford a full-time babysitter. An only child, Grandpa George found odd and sometimes disturbing ways to entertain himself. He once put a relative's dog into a soaped-up claw-foot bathtub before tossing a feral cat into the slippery arena to see what would happen. The dog didn't fare so well but managed to survive. Grandpa George probably took a beating for that one.

During those rambunctious and somewhat troubling pre-teen years, he spent a bit of time with an aunt and uncle, but at age eleven he overheard them talking about how hard it was to live with a "stranger" in the house. That comment compelled him to run away to try and find his mother. He succeeded, but the reunion didn't last. She immediately sent him back, and for that, he never forgave her.

After high school, Grandpa George started working for Paris Cleaners, his cousin's business. During WWII, they cleaned uniforms from Fort Campbell in Kentucky and were considered a part of the war effort.

An internal squabble between Grandpa George and his cousin caused him to quit or get fired. After that disappointment, he moved on to Sterling Cleaners and then American Cleaners and, by 1947, had become an expert spotter and cleaner. Not wanting to depend on anyone, he decided to venture out on his own, or mostly his own, with the help of a man named Jim Gerard, whom he had met at American Cleaners. Jim understood the money side of the business, so the partnership made perfect sense. They named the business Rainbow Cleaners because a rainbow represented how bright, clean, and colorful their customer's clothes would become after proper cleaning and pressing.

A few blocks from the Rainbow Cleaners break-in and the funerals at Ziemer Funeral Home, Mom's family prepared for a Christmas Day morning celebration. Mom turned fourteen that Wednesday. Perhaps Aunt Mary Alice sang "Happy Birthday" to her. Uncle Charlie, an accomplished football player, considered enlisting in the navy as he enjoyed Christmas break before his last semester in high school.

As usual, Grandpa Al and Grandma Bessie didn't buy Mom birthday gifts, even though they now had the money to do so. Instead, they let a few Christmas gifts serve both celebrations. For Mom, that was okay. At least she didn't get the lumps of coal Uncle Bill continued to receive.

While Mom's family celebrated in the house on Harriett Street, Dad's family sat at a small round table eating breakfast when, just like Christmas Eve the night before, the phone rang. Grandpa answered.

"What? Again? Goddammit."

Grandpa George slammed the heavy black receiver onto the telephone base.

"The goddamn alarm is going off again."

"George, watch your language on Christmas," Grandma Mil implored.

"Can I go?" Dad asked.

"No, stay here with your mom and sister."

Grandpa George exited the back of the house and walked down the five concrete steps toward the car. Arriving at Rainbow Cleaners, Grandpa George relived the previous day. A broken door. Nothing taken. Simple as that. That's what he told the police before they told him, "Burglaries sometimes go up during Christmas time. Everyone's trying to get someone or maybe themselves a gift, and they don't always have the money to do so."

I'll bet Grandpa George felt like throwing whoever broke into the cleaners into the firebox of the coal-fired boiler. That would send them straight to hell—or at least a place just like it.

The firebox door, heavy and made of iron and secured with a large latch, closed almost like hatches on a submarine. Dad or Grandpa George wore thick work gloves, not the rubber gloves they used to grab the chemically soaked clothes, when grabbing the iron latch and opening the firebox door.

I never got the chance to open that door. However, I used to look inside when Dad or Grandpa George opened the entrance to bright orange flaming embers, much lighter and brighter than my fiery auburn hair.

When I did look, the smell of burning coal, first cousin to hot asphalt, penetrated my nose as my face flushed with a desert-dry heat that warmed my lips, nose, and eyes while penetrating my clothes to add warmth to my shoulders, chest, stomach, and thighs, but leaving my back cold. I wanted to stand there for hours, to watch, to feel, to smell and perhaps turn around so my back could enjoy the heat, but that never happened. The door only remained open just long enough to check the fire, and then with a clank and a grating slide of the latch, the glow vanished behind the door, and the warmth rose toward the ceiling liked a blessed soul before I turned and walked toward the cold my back had felt all along. When Sam, Amy, or Andy told me, "You're going to hell if you don't stop..." doing whatever I was doing to drive them crazy, I remember thinking, "At least I know what it looks like."

Grandpa George gained a reputation for cleaning fine suits like those Rudy Ziemer wore while comforting mourners feeling the cruel grief of Christmastime deaths, a far more painful blow than nuisance break-ins. Mom and Dad had not yet met, and no one in the family really knew Rudy Ziemer, but their seemingly disconnected and divergent threads would soon converge at a river camp.

MORE TROUBLE

● ● ● ● ●

Grandpa George's business partner, Jim Gerard, like many in Evansville, enjoyed the Ohio River. He loved it enough to either own or rent a house on Roth Road very near Rudy Ziemer's second home. Roth Road, a narrow strip of asphalt running parallel to a wide portion of the river, is home to twenty or so lots with houses or trailers, some on stilts, where locals launch speedboats, flats, and skiffs.

Grandma Mil, Grandpa George, Dad, Great-Uncle Bud, and Aunt Kate often spent spring and summer Sundays at Jim Gerard's "river camp." Kate even got to take a ride in Rudy Ziemer's sixteen-foot Truscotteer speedboat in the summer of 1949, telling everyone how nice Rudy was to let her do that.

Luckily her ride wasn't on a particular Sunday that year when Rudy allegedly crashed into another boat. Wilbur Kinder claimed Rudy's Truscotteer struck his boat, knocking him unconscious and into the dark waters of the Ohio River. Another boater pulled Kinder from the water and took him to Deaconess Hospital. The accident totaled Kinder's craft.

Rudy denied hitting Kinder's boat and told news-paper reporters, "We had just left the boat club above the Water Works when we came up to Dress Plaza. His boat was a little in front of mine. Then I noticed we were too close to shore, and he evidently did too. He turned toward the middle of the river, and I had to turn sharply to avoid hitting him. The wash from my boat split his boat, and my boat went up on the rocks."

Rudy said Kinder jumped from his boat when he knew it was sinking and was not knocked unconscious due to an accident. Rudy finished his story with report-ers by telling them, "My boat couldn't have been in a collision because it doesn't have a mark on it. It is at the boat club now, and anyone is welcome to inspect it."

Kinder sued Rudy for $5,000.

One story about those river camp days I've heard more than once is that Rudy, stumbling drunk, slipped and fell into a mud puddle while wearing a white suit. Who wears a suit at a river camp? The same man who wore a dress shirt and tie while piloting a speedboat. Perhaps the day he became a muddy mess is also the day Rainbow Cleaners started cleaning Rudy Ziemer's clothes.

Rudy rarely picked his clothes up as Rainbow offered home delivery. One of Grandpa George's drivers left his clothes hanging in a covered walkway between Rudy's well-maintained white brick single-story house, with a large, finished basement, and the unattached garage.

Money, dry-cleaning tickets, receipts, and any other transactional paper would be exchanged later, if at all.

Later that year, in December, the Brinkley VFW post appointed Great-Uncle Bud chairman of the post's Christmas party. The group planned to host a group of underprivileged children that year. Siblings Great-Uncle Bud and Grandma Mil had been underprivileged children themselves. Their dad, Francis Carr, essentially abandoned his family, preferring to hobo and train hop from Indiana to Massachusetts and back. His whereabouts were largely unknown to the children, who lived with their mom and struggled to make ends meet without a man in the house.

Two days after Great-Uncle Bud turned eighteen in 1930, his mom died, leaving the two young siblings on their own. Great-Uncle Bud immediately found a job working for Strouse & Bros. as an elevator operator. For a short time, they moved in with their maternal grandma, Sophia, whose dementia was so severe that before she went to school, Grandma Mil would hide her grandma's shoes because that was the only way to prevent her from leaving the house and wandering the streets. Grandma Sophia died in 1931. At nineteen and sixteen, siblings Great-Uncle Bud and Grandma Mil were on their own, their dad nowhere to be found.

As the story goes, it was love at first sight for Grandpa George when he met the short, petite young woman with auburn hair and freckles. He wanted to take Grandma Mil on a picnic but didn't have a car, so he traded most of his fishing gear for a full-day use of his friend's car. Grandpa George asked her out, and she said yes, and the rest, as they say, is history—a muddled history, however. Muddled with smudged dates and a confusing marriage license.

HUSBAND AND WIFE

George Melchior AND Mildred Carr and for doing this shall be his sufficient authority.

In Testimony Whereof Chas. H. Salm, Clerk of the Spencer Court, hereunto subscribe my name and affix the seal of said Court this 2nd day of April 1933.

The State of Indiana, to wit: Spencer County, ss.

This certifies that I joined in marriage as husband and wife

George Melchior and Mildred Carr on the 2 day of April 1934. Revalidated in St. Joseph's Rectory, April 11, 1934.

Dad was a bastard. 1933 is clearly smudged and rewritten by someone, but who? Grandma Mil, Grandpa George? Who knows? Again, we are, after all, a private bunch.

By September 1950, Doris Mae Carr, sixteen years younger than Great-Uncle Bud, filed for divorce. Apparently, she had an affair with another Strouse employee. At least, that's the story we heard. O. H. Roberts Sr.'s law firm, the one that represented Rudy after he allegedly crashed the boat that Aunt Kate rode in, represented Doris Mae. Great-Uncle Bud did not attend the proceedings. He preferred to drown his sorrows at Roy's Tavern, Old Kentucky, or the Fraternal Order of Eagles with new friend Rudy Ziemer and closest friend Forrest Arvin. Great-Uncle Bud enjoyed Gobi-dry martinis instead of beer, the family favorite.

For a couple of years, Rudy managed to steer clear of trouble, until Halloween Eve 1951, when he drove his car into the parking lot of the Fraternal Order of Eagles near downtown Evansville. The rounded, almost bulbous fenders and chrome bumpers of the 1947 Cadillac shined underneath parking lot lights. Whitewall tires gleamed like polished shoes. A white fluorescent sign rested atop two steel poles. On the sign, the words Liberty, Truth, Justice, and Equality encircled the glowing image of a bald eagle with its talons out, ready to pounce.

Outside the brick Fraternal Order of Eagles building, men and women milled about the parking lot. Rudy's slick car and fine clothes attracted the attention he craved. Rudy got out of the car and strode toward the entrance. Before he could open the door, he met two men who he convinced to go with him to his Roth Road river camp home for beers rather than going inside the Fraternal Order of Eagles.

Once inside the home, the two men viciously beat and robbed Rudy of his beloved Cadillac. Rudy suffered severe facial injuries. After a brief investigation, Rudy could not or would not identify his assailants.

October 30, 1951
Area Man Is Beaten Then Robbed of Auto
Rudolph Ziemer, 45, is being treated at St. Mary's Hospital

Less than a year later, authorities charged Rudy with having "unnatural relations" with a boy aged seventeen and another boy aged sixteen. The sixteen-year-old boy implicated Rudy. Evansville residents began referring to Rudy Ziemer as the "Queer Undertaker."

July 16, 1952
ZIEMER TO BE ARRAIGNED MONDAY IN MORALS CASE
Rudolph Ziemer, 45, co-owner of the Ziemer funeral home

Dinner table or get-together conversations often centered on Rudy and his exploits. One such conversation took place during Grandma Mil's Clabber Club, a monthly card game with friends. Cigarettes and beer crowded the table as the four women took tricks. Grandma's closest friends heard Rudy had been offering high school boys money for sex, and some took him up on the offer. This appalled everyone, including Grandma Mil, although she doubted the validity of the stories and told her friends, "Well, maybe if we teach our boys what we teach our girls, that they should wait until marriage to have sex, and we also stop teaching them how goddamn important money is, maybe they wouldn't take his offer. Maybe they would value themselves a bit more." The card game ended early that night.

While rumors swirled about Rudy and the other Ziemers living in the house on Lincoln Avenue, Dad continued at Reitz Memorial Catholic high school, as did Ted and Jerry Ziemer, Rudy's nephews, who lived on the "other side" of the Ziemer family, the side that didn't live in the house on Lincoln. That's also about the time Grandpa Al got an even bigger break than his job at Sunbeam. He had landed a job working in the metal pressing shop at Whirlpool on Highway 41. Evansville was considered the "Refrigerator Capital of the World," and Whirlpool produced the finest refrigerators. Grandpa Al suddenly had a steady, good-paying factory job that would provide him with a pension for life if he made it to retirement.

As Grandpa Al stamped metal, Rudy fought the charges through a series of legal maneuvers. Rudy sought to have the charges dismissed because an amended affidavit was filed before the original affidavit was dismissed. In the new affidavit, the date of the alleged offense had also been changed. Rudy Ziemer never faced trial for the two sodomy charges.

In May 1953, police arrested Rudy again and charged him with drunken driving after a two-car collision. By this time, Ted Sr., Rudy's brother, had seen enough. He sold his stock in Ziemer Funeral home to Rudy. Rudy continued to run the funeral home with his mom Anna, sisters Elizabeth and Agnes Mary, and priest brother George.

Ted Ziemer's Fountain Terrace sprang up on the east side of Evansville. The two brothers stopped speaking. A judge fined Rudy $300 and revoked his driver's license for two years for the drunken driving charge. The judge suspended a 180-day sentence.

Rudy continued to buy clothes from Great-Uncle Bud and have his clothes cleaned at Rainbow Cleaners. Grandma Mil, Grandpa George, Great-Uncle Bud, and Dad considered Rudy a friend, albeit a troubled one. Other than cleaning Rudy's clothes he bought from Great-Uncle Bud, what they enjoyed most about Rudy is he liked to have a good time, something my family always loved to do. They knew he was gay and could not have cared less except for their belief that being gay in the Crossroads of America probably made for a very difficult life.

A MARRIAGE, A BIRTHDAY,
AND A MAD DOG

● ● ● ● ● ● ●

Friends and family of Mom and Dad, wearing sharp suits and dresses, milled about the sidewalks surrounding the Sisters' home and school. Assumption Cathedral's towering spire basked in partly cloudy, eighty-degree sunshine on Saturday, April 24, 1954. As the home to Evansville's first Catholic parish, the glorious Romanesque brick structure with stone trimmings shone like a diamond a mere mile from Rainbow Cleaners.

As guests filed into the cathedral, taking seats on the bride's or the groom's sides, Mom, wearing a waltz-length, white satin and lace gown, nervously posed for pictures. Dad and the groomsmen wore black suits, white shirts, and black neckties. Dad's sister, Kate, and Mom's sister, Mary Alice, served as bridesmaids. Dad chose Mom's brother, Charlie, the spitting image of Grandpa Al, and a couple of his friends, including Jack Gruebel, a drummer and promising professional musician, as his groomsmen. Jack served as his best man.

Earlier that morning, Mom, Grandma Bessie, and Aunt Mary argued about crinoline. Mom had quietly saved enough money to buy the special fabric for her dress so that it would hang with the proper fullness a wedding gown deserved. Mom also bought crinoline for Aunt Mary, as a fifteenth birthday present. The crinoline Mom bought for Aunt Mary was not as nice as the crinoline she bought for herself.

Being the youngest, Aunt Mary often pouted and fussed if she didn't get her way, and that day, Mom's wedding day, Aunt Mary wanted the nicer and more expensive crinoline. As Aunt Kate looked on while everyone dressed, Grandma Bessie insisted that Mom give the nicer crinoline to Aunt Mary. In that brief but chaotic moment, Aunt Kate began to understand the Evans family dynamic. Grandma Bessie asked Mom to take a back seat to her younger sister even on her wedding day. Grandma Bessie reasoned, who would know that Aunt Mary had the nicer crinoline, and what difference did it make? Is it a sacrifice if no one knows? Aunt Kate knew—and never forgot it.

As the organist played "Bridal Chorus," Grandpa Al gladly walked his oldest daughter toward the altar and into marriage. Mom carried white orchids and baby's breath. She wore the single strand of pearls Dad had gifted her during her last year of high school. A reception followed at the Evans family home, the two-story shotgun on Harriet Street.

After the reception, Mom and Dad embarked on a "southern honeymoon." Leavenworth, Indiana, a ninety-minute drive from Evansville and home to The Overlook Restaurant, Dad's favorite because of the view, sat at a horseshoe bend in the Ohio River similar to the one in Evansville. Never venturing too far from familiar haunts, Mom and Dad spent three days in Leavenworth before returning home to begin their life together. Mom thought, "We have our whole lives ahead of us."

A few weeks after the wedding, Mom walked to pick up wedding pictures and keepsake black-and-white wedding-party postcards. The inscription on the postcards read, "The Wedding Party of Dan and Dolores Melchoir, April 24, 1954," misspelling her new last name. A typo and cheaper crinoline. Who's going to notice?

Mom and Dad rented an apartment at 625 Reis Avenue, only three houses down from Grandma Mil and Grandpa George and a far (pronounced fur) piece from Grandma Bessie and Grandpa Al. Al and George only lived one and a half miles apart, but in Evansville, and to Mom, who didn't drive, a pretty far piece.

They chose the apartment because Mom helped raise Dad's youngest brothers, Tom, and Dave, born in 1949 and 1952, respectively. Tom had asthma and eczema, like my Uncle Bill. Although some on Dad's side thought he could do better than Mom, including

Great-Uncle Bud, who flat out said, "Dan, you can do better," they all agreed, "That Dots is a hell of a worker." Mom got her nickname from her grade-school friends, and everyone on Dad's side of the family called her Dots. Most in her immediate family called her Dolores or Dotsie.

When she wasn't working at The Baby Shop, a popular store on Main Street for new and expectant mothers, Mom walked the couple of hundred feet between the two Reis Avenue houses to care for Tom and Dave while Grandma Mil worked with Grandpa George, at Rainbow Cleaners. Mom practiced her parenting skills on Tom and Dave and spent time learning to cook like Grandma Bessie and Grandma Mil, which meant she learned to cook round steak and onions, beef and noodles, chicken and dumplings, liver and onions, fried chicken, and brain sandwiches.

Brain sandwiches are an Ohio River Valley delicacy sold mostly in Evansville and St. Louis. Preparing calf brains is relatively easy except for cleaning the brains, which involves soaking them in salt water and then removing the membrane and veins. With Mom's large, strong hands, she was able to make quick work of the process. She mixed the brains with flour, baking powder, eggs, salt, and pepper to form a batter similar in texture and look to pancake batter. She used a ladle to pour a large dollop of batter into an iron skillet bubbling with hot, but not too hot, grease. Brains need to fry slowly to ensure they are cooked throughout and have the time required to rise and become fluffy. The consistency of cooked brains is similar to scrambled eggs except for the golden-brown crust, which, when appropriately cooked, is pleasantly crunchy. Most everyone on both sides of the family enjoyed brain sandwiches, and Mom loved nothing more than fixing a meal everyone enjoyed. "That Dots is a hell of a worker" quickly expanded to "That Dots is a hell of a cook."

Mom and Dad settled into a comfortable routine of work, time with Dad's family, and occasional but far less frequent time with Mom's family. They wanted kids, probably four or five, they thought, but a few early miscarriages signaled a rougher start to building a family than they had hoped. Despite that, they enjoyed each other, and Mom took pride and care in helping to raise Tom and Dave.

On the morning of December 3, 1954, Evansville residents opened their morning newspaper to the news that Pope Pius XII had collapsed in the Vatican. Great-Uncle Bud wouldn't have cared less and Mom probably worried and felt sorry for him, but that headline took a backseat to the glaring all-caps headline:

December 3, 1954
**OWNER'S WIFE SHOT TO DEATH,
ROBBED IN LIQUOR STORE ON
BELLEMEADE AVE.**

Bellemeade Liquor Store, advertising "Wine * Gin * Beer," stood three miles from Mom and Dad's apartment. A. C. "Doc" Holland found the body of his wife, Mary Holland, thirty-three, stuffed in a bathroom at the back of the liquor store. Three months pregnant, Mrs. Holland's body had been wedged so tightly into the small bathroom enclosure that the first officer on the scene had to wait for backup to arrive and help him extract her from the stall. The robber had shot Mrs. Holland in the right temple. Police interviewed residents in neighboring homes, but no one heard anything indicating that a crime had taken place. Police did not have a clue but did not consider her husband, Doc, a suspect.

The brutal crime shocked residents and put some on high alert, especially those who worked in other late-hour establishments, like the Standard Oil gas station, two miles from Mom and Dad's apartment, at the corner of US 41 and Franklin Street. The gas station operated twenty-four hours for the midnight truck drivers who navigated the north-south route through Stoplight City.

Days after the brutal slaying of Mary Holland, as snow flurries danced in the wind and glistened in the glow of after-midnight streetlights, Whitney Wesley Kerr, a WWII paratrooper who fought at the Battle of the Bulge, where his feet froze so badly that only very skilled doctors and a six-month stay in the hospital prevented amputation, looked out a window of the Standard Oil gas station. He noticed smoke coming from the brakes of a gasoline truck slowing at one of the many stoplights. Kerr raced out of the gas station with a fire extinguisher in hand and flagged down the driver, who stopped. Kerr proceeded to engulf the brakes in the extinguisher agent. The incident most likely provided a rare bit of excitement for Kerr on his otherwise quiet graveyard shift.

As the end of the year approached, Kerr's friendly demeanor and courtesy with Standard Oil customers had earned him a Christmas turkey, but that wasn't the only thing Kerr received during the 1954 holiday season. A few days before Christmas, when Kerr arrived for his shift, he discovered a package had been left for him. He opened it to discover a hand-made leather wallet with the word *Mexico* embossed across the front. Later, during a car ride with his wife Peggy and his mom, Kerr told his mom, "You aren't the only one with a Mexican purse. Look at this." He handed her the wallet so she could compare it to the handbag she owned. Both were reddish-brown and, except for the size, nearly identical.

On December 23, with the Mexico wallet in his pocket, Kerr arrived for his graveyard shift. During that shift, a man from Atlanta purchased gas and asked Kerr if he could park his car in the back of the station so he could get some sleep. That Kerr said yes wouldn't have surprised anyone. While the man slept, sometime between 1:30 and 1:45 a.m., a person entered the gas station and demanded, at gunpoint, that Kerr open the cash register, which he did. After being handed six-ty-eight dollars, the robber walked Kerr to a restroom with an outside entrance. In that restroom, the robber placed the gun against the back of Kerr's head and shot him. The bullet lodged in his skull, just above his right eye. The two Christmastime murders and their similarity shocked the police.

December 24, 1954
POLICE SEARCH FOR "HOMICIDAL MANIAC"

That Christmas Eve, Grandma Mil made sure Mom received a proper birthday gift and card, along with a few Christmas presents. Although not very religious herself, Grandma Mil loved Christmas like no other holiday, and she made sure to include Mom in the preparations and festivities. The murders of Mary Holland and Wesley Kerr would have upset Mom to no end. She despised violence and would often, like a frightened puppy, visibly shake when arguments got out of hand. Perhaps her reaction stemmed from her Grandpa Charles unloading all six bullets from a revolver into the living room floor on one of her Christmas Eve birthdays. As Christmas lights twinkled and children waited for Saint Nick, adults in Evansville feared a killer among them.

Police Chief Kirby Stevens canceled all days off for Evansville police officers, who, often using their own cars and street clothes, chased down all leads in both cases. Mayor H. O. Roberts convened a special meeting of the Safety Board to hire five new police officers who would be assigned to parking patrol and promote five parking patrol officers to help with the investigation.

Interestingly, H. (Hank) O. Roberts, the Republican mayor, was not related to O. H. (Herb) Roberts Sr., a Democrat who had represented Rudy Ziemer in the civil suit that resulted from Rudy's 1939 car crash. That the mayor and one of Evansville's most prominent lawyers would have such similar names while being on opposite sides of the political spectrum provided one more quirk in Evansville's colorful history.

Almost ninety days after Mom's twenty-first birthday, two days of heavy rain and sixty-degree temperatures surrendered to a cold snap hovering in the mid-thirties to low forties. Twenty miles west of Evansville, near Mt. Vernon, a river town of about six thousand, around 4:15 pm, seven-year-old John Ray Sailer exited the school bus that brought him home. As usual, he ran toward the house. Once inside, he noticed that his mom and dad's noon lunch plates had not been cleared from the table.

Five minutes later, John Sr. drove up the driveway and parked near the garage. John Jr. cried to his dad, "Mommie's on the floor and won't get up!" Mr. Sailer ran into the house and found his wife, Wilhelmina

Susan, forty-seven, lying in a pool of blood, her hands tied behind her back with her own apron. She had been shot in the right temple. The scene in the kitchen, bedroom, and hallways indicated Mrs. Sailer had attempted to fight off the intruder, who had ripped her dress and tore off her undergarments. Several tubs of wet clothes sat beneath laundry drying on an indoor clothesline. Pulled-open kitchen drawers and other out-of-place items in the always-tidy home were evidence of a gut-wrenching, violent end to Wilhelmina Sailer's gentle, quiet farm life.

Mom and Dad never owned a gun, and Grandpa George's only gun, an octagon-barrel .22 caliber rifle, never seemed to leave its place on the wall in the back bedroom. Others in Evansville that owned guns imme-diately loaded them and greeted anyone that came to the door with shotguns, handguns, or rifles. Those without guns often kept a baseball bat or a lead pipe near the door. While most everyone felt saddened by the Christmastime murders of Holland and Kerr, those murders occurred in places of business and seemed less worrisome. The fact that a killer entered a peace-ful home put Evansville and the surrounding area on a knife's edge. Farmers, hunters, and fishermen suddenly felt more like prey than trackers. City violence had moved to the county.

A nervous worrier, Mom hustled between the two Reis Avenue houses as she cared for Dad's brothers.

A killer without much of a pattern was on the loose in Evansville. If, when, and where he might strike again caused panic for many, Mom and Grandma Mil included. Aunt Kate received a blistering scolding when Grandma Mil came home to find the doors unlocked, the windows open, and Aunt Kate lounging about. Aunt Kate, more carefree than Mom or Grandma Mil, was not overly concerned. Why worry? A week later, worry crept into everyone's mind, including Aunt Kate's.

Henderson, Kentucky, a town of just over sixteen thousand residents at the time, sits right across the river from Evansville and, more specifically, across from the southeast side. In 1955, a single bridge crossed the Ohio River, connecting the two towns. Ralph and Danny Ball and Wallace Brown rode in Ralph's pickup truck along a gravel road near Geneva and Corydon, two tiny towns southwest of Henderson. Due to recent heavy rains, a muddy slough framed the gravel road. Looking out the passenger window, Wallace shouted, "I believe there's somebody over there." Ralph stopped his truck, and the three men got out to investigate. Two bodies, both men, lay face down in four inches of dark mud. The three men walked back to the truck and drove to Corydon and informed authorities, who immediately rushed to the gruesome scene.

Upon arrival, Sheriff Williams recognized the bodies as those of his close friends Goebel Duncan and Goebel's twenty-one-year-old son, former high school basketball star Raymond. Raymond had just become a father to a newborn son for the first time the day before. Goebel Duncan's head rested on the fork of a fallen tree. Deputy Coroner Stokes retrieved the bodies and began transporting the murdered father and son to Henderson, while Sheriff Williams went to the Duncan home to inform Mrs. Mamie Duncan of the horrific murder of her husband and son.

Sheriff Williams knocked on the door but did not receive a response, so he opened the door and walked into the small house. Upon entering, he saw two-year-old Shirley Faye Duncan sitting on a bed next to her mother, Goebel's daughter-in-law Elizabeth, who was lying face down and diagonally across the bed. Elizabeth was married to Goebel's son Dorris Ray. She had been shot in the back of the head. Little Shirley Faye was not harmed. Sheriff Williams yelled for his deputy, Cleo Gish, who, upon entering the house, looked at Sheriff Williams and said, "My God."

They walked farther into the house and, in an adjoining room, found Mrs. Mamie Duncan lying face down on another bed. She, too, had been shot in the head. The men returned to the first bedroom and carried Shirley Faye out of the house. Sheriff Williams immediately radioed for additional officers. Neighbors, who gathered at the house like flocks of crows, took Shirley Faye as Sheriff Williams returned to the house. As the sheriff attempted to turn over Mamie Duncan,

Mrs. Duncan raised her head slightly and groaned. She was alive!

At Methodist Hospital in Henderson, Mamie Duncan clung to life as investigators attempted to understand why such a brutal crime could have been perpetrated and who on earth was responsible. Doctors discovered Mamie had been shot twice, once in the head and once in the back. The shot in the back was superficial and did not impact her well-being. The bullet that entered her right temple passed through her head completely and exited the left temple. Doctors feared the bullet most likely severed or severely damaged her optic nerves. During a two-hour surgery, doctors removed bone fragments and damaged tissue. Mamie Duncan's eyes were swollen shut, so they could not determine if she had been permanently blinded. She did recognize the voices of family members.

Mrs. Duncan did not remember being shot or anything else about the day her husband, son, and daughter-in-law were killed. In fact, she told doctors that Mr. Goebel would be there to pick her up in the evening. Police stated that Mamie Duncan's recovery "is our only hope right now."

On April 10, reporters discovered that Evansville police had detained a suspect in the Duncan family murder. An Evansville convict, whose trademark burglary technique was discovered at the Duncan home, was being questioned by police.

Under ultra-tight security and a veil of secrecy, police took the suspect to Indianapolis so he could take a lie detector test. Reporters learned the man had confessed to twenty-four burglaries in four Indiana counties. After the ninety-minute test, authorities continued to believe he was a "hot" lead and moved forward with their investigation.

While the suspect was initially held in the Duncan family slaying, authorities charged him the next day with another murder. The charge was the result of the right question asked of the right person by a brilliant reporter.

A newspaper reporter had learned of Wesley Kerr's unique Mexican wallet but asked Evansville Police whether he should mention it in his story. The police instructed him not to mention it, as that might cause whoever had committed the crime to throw it away if they even had it. It was a long shot but one worth taking. The reporter did not mention Kerr's wallet in any of his stories.

In the early morning of April 14, under continued intense questioning by Prosecutor Paul Wever and Detective Chief Dan Hudson, who knew the suspect and considered him to be a friend, and the one who the suspect spoke to most freely, a thirty-year-old convict and steam pipe insulator confessed not only to the murders of Goebel, Raymond, and Elizabeth Duncan but also to the murders of Mary Holland, Wilhelmina Susan

Sailer, and Whitney Wesley Carr. The suspect, who had served nine years in the state prison at Michigan City and seemed to have a "deathly fear" of ever being confined again, showed no repentance. When police had apprehended the suspect, they found in his possession a leather Mexican wallet. The United States Supreme Court would eventually learn the name Leslie Irvin.

"STATE OPENS FIRE ON IRVIN TODAY," read the headline in the *Evansville Courier & Press*. State attorneys Paul Wever, Loren McGregor, and Howard Sandusky planned to call "six to eight" witnesses to testify against Irvin regarding the murder of Wesley Kerr. James Lopp represented Irvin. The state hoped to "strap Leslie Irvin to the electric chair."

On Friday, December 16, jurors leaned forward and listened as Howard Sandusky read Leslie Irvin's confession to the murder of Wesley Kerr. Prosecutors fought intensely to be able to read the confession during the trial and scored a huge victory when the judge ruled in their favor. It was a confession that Irvin had never signed.

During the trial, defense attorney James Lopp offered up a two-and-a-half-hour summation in which he told jurors, "In my opinion, no one has the right to take the life of another human being. That is God's right and God's alone. If he [Irvin] took a life, then it is wrong. But that doesn't give you the right to take his life." Religion also played a role during jury selection when Lopp insinuated that any person who could order the death penalty was unchristian. During his summation, Lopp continued, "In each of you is the breath of God as He breathed life into Adam. And that breath of God is in this man's body [pointing to Irvin]."

Holding up to the jurors a volume of the Indiana Criminal Code, Lopp continued, "That's not justice. Not justice in the word of the Master. For at no time during those thirty-two years that he lived on this earth can I find where he took part in governmental affairs."

"At Jesus's trial, they cried, crucify Him. Crucify Him, just like many people are crying in this case."

Referring to the confession, Lopp said, "This thing is so full of holes it's ridiculous. They wanted an oral statement, and they couldn't get one. They wrote one themselves. Is that how low they stoop?"

Howard Sandusky countered with a blistering attack on Irvin and, at one point, turned to the defendant and shouted, "You didn't have to kill him if you didn't want to." Sandusky pivoted toward the jury and said, "He had murder on his mind." Irvin, calmly chewing gum, stared at Sandusky.

Later, Sandusky told the jury, "You gentlemen have a job that's not easy. You have an obligation to society. Society needs some protection, and society has some rights. Is there any reason why this man who sowed the seeds of murder should reap anything but the supreme penalty? A life sentence for Leslie Irvin will be a triumph for him."

Taking a very small role in the state's summation, prosecutor Paul Wever, pointing at Irvin, said, "This man is no different than a mad dog in a community, and we've got to get him out of the community." That summation would not be the last time Evansville residents heard the term "mad dog" when referring to Leslie Irvin.

A couple of days shy of the one-year anniversary of Wesley Kerr's murder, a jury found Leslie Irvin guilty and recommended the death penalty. Formal sentencing was delayed as defense attorneys immediately signaled their plan to file a petition for a new trial. Irvin sat next to his mother, who cried uncontrollably when the clerk of the court read the verdict. On Monday, January 9, Judge A. Dale Eby sentenced Leslie Irvin to die in the electric chair. The judge scheduled his execution for June 12.

Mrs. Mamie Duncan, who had managed to survive being shot twice, could not read the trove of newspaper articles about her assailant and the murderer of her family. The wounds to her head had permanently blinded her. Some Evansville residents, including Mom, wondered whether she'd have been better off being killed. Blindness or death, a crying shame.

Twenty-nine days after being convicted of murdering Wesley Kerr, Leslie Irvin, who once boasted, "There isn't a jail that can hold me," escaped from the "escape-proof" Gibson County jail. On top of a shower stall in the jail, state police and FBI agents found a key made out of cardboard, magazine covers, tin foil, and glue. The key measured three and one-half inches long and was less than one-eighth thick. The end had been covered in soap to make it easier to work within the lock.

As Valentine's Day approached, a handsome piano player dressed in a sharp new suit and sport shirt walked into a San Francisco pawn shop so he could pawn two diamond rings for $1,000. As he attempted to pawn the rings, two police officers entered the shop to perform a routine check. The musician stated that the rings were a gift from his grandmother, a story the pawnbroker did not buy. He quietly alerted the police officers, who confiscated the piano player's identification. A check with the police determined the identification of Victor R. Davis had been stolen. Victor Davis, part of a Hollywood band, had given the man a ride from Las Vegas to Los Angeles. As the officers arrested the calm, sharply dressed man for the stolen identification, he told them, "I'm Leslie Irvin, and I'm wanted in Indiana for six murders. I've been convicted of one, and I'm not guilty of any."

"In a way, I'm glad it's all over with. You don't know how hard it is on the road," Irvin told the San Francisco police. When asked if he was coming back to Indiana, Irvin replied, "Yessir, I guess I'll have to come back." About his arrest, Irvin said, "I wasn't too surprised. I've been expecting to get picked up for quite a while. Getting out of jail in Princeton wasn't too hard.

I made some keys out of cardboard backs of books and went through three doors." He said he made the keys "after three days of experimenting. I escaped from army stockades seven times."

On the run, Irvin had walked, jogged, hitchhiked, and driven crossroads through Mt. Carmel and Cairo, Illinois; West Plains and Springfield, Missouri; Des Moines, Iowa; Cozad, Nebraska; Cheyenne, Rawlings, and Laramie, Wyoming; Salt Lake City, Utah; and Las Vegas, Nevada.

Asked about his execution date of June 12, he said, "Well, that's the reason I left. The whole jury believed I was guilty, even while they were picking the jury and before the trial started," Irvin stated in his conversation with the police.

"My lawyers, Theodore Lockyear and James Lopp, are trying to get me a new trial, but I don't know how that's going to turn out."

That summer, as temperatures hovered near the nineties in Evansville, in Washington, DC, the United States Supreme Court, via a unanimous decision, despite his escape, overturned Leslie Irvin's death sentence. The decision said that Irvin remained subject to retrial for the murder of Wesley Kerr and trials for the five other murders he admitted to after his arrest in 1955. Vanderburgh County prosecutor O. H. Roberts indicated they would rethink their strategy and might try him for the other murders as well. Authorities ensured he would be held in maximum security during his wait for a new trial.

Uncle Bill started to get in a bit of trouble himself, although nothing like the trouble Irvin caused. Uncle Bill had started to drink at an early age, and by the time he turned twenty-one, he knew his way around coolers, beer halls, and taverns. On May 27, 1956, around midnight, at the intersection of Riverside and Kentucky and near The Old Kentucky BBQ, Uncle Bill rearended a car that was sitting at the intersection. Doctors treated Uncle Bill for a possible right knee fracture at Deaconess Hospital, where Grandma Bessie worked in the cafeteria. Alcohol almost certainly played a role in Uncle Bill's Saturday night crash. Mom had learned of Uncle Bill's troubles from Grandma Bessie. Not living under the same roof as her younger brother caused Mom to worry even more about "Poor Bill."

THE BOMB PLANT

● ● ● ● ●

Later that year, as the marigolds began to wilt and Mom and Dad's favorite season settled into the Crossroads of America and they looked forward to wearing sweaters, a letter arrived at Grandpa George and Grandma Mil's house. The letter looked official, so they immediately took it to Dad. His heart sank when he saw the envelope and the return address. Nervously opening the letter, he unfolded it and read:

> *You are hereby ordered for induction into the Armed Forces of the United States and to report at Court House Basement, Evansville, Ind., at 4:30 a.m. on November 6, 1956.*
>
> *It is suggested that you bring with you the following items to take to your first duty station:*
>
> *1 Bath Towel, 1 Face Towel....*

Just over two years after their marriage at Assumption Cathedral, Mom and Dad's comfortable routine ended. Mom cried as Dad stared blankly at the letter. His work at Rainbow Cleaners, "the plant," in no way prepared him for what he was about to experience in Williston, South Carolina.

After basic training, the army assigned Dad to the Savannah River Defense Area, a site near Williston, South Carolina. Known by locals as "The Bomb Plant," the site was constructed in the 1950s by the government in conjunction with DuPont and other private-sector companies to refine plutonium and tritium to be used in America's Cold War nuclear arsenal.

In 1950, the town's population was a mere 896 people. As nuclear production and research peaked, the population of Williston and surrounding areas swelled to more than ten thousand. Many of those new residents labored as employees of DuPont or as contractors, not army personnel. The employees and contractors earned far more than their military counterparts, and Dad resented their good fortune.

Dad worked in the offices of the plant when not manning a 90mm anti-aircraft gun. Soon after his assignment became permanent, Mom joined him, and they moved into a small house just off the base. Mom didn't work outside of the home during their time in Williston. Instead, she decided to keep a neat and tidy house and make sure Dad had decent meals when he retired for the evening. The army's meager pay and their choice to live off-base meant they often couldn't afford the type of food Mom liked to cook.

On many occasions, she got out the ten-cup Mirro aluminum pot with a straining lid that she and Dad received for a wedding gift. Along with that, she put on the counter a bowl of bacon grease. Using a tablespoon, she scooped a large dollop of the grease out of the bowl and dropped it into the Mirro with a crack of the spoon against the side of the pot. She turned on the gas burner and waited for the bacon grease to melt and then slightly smoke. Upon seeing the smoke, she dropped in a third of a cup of popcorn before putting on the lid and securing it with the straining latch. Keeping one of her too-large-for-her-body hands on the handle, she gently shook the popcorn until she heard *pop...pop...pop...pop...pop, pop, pop, pop, p-p-p-pop, p-p-p-p-p-pop* and then she shook vigorously like an overzealous craps player until the popping died down to a *pop.........pop.........pop.* Popcorn for dinner: popcorn and tap water.

Because Mom had time to explore Williston via bus rides or long walks, she witnessed the hatred directed toward African Americans and was often, although white as ivory, the target of similar hatred because she chose to clean her own house and perform menial chores that locals considered beneath white people. She was called "n*****" on more than one occasion for doing such work.

While she hated being called vile names, she was more appalled by what she experienced when shopping downtown. "Black people would step off the sidewalk and stop while we passed. I never thought that was right. Why should they step off and stop for us?"

While Mom witnessed firsthand the hate Grandpa Al taught her, Dad trained to use an M1 rifle, a .30 carbine, a submachine gun (SMG), a rocket launcher, and the 90mm anti-aircraft gun to protect the Savannah River Defense Site from a potential attack by America's Cold War enemy, the Soviet Union. Dad also learned how to drive half-ton and two-and-a-half-ton trucks. He came home virtually every night with dusty clothes. Ever the cleaner, Mom went outside and shook the clothes before washing them with soap and water. When Aunt Kate went to Williston to visit Mom and Dad, the dustiness of Dad's clothes shocked her. "It's like he's working in a woodworking factory."

Dad exaggerated and embellished stories like a fisherman. Whenever he took off an acrylic sweater in the winter, like the night we looked at pictures, he used to say that it shot a three-foot electrical arc. He claimed that when he was a kid, he could take a quarter to the movie house, watch a double feature, get a large popcorn and soda, and after the movie, a sack of hamburgers, and still have change left. He once claimed a hammer he bought for five dollars was the "deal of the century." His exaggerations made us laugh but also made us doubt many of his stories, including the ones about "The Bomb Plant."

He spoke of ponds that glowed in the dark and dustiness that hung in the air like clouds of mosquitos in the

Okefenokee Swamp where he and a few fellow soldiers encountered an alligator and shot it with a .22 caliber rifle, only to have the bullet bounce off the prehistoric creature. Depending on how far away they were from the alligator, that is, I believe, conceivable.

Dad's exaggeration contrasted with Mom's pragmatism and honesty, so no one ever doubted her depictions of hatred, bigotry, and loathing of black or brown people. When telling those stories, her eyes moistened and stared through the table, the floor, or the wall as if she could see the bigots and their victims in our kitchen.

On November 6, 1958, Dad's active duty ended, and he and Mom, seven months pregnant, returned home. They could not have been happier to leave the South and to have a little one on the way. Back in Evansville, everyone in the family, including Mom and Dad, referred to Rainbow Cleaners, not the Savannah River Defense Area, as "The Plant."

Mom's worries for Uncle Bill proved worthy as the solidly built fireplug of a young man got into trouble several more times. He made the front page for stealing two twelve-can packs of beer.

April 1, 1959
Police Hold Man Injured During Chase
Driver Pursued

The story wouldn't have garnered much attention except that after leaving the tavern with the stolen beer, he led police on a two-county car chase after being involved in a hit-and-run. He suffered head injuries after finally crashing his car on Highway 62, five miles east of Boonville, a nearby town. Uncle Bill spent a night in the hospital before being arrested by police upon his discharge the next morning.

Mom's worries about Uncle Bill were soon joined by worries about her not-quite-three-month-old son, David Samuel. My brother Sam, as everyone called him, the firstborn to Mom and Dad after several miscarriages, garnered lots of attention from both the Melchior and Evans sides of the family. Finally, something they could all agree on: Sam's a cute kid. Mom was over the moon.

She doted on Sam: bathing, holding, kissing, hugging, smiling, and laughing with him. She showed him off to friends and family and, although a worrier, allowed others to hold him too. Mom had found her calling. "That Dots is a hell of a worker" and "That Dots is a hell of a cook" continued to evolve. "That Dots is a hell of a mom," they now said.

Mom's natural energy and fast walking passed straight through to Sam as he grew into a rambunctious rascal with enough energy for two kids. While Mom doted on and chased Sam around, Uncle Bill continued courting trouble, including one disturbing incident.

May 5, 1961
Man Calling on Housewife Is Arrested in Harassment

Police again arrested Uncle Bill, this time for calling a woman over the phone more than six times and asking her if he could meet her somewhere for a date. When the woman complained to the police, they set up a sting at her house. Uncle Bill showed up, and the police arrested him for harassment. He denied calling the woman and said he was only there to inquire about buying a beagle. He also told the police his name was Don, not Bill. Don happened to be his best friend's name. Some friend Uncle Bill turned out to be.

With a couple of arrests under his belt and belligerence in his heart, doctors, authorities, or perhaps Grandma Bessie or Grandpa Al decided to send Uncle Bill for treatment. According to Mom and Dad and Aunt Mary, who once worked at the Evansville State Hospital, that treatment included electroshock therapy.

THE OLD KENTUCKY

● ● ● ● ● ●

The border between Indiana and Kentucky twists and turns before eventually bending into the horseshoe at Dress Plaza in Evansville. Shifting courses of the river mean that one can stand on the northern side of the river and be in Kentucky and near Ellis Park, where horse racing is legal and nearly a religion. This explains why Evansville gamblers who prefer horses to betting black or red or hoping for a blackjack don't have to cross the river to bet the horses at Ellis Park.

In May '62, after one of his frequent nights of bar hopping, Rudy Ziemer drove his new-model Cadillac across the bridge connecting Indiana and Kentucky. Cruising downtown Henderson, a familiar haunt because he often kept his Truscotteer docked at the Henderson Yacht Club, an inebriated Rudy turned down Horseshoe Bend Road and drove toward the eponymous twist in the Ohio River.

At the end of the road, Rudy's car became mired in thick, claylike floodwater mud. Rudy sat in the driver's seat, gunning the engine, asking for all its horsepower to no avail as the back tires spun like tops. As he desperately continued mashing on the accelerator, the engine overheated and burst into flames that shot out from beneath the dashboard. Drunkenly reaching for the handle, Rudy managed to open the door and roll out of the car into the mud but not before suffering first and second-degree burns on his face and hands. Rudy crawled backward through the mud as he watched an orange and yellow inferno destroy his treasured car. Despite his burns, Rudy had no choice but to walk almost twenty miles back to downtown Henderson.

In the *Evansville Press* account of the car fire the following day, the trooper who had picked up Rudy after noticing him wandering the streets described Rudy's Cadillac as a total loss, except for one tire. Under the care of a doctor, Rudy recovered from the burns at home. Little did he know, trouble with Ohio River floodwaters would begin bouncing around him like a pill on a slowing roulette wheel.

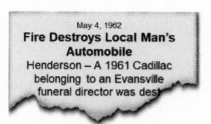

May 4, 1962
Fire Destroys Local Man's Automobile
Henderson – A 1961 Cadillac belonging to an Evansville funeral director was des[...]

Only a few miles from the bridge where Rudy had crossed into downtown Henderson, Evansville's south-east side offered several restaurants, including the drive-in Hamilton's, a family joint called The Farmer's Daughter, and The Old Kentucky, a bar and restaurant that didn't always check identification and therefore was popular with partiers, some underage as well as older folks like my Great-Uncle Bud and Forrest Arvin. Ten months after the fire and fully recovered, Rudy drove around the southeast side in his new Dodge station wagon, a car that might not be as jinxed or attract as much attention as his preferred Cadillacs.

While Rudy cruised, Carole Sue Gentry, a recent graduate of Benjamin Bosse High School, and her friend Melvina "Mel" Shutt got ready to go out and meet a few boys. Carole's petite stature and short hairstyle matched her understated nature. She participated in the Seventeen Club, whatever that was, and helped in the nurse's office. Carole and Mel planned to spend the night, like Rudy, cruising the southeast side before meeting up with a group of army paratroopers on leave from Fort Campbell, Kentucky. The women had been on a few dates with two of the group, Bill Thompson and Pat Pirrie, and expected to see them that night. Thompson, originally from East Gary, Indiana, enlisted out of high school, as did Pirrie, who hailed from Southgate, California.

Carole and Mel stopped first at Hamilton's and sipped on Cokes while sitting in Carole's car. As their loud slurping straws signaled their last drops of Coke, they noticed a Chevy convertible that, despite cooler temperatures, rolled into the parking lot with the top down. Thompson and Pirrie sat in the passenger seats as their buddy, also an army paratrooper, Bob Greymont, drove.

Greymont backed his car next to Carole's, and Carole and Mel stepped out of their vehicle to chat with the three young servicemen, all in their twenties. After a bit of small talk and some convincing, the women decided to go "convertible riding" with Greymont, Thompson, Pirrie, and a fourth paratrooper that Carole and Mel did not know. Twenty minutes of chilly driving proved enough for Carole and Mel, so they convinced the paratroopers to take them back to Hamilton's. Attempting to park his car, Greymont backed it into a ditch behind the restaurant. Like Rudy's car ten months earlier, the Chevy proved a stubborn beast.

Carole and Mel decided to go to Mel's house to get some chains that might help them get Greymont's car out of the ditch, but by the time they got back to Hamilton's and Greymont's car, there was no sign of the paratroopers, just the disabled Chevy convertible.

Driving away from Hamilton's in Carole's car, the two women cruised around looking for the paratroopers. After driving by Hamilton's and The Farmer's Daughter came up empty, they drove to The Old Kentucky. Carole pulled into the parking lot as an old beat-up black car stopped near the side of the road. Greymont, Thompson, Pirrie, and the fourth paratrooper, whom they later learned was Frederick Easton, filed out of the clunker like they were jumping from a plane. Carole and Mel didn't drink, so they sat in the parking lot and waited as the boys went inside to have more drinks. Outside, directly in Carole's line of sight, Rudy Ziemer's station wagon gleaned like a diamond under the glow of a streetlamp.

The Old Kentucky, a dining room and tavern, bustled that night, according to Margie Stephenson, a career waitress who had been working there for the past five years. As the solo waitress working that night with bartender Arnold Jewel, she didn't have time to notice everyone or everything going on in the place, but a few customers did bring to her attention a man sitting at the bar because of the way he drank a glass of water. Margie Stephenson knew that man as Rudy Ziemer.

Rudy's sartorial choices, as consistent as his barhopping and drinking, meant, on this night as virtually all others, a suit, white dress shirt, and impeccably tied tie. His stylish wardrobe, rather tall stature, coiffed if slightly receding hair, and prominent chin dimple meant Rudy looked every bit the part of a successful businessman except for his two-handed, clumsy, and unsure sips of water.

He had been in the bar since nearly nine o'clock. Bartender Jewel knew Rudy as a regular at The Old Kentucky. Jewel didn't serve Rudy that night because, to him, it seemed Rudy had indulged in enough alcohol somewhere else. While Rudy drank from his water glass using both hands, Greymont, Thompson, and Pirrie sat at a table singing, laughing, and talking loudly enough to offend dining families.

As their antics continued, Jewel told Stephenson not to serve the paratroopers any more alcohol. Nevertheless, the paratroopers stayed on as diners continued leaving. As Rudy stared blankly at the bar, Easton, near pass-out drunk, stumbled toward him. Greymont followed Easton, and within a few minutes, Jewel noticed Rudy, still drinking water, "having trouble with two Fort Campbell paratroopers." As Jewel walked toward Rudy, he noticed one paratrooper had a hold of Ziemer.

While Jewel did not recognize Easton, he did know Greymont, Thompson, and Pirrie from their previous outings at The Old Kentucky. Easton was new to the crew.

Jewel reminded the paratroopers he would not serve them any drinks and to leave Rudy alone. After a trip to the bathroom, the frustrated and angry paratroopers exited The Old Kentucky through the front door while Rudy continued to sit at the bar holding his water glass.

In the parking lot, Easton stumbled toward Carole's car, opened the back door, and immediately passed out in the back seat near Mel. Looking out of the windshield, Carole noticed Pirrie standing near Rudy's station wagon when the door of The Old Kentucky swung open, and Rudy staggered out. At his car, Rudy leaned against the driver's side door when Pirrie approached. Carole watched Pirrie and Rudy exchange words she could not hear. Pirrie opened the door to Rudy's car and helped Rudy get in. He looked toward Carole and then The Old Kentucky as Thompson walked across the back of Rudy's car and got in the front passenger seat. Before getting in the car, Pirrie looked once more at Carole and motioned for her to follow. Greymont sprinted in front of Carole's car, opened the door, and sat in the passenger seat.

Carole watched as Pirrie slowly backed Rudy's station wagon out from under the glowing streetlight. With Rudy squeezed between himself and Thompson, Pirrie drove Rudy's car out of The Old Kentucky parking lot. As instructed, Carole followed. The two cars headed north on Riverside Drive.

Carole Sue Gentry followed closely behind the white station wagon as Pat Pirrie drove Rudy's car down Lodge Avenue near the Colonial Apartments and Holy Spirit Catholic Church. Unfamiliar with Evansville streets, he slowed Rudy's car to a crawl at a dead-end on Marshall Street and Ridgeway Avenue, near where Great-Uncle Bud lived in a townhome filled with classical, jazz, opera, and blues albums, books, Playboy magazines, and plenty of booze. A bachelor since Doris Mae divorced him, Great-Uncle Bud had morphed into a '60s bachelor who knew his way around a kitchen. He shared the moniker "one hell of a cook" with Mom.

As the car stopped, Rudy pawed Pirrie's thigh and attempted to kiss him. Startled and enraged, Pirrie struck Rudy in the face with the back of his right hand.

Infuriated at Rudy's advances toward Pirrie, Thompson then punched and karate-chopped Rudy in the face and neck. While Thompson continued viciously beating Rudy, Pirrie turned on the light. Carole stopped directly behind Rudy's car. She noticed Thompson "striking at something" in the shadowy car, she later testified. Thompson continued beating Rudy about the face and neck, breaking his glasses, and eventually rendering him unconscious. As Rudy slumped in the bench seat and gasped for air, Thompson reached into Rudy's jacket pocket and lifted his wallet. A few yards away, Carole, her girlfriend, Mel Shutt, and Bob Greymont watched as Pirrie and Thompson quickly exited Rudy's still-running station wagon and ran toward Carole's car. Pirrie squeezed in the back while Thompson pushed Greymont into the middle and jumped in the front before slamming the door. Stuck at the dead-end, Carole T-turned out of the parking lot road. Rudy's Dodge idled in the glow of a streetlight as he lay unconscious in the front seat. While Rudy struggled for breath and consciousness, Great-Uncle Bud slumbered into the night.

As Carole drove, Pirrie and Thompson argued about fingerprints while Thompson searched Rudy's wallet. Thompson looked at Rudy's driver's license and identified him by name. Not being from Evansville, the Ziemer name registered like Smith, Jones, or Johnson to the army paratroopers. Evansville-born Carole or Mel must have certainly recognized it from the prominent funeral homes and frequent newspaper articles about Rudy. Whether it was the fear of leaving behind fingerprints or the attention that beating and robbing a locally famous man would generate, the group decided they had to go back, so Carole steered her car toward Marshall Avenue. Arriving back at Rudy's car, Carole noticed Rudy now hanging halfway out of the driver's side door, his head dangling toward the pavement. Carole stopped her car as Thompson jumped out and ran toward Rudy's car. Carole watched as Thompson shoved Rudy back into the car, got into the driver's seat, and began driving. Carole waited for Thompson to exit the dead-end and once again followed the station wagon. Thompson drove around aimlessly for twenty or so minutes, unsure where to go or what to do, while Carole followed. Frustrated at the confusion and aimless direction, the group in Carole's car argued before both cars stopped. After a short argument, Thompson followed Carole.

Near the top of the Weinbach levee, built after the 1937 Ohio River flood, Carole pulled her car off the side of the road as Thompson drove Rudy's car to the top of the levee near a barricade. Pirrie and Greymont got out of Carole's car and moved the barricade to the side of the road so Thompson could drive Rudy's car down the south side of the levee. As Carole and Mel watched, the glowing red taillights of Rudy's station wagon disappeared like setting suns as the car rolled toward the bottom of the earthen bank.

After a few minutes, Pirrie and Greymont trudged back up the levee and stood on top before walking back to Carole's car. Minutes later, Thompson, his pants dripping with Ohio River floodwater, slowly walked toward them. He sat down in the front passenger seat and instructed Carole to drive.

Packed in Carole's car, the group decided to go to the apartment of Kay Goble, another of Carole's girl-friends. Kay had dated Greymont a few times and knew the group well. Along the way, the group of two women and three men—Easton remained passed out—decided not to talk about what happened. Upon their arrival, Kay noticed Thompson's shoes were muddy and his pants soaked; complaining he was cold, Thompson asked Kay for a blanket. She loaned him one. Thompson told Carole "that he was no good for her in view of what had happened that night." Mel left the apartment shortly thereafter.

Around midnight, with Easton still passed out in the back seat, Carole drove the men back to Greymont's stuck-in-the-ditch convertible. The three men eventu-ally freed the car, woke Easton, and returned to Fort Campbell, Kentucky, the long night in Evansville finally over.

FOUND

● ●

The following day, the Ohio River crested at nearly forty-three feet, just above the forty-two-foot flood stage. For Evansville residents, the Ohio River waters, flowing east to west toward the horseshoe bend, wrapped the city, especially downtown, in a beautiful bow, a bow that sometimes became a lasso or, worse, a noose, choking the city.

Three boys walking along the Weinbach levee, an earthen portion of Evansville's protection against floodwaters, found personal papers belonging to Rudy Ziemer. They alerted authorities, who immediately formed a search team, including a dragging party and skin divers. Chief Deputy Jerry Riney said that a deputy suspected Rudy Ziemer and his car rested beneath the brownish floodwaters lapping at the earthen levee.

As police and other officials combed the Weinbach levee where the boys had found Rudy's personal papers, one searcher spotted an aerial antenna jutting out of the floodwaters. Firemen attempted to attach hooks to the submerged vehicle but failed, so a State Police scuba diver dove beneath the waters and attached lines to it.

As the searchers watched, a tow truck pulled a 1962 white Dodge station wagon from the waters. Mud streaked down the sides of the car like running mascara. Inside the car, Rudy's lifeless body slumped against the driver's-side door. His necktie, like a noose, had been pulled tightly around his neck.

While authorities drove Rudy's body to his own funeral home, police retraced Rudy's stumbles through Evansville, spoke to witnesses, and eventually drove one hundred miles south to Fort Campbell, Kentucky, where they interrogated Thompson, Pirrie, Greymont, and Easton. In a matter of hours, William Thompson confessed to driving Rudy's car into the Ohio River flood waters on the south side of the levee. Police arrested Thompson, Pirrie, Greymont, and Easton. They later released Easton after learning from the other paratroopers he had passed out after leaving The Old Kentucky and never woke up until the long drive back to Fort Campbell.

Headlines informed locals of Rudy's potential demise. Beneath the headlines, lurking in small paragraphs, Rudy's troubled history began to emerge like the cicadas that occasionally swarm Indiana. Reporters reminded Evansville's conservative residents that "court records show that three times in the last seventeen years, Ziemer faced court charges stemming from alleged unnatural sexual relations. None of the cases, which originated in 1946, 1948 and 1952, resulted in convictions, but on

one occasion, he voluntarily entered a St. Louis hospital for treatment."

That paragraph reignited debates, or more accurately arguments, like Grandma Mil's with her Clabber Club friends. Shouts bounced off metal kitchen cabinets and hung among the cigarette smoke, beers, and snacks.

"They killed him. They killed him. Did he deserve that? Is that what you wanted?"

"They had a right, a right to protect themselves from a pervert, which he obviously was."

"They had a right to kill him. That's what you're saying?"

"Yes, they had a right. Who knows what he might have done to those boys?"

"One man against three paratroopers. Do you really think he could've done anything to those men? They were men, not boys."

"Well, we'll have to disagree. If I were them, I would've done the same thing."

"You would've killed him? They killed my friend, and you would've done the same thing? That's what you're saying?"

"Yeah, that's what I'm saying."

"You knew Rudy, too. And you're saying you would've killed him?"

"Yeah, I guess so."

"This game is over. You need to leave."

Conversations like that occurred throughout the city. Rudy had some friends but a lot more detractors.

Three paratroopers against one man, three friends in a Clabber game against one woman, and three boys walking along a levee. Three sodomy charges against Rudy, never a conviction. Three horses lived to graze another day.

Rudy Ziemer drowned, plain and simple. While he had cuts in his mouth caused by an external force and bruises on his nose near where his glasses rested, and discoloration of the neck near the collar line, Rudy Ziemer's death was definitely due to asphyxiation by drowning. This according to the pathologist and coroner who performed the autopsy in the basement operating room of Ziemer Funeral Home.

On Tuesday, March 19, 1963, a couple of months after Mom had given birth to Amy Louise, morning rain showers subsided and gave way to cloudy skies and temperatures warming to nearly sixty degrees. Grandpa George had completed the "In by Ten out by Two" bundles of clothes that very few Rainbow Cleaners customers retrieved the same day. Six o'clock closing time gave him, Grandma Mil, Mom, and Dad enough time to go home, clean up a bit, change clothes, and head over to Rudy Ziemer's visitation that was scheduled to begin at 7:00 p.m. Because Great-Uncle Bud wore suits to work every day at Strouse & Bros., Evansville's finest men's store, he could head directly to the funeral home.

The parking lot and adjacent streets were filled with clean and shiny cars because no one should drive a dirty car to a visitation or, God forbid, to a funeral procession in Evansville, where church-going citizens respect the departed.

I imagine Great-Uncle Bud in his Hickey Freeman suit with a Countess Mara tie, and Dad and Grandpa George in dark ensembles with thin black ties. Mom and Grandma Mil would have worn conservative, perfectly pressed dresses. The spotless and wrinkle-free clothes of the group fit them well. That is a certainty. Another certainty is that they wouldn't be late.

Members of St. Anthony parish and St. Henry Society recited the Rosary at 7:00 p.m., and the Men's Club of Christ the King Catholic Church did the same at 7:30 p.m. By 1963, Grandpa George's faith had evaporated like the steam he used to remove spots on clothes, and Great-Uncle Bud despised religion and often told anyone who would listen that heaven sounded like the most boring place imaginable—even if he was given the job of holding God's left nut, as he not-so-delicately put it—so not being late was simply a matter of courtesy, not devotion.

Rudy's sisters dressed his body in a suit, white shirt, and tie, all cleaned and pressed at Rainbow. After the visitation, the family of five sharply dressed mourners went to Grandpa George and Grandma Mil's house on Reis Avenue. In the small kitchen at the back of the bungalow, they sat around the round table with a red and white checkered tablecloth, drinking PBRs, smoking cigarettes, and wondering how such a tragedy had happened to their friend.

Because Grandpa George considered shutting Rainbow Cleaners for even a few hours unthinkable, they did not attend Rudy's funeral the next morning with the three hundred or so mourners who did. After high mass, shiny, gleaming cars slithered and snaked their way along the two-mile route to St. Joseph Catholic Cemetery on Evansville's west side and adjacent to Mesker Park Zoo, home of Bunny the elephant. Bunny often spent much of her time in a too-small cage resembling a jail cell.

After interment, the priest performed a graveside rosary service because Rudy needed all the prayers he could get. The mid-fifties temperature and slight breeze made the long ceremony more bearable. A few miles away, Ted Ziemer handled funeral services for another family at Fountain Terrace Chapel. He did not attend his brother's funeral, nor did his wife or children.

A few months later, on July 2, despite a confession, a judge released the three paratroopers on $10,000 bail each. All three returned to their respective homes in Indiana, Massachusetts, and California.

As farmers harvested their crops, high school football teams practiced and played, and residents unpacked sweaters as temperatures cooled and skies greyed, many Evansville residents worried more about their beloved

Indiana University Hoosier basketball team than a dead undertaker. They learned that Dr. Moehlenkamp had offered Evansville high school basketball player Tom Niemeier, who had received scholarship offers from both Indiana University and Purdue University, a three-hundred-dollar-a-month clothing allowance if Niemeier would play at Indiana. The six-foot-eight, tow-headed Niemeier had also received an offer of one hundred dollars a month for working in a frat house kitchen from then-coach Branch McCracken. Niemeier had commented to some that he was confused by Dr. Moehlenkamp's offer as he had no idea how he could spend so much money on clothes. Niemeier eventually chose Purdue, but an investigation followed into both schools' efforts to recruit the basketball star. College officials did not discipline Moehlenkamp for his attempt to influence the all-star recruit.

The next year, just after Mom gave birth to Andrew George, named after Grandpa Al and Grandpa George, Dr. Moehlenkamp drove east on West Mill Road, north of the horseshoe bend in the Ohio River. He did not see three-year-old Joseph Arthur Beckman, running with his older brother to a Stringtown Road playground. Moehlenkamp's car, traveling thirty miles per hour, struck the young boy after he darted into the street. The impact hurled Joseph's body thirteen feet from the impact. According to witnesses, Dr. Moehlenkamp immediately began artificial respiration and heart massage but was unable to resuscitate the young boy. According to Deputy Coroner Stonestreet, Joseph died of a broken neck and internal injuries. The death was ruled an accident, and authorities did not charge Dr. Moehlenkamp. He had escaped discipline and scrutiny in the recruiting scandal and in the death of a young boy but would soon find trouble with the law amid many encounters with my Uncle Bill.

CHANGE OF VENUE

● ● ● ● ● ●

Attorney Howard Sandusky, representing defendant Robert Greymont, requested Rudy Ziemer's murder trial be moved out of Evansville's Vanderburgh County because he believed Greymont could not receive a fair trial in the county due to the extensive news coverage the case received. Attorneys for William Thompson and Patrick Pirrie did not object to Sandusky's motion.

Boonville, Indiana, rests among mostly flat, sometimes slightly rolling farmland almost twenty miles northeast of Evansville. The 1960 census put Boonville's more than 97 percent white population at just under five thousand people. Another twenty miles to the east sits Lincoln City, named after Abraham Lincoln's family and where young Abe spent many of his formative years. The future sixteenth president spent time in Boonville, coming to town to borrow books from attorney John Adams Brackenridge and to watch Brackenridge argue cases. These facts earned Boonville the moniker "where Lincoln learned the law."

Thompson, Greymont, and Pirrie, out on bail more than six hundred days since Rudy Ziemer's murder, had traveled to Evansville for the trial from their homes in East Gary, Indiana, Needham, Massachusetts, and Southgate, California. The trio now made a daily trek east along the lazy, rolling two-lane Highway 62 toward Boonville, the same highway Uncle Bill had used to try and evade police for stealing two twelve-packs of beer.

Many residents of Boonville worked on their farms or at the nearby Alcoa aluminum smelting pot in Newburgh, Indiana, while some, labored at both. The trial's move to Boonville surely caused excitement for some residents, but for others gave rise to fear they would be taken away from their necessary work to serve as jurors on a trial they cared little about. Five hundred twenty-four prospective jurors, more than 10 percent of Boonville's population, received jury notices.

While the five-hundred-plus residents worried about their fate serving on a jury, acting US attorney general Nicholas Katzenbach hinted that the murders of civil rights workers James Chaney, Michael Schwerner, and Andrew Goodman, killed in Philadelphia, Mississippi, would finally be solved.

In Evansville and Boonville, the week began with unusually high temperatures near the seventies, while in New York City, heat of a different type emerged. The United Council of Harlem Organizations, made up of eighty-two organizations, including the NAACP, called the ruling of the police shooting of a fifteen-year-old boy a "whitewash." A council spokesman said, "Harlem is seething with resentment and unrest."

While headlines from New York and Washington, DC, made Evansville's papers, the trial of three active-duty paratroopers charged with killing a gay funeral home director either did not warrant space in big city newspapers such as the *New York Times* or the *Washington Post* or no one outside of the Ohio River Valley had ever heard of the case.

As the defendants sat quietly, jury selection commenced with the questioning of twenty-four prospective jurors. By noon, more than twenty of the twenty-four had been excused.

As potential jurors came and went, the three defendants sat at a table, flanked by their attorneys. Over and over and over, they heard prosecutor O. H. Roberts, whose dad, O. H. Roberts Sr., had once represented Rudy Ziemer in a civil case regarding his 1939 car crash and considered Rudy a friend, ask each juror, "If the evidence justifies it, would you put these men to death?" Or framed another way, "Would you oppose the death penalty?"

One after another and another, they stated:

"Yes, I don't believe in capital punishment."

Or:

"I'm against capital punishment."

Or:

"I'm for the death penalty."

While Roberts vetted jurors for their opinion on the death penalty, defense attorneys asked jurors again and again and again, "If Ziemer were so drunk at the time that there was confusion as to the cause of death, would you give the defendants the benefit of the doubt?"

Or:

"Have you ever been approached by a pervert?"

Or:

"Do you think a person has a right to protect himself from a homosexual attack?"

Or:

"Are you familiar with the reputation of Rudolph Ziemer?"

In all, 154 potential jurors answered the same or similar questions over the course of four days. By the end of the fourth day, O. H. Roberts and the defense attorneys seated a jury of twelve white men, one of those being farmer and Alcoa worker James J. Wathen. Two alternates, also white men, were selected and sat near the twelve-seat jury box.

As Wathen and other jurors prepared for what could be a long trial, Carole Sue Gentry sat in her apartment contemplating whether to testify. Alone with her thoughts, Carole decided to go to her girlfriend's apartment. What she didn't know as she left her apartment was that her one-time friend, Melvina, now Mrs. Patrick Pirrie, and Patrick himself were scouring Evansville in search of Miss Gentry.

BEST KNOWN QUEER

● ● ● ● ● ●

Six hundred fifteen days after Rudy Ziemer drowned in the Ohio River floodwaters, the three defendants' trial began. Cloudy skies and another spell of unseasonably mild, mid-seventies temperatures greeted the attorneys, jurors, friends, family, and curious onlookers as they climbed the courthouse stairs.

Across four equal-length streets, shops, restaurants, and an ice cream parlor surrounded the three-story, four-columned brick courthouse. Erected two years before Rudy's birth, the courthouse anchored downtown Boonville like a block of granite. Walking up the stairs, Robert Greymont, Patrick Pirrie, and William Thompson wore almost-matching dark suits, white dress shirts, and thin dark ties. Their closely cropped hair matched the crispness of the creases in their trousers. Three clean-cut all-American boys could not have been a more accurate description, and the handsome trio could not have found a more welcoming town than Boonville.

O. H. Roberts had decided to try all three defendants together, though different verdicts could be found for each defendant, who were all represented by their own Evansville-based attorneys. Howard Sandusky represented Greymont; James Lopp, one of Leslie Irvin's attorneys, represented Pirrie; and Paul Wever represented Thompson. The sharp-dressed defendants, looking more like interviewees for a bank manager-trainee job than defendants in a murder case, sat at the defense table in the third-floor courtroom with their hands properly folded as if they were about to answer the question, "So, why do you want to be a banker and where do you see yourself in three years?"

In his opening statement, Roberts told the all-male, all-white jury that Thompson, Greymont, and Pirrie "intentionally and with premeditation" killed Rudy Ziemer. Roberts and his prosecution team, Terry Dietsch and Boonville prosecutor Burley Scales, then began the testimony phase by calling as their first witness the scuba diver who located Rudy's 1963 Dodge station wagon. The diver testified that both front windows of the car were rolled down when he located the car some seventy yards from the edge of the Ohio River floodwaters. Under cross-examination, the diver said he could not tell where the car entered the water or who had put it there.

Prosecutors continued their strategy of focusing on the facts of the case, most notably Rudy's car, his body in the car, and the cause of death. A state trooper testified that the car's ignition was turned on and that the car was in drive when searchers found it. As Sandusky cross-examined the trooper, the defense strategy became crystal clear to everyone in the third-floor courtroom. Sandusky asked the trooper if the Rudy Ziemer found in the car was the same Rudy Ziemer that had been charged with sodomy years before. Roberts and his team immediately and vehemently objected to that line of questioning and reminded the jury and judge that Rudy Ziemer was not on trial.

Judge Addison Beavers sustained the objection and asked the jury to disregard the question. That disregarded question marked the beginning of an aggressive defense.

The defense's smear campaign did not focus solely on Rudy's reputation as a "pervert" homosexual who had thrice been charged with sodomy. The three seasoned attorneys also planned to attack his reputation as an alcoholic. Judge Beavers allowed testimony along those lines, including Rudy's multiple arrests and convictions for driving under the influence. That testimony, deemed relevant, bolstered the defense strategy of suggesting that perhaps Rudy died of alcoholism and not drowning as the coroner in the case had ruled. Deputy Coroner Verner Stonestreet, who assisted with the autopsy, testified that Rudy's .28 blood alcohol level at the time of his death indicated he was drunk when he died.

Day two of the trial saw an increase in the number of spectators as the previous day's newspaper accounts and gossip surrounding the three handsome defendants swirled about Evansville and Boonville. Robert Flynn, an *Evansville Press* reporter, wrote:

> *For the growing audience in this stuffy courtroom presided over by Judge Addison Beavers, the young defendants present a center of attention.*
>
> *The people came to see three obviously tough young hoods capable of living up to Roberts' opening speech—that they were the men who beat up Ziemer, robbed him and then two of them stood by while the third one drove the unconscious victim into the floodwaters.*
>
> *Instead, they are seeing three clean-cut young men, who, as one prospective juror put it last week, "don't look like murderers." That prospective juror was finally excused by the prosecution when he insisted that he had a fixed opinion in the case. He said he just couldn't believe that the defendants were guilty.*

Spectators in the courtroom included Greymont's wife and mother and Thompson's parents. Also in the courtroom, sitting behind the defendants, was the former Melvina Shutt, now Mrs. Patrick Pirrie, holding the couple's young son, Danny. Judge Beavers ordered Mrs. Pirrie out of the courtroom during certain testimony because she was scheduled to appear as a witness for the prosecution.

The cause of Rudy's death continued to be the topic of testimony during day two of the trial. Dr. Donald Godwin, the pathologist who performed the autopsy, testified that Rudy drowned. He also detailed the numerous bruises and cuts around Rudy's mouth, nose, and collar line but did not offer an explanation for those injuries.

Carole Sue Gentry kept her head low during most of her testimony. She also fought to maintain control of her voice.

"Now you say you've known these three, uh, defendants, Carole. Have you been out with any of them socially?" O. H. Roberts asked.

"Yes."

"Who?" Roberts continued.

"Bill Thompson."

Roberts continued to question Carole as the three defendants and their supporters watched the diminutive and nervous twenty-one-year-old. She testified that she, along with Melvina Shutt and the defendant soldiers, went to The Old Kentucky Barbeque multiple times the night of Rudy Ziemer's murder. Roberts asked Carole about the group's first visit to The Old Kentucky.

"Carole, did anyone that went into The Old Kentucky Barbeque bring anything back to the car with them?"

"Yes."

"What was it?"

"They purchased some wine."

Carole explained, after an ill-fated convertible ride that resulted in Bob Greymont's Chevrolet convertible getting stuck in a ditch, the group eventually all met back at The Old Kentucky BBQ.

"As we were pulling into the lot, there was an old black car leaving, and it stops, and the three defendants got out of the car."

"Alright, then, what happened?" Roberts asked.

"Well, I parked mine up next to The Old Kentucky, and I got out of the car, and I walked over towards them away from The Old Kentucky," Carole continued.

"And what did you do then?"

"I stopped, and I talked to Bill Thompson for a while."

"And after you talked to him, what did you do?"

"Well, we walked back towards my car, and I got back in my car."

Roberts continued to question Carole as she kept her head low and avoided eye contact with any of the defendants. Roberts eventually asked her about seeing Rudy Ziemer's car.

"Pat was standing over by the Ziemer car, what I know now as the Ziemer car."

"What kind of car was it?" Roberts asked.

"It was a new-model station wagon."

"Who was standing by the car?"

"Pat Pirrie."

"Was anyone else there?"

"There was a man in the front seat."

"There was a man in the front seat of the car?"

"Yes."

"Did you notice anything unusual about the actions of the man in the seat of the car?"

"I noticed he was drunk."

"Were you in your own car at that time?"

"Yes."

"Who else was in your car at that time?"

"Bob Greymont got in my car, and Mel Shutt was in the back seat, and Fred Easton got in the back seat."

"Was Easton another paratrooper?"

"Yes, he was."

"What was his condition when he got in the back seat of your car, Carole?"

"Very, very drunk."

Carole stated that while Easton slumbered, she continued to watch as Pirrie and Thompson loitered around Rudy's car, but not before being interrupted by another girlfriend who wanted to talk.

"And then what happened?"

"I don't exactly know what went on then because a girlfriend of mine pulled up alongside of me, and I was talking to her."

"And, uh, when did you next observe the Ziemer car, Carole?"

"Pat was signaling for me to—for some reason—to follow him."

"Where was Pat at that time when he was signaling for you to follow him?"

"He was getting in the car, the Ziemer car."

"What side was he getting in?"

"The driver's side."

"And, uh, who else was in the car?"

"Well, Ziemer was in the middle, and Thompson was getting in on the passenger side."

"Were they all in the front seat?"

"Yes sir."

"Now, uh, what happened then, after he signaled to you, Carole?"

"He left with the car and...."

"Which way did he go?"

"He headed north on Forty-One."

"Towards what street?"

"Riverside."

"And what did you do then?"

"I followed."

Carole explained to the jurors and the prosecutor that after a short drive, including one stop along the side of the road when Pirrie pulled Rudy's car over, and Carole pulled beside them on the passenger side, Pirrie drove Ziemer's car to the edge of a dead-end street. It's there that Carole noticed the interior light of Rudy's car came on, and in that light, she saw Thompson. "It looked like he was striking at something," she testified.

Carole recalled that Pirrie and Thompson then got out of Rudy's station wagon and came back to Carole's car. After the two men got in her car, Carole drove off, leaving Rudy in his still-running, illuminated car. As Carole, Melvina, Pirrie, Thompson, Greymont, and Easton, still passed out, all rode around, the group talked of fingerprints and Rudy's wallet.

"Carole, did you hear any specific conversation between the defendants during that time?" O. H. Roberts asked.

"Yes."

"What did they say, if you can remember?" Roberts continued.

"As I said before, exact words I can't say, but it was in relation to...they were talking about his condition and fingerprints being around on the car and such."

"Whose condition were they talking about, Carole?"

"Ziemer's."

"Carole, do you know if they had any of Ziemer's belongings with them when they came back to the car?"

"They had his billfold."

"Did you see the billfold?"

"No, not actually."

Carole went on to explain that she heard them talk about it, especially that it didn't have any money in it, just personal papers. Roberts then asked her a couple of questions that Carole answered, uttering perhaps the most damning words—not to the defendants but to herself.

"Then what happened, Carole?"

"I turned around and went back," she confidently answered.

"Did anyone ask you to turn around and go back?" Roberts inquired.

"It wasn't...no, no one specifically came out and told me to turn around and come back."

"Did you go back to the scene where the Ziemer car was then?"

"Yes."

Upon arriving back at the scene, Carole remarked that she noticed that Rudy had managed to crawl his way partially out of the car.

"Ziemer was laying halfway out on the ground," she testified.

That's when Thompson went back to Rudy's car, shoved him inside, and drove off with Carole following closely behind. After a confusing ride around the southeast side of town, both cars stopped, and Carole testified that "the majority ruled that he [Thompson] should follow me."

Upon reaching the Weinbach levee, lifelong Evansville resident Carole testified, "I couldn't say exactly where it is, and I couldn't take you there."

Carole testified that Greymont and Pirrie exited Carole's car and moved a barricade blocking the road. With the barricade moved, both cars drove over the levee. At that point, Carole let Greymont drive her car so he could turn it around in the tight confines of the levee. With her car and Rudy's car facing in opposite directions, Carole looked back and saw the taillights of Rudy's Dodge. She claimed that during the ordeal, Greymont and Pirrie were away from her car for about five minutes. Thomspon, the man she had dated, was the last to return from Ziemer's car, and when he did come back, he was soaked below the belt.

While the details of that night proved interesting, those details paled in comparison to the bombshell Carole dropped later during her testimony.

Less than a week before her testimony, as jurors were being selected and Carole contemplated at a girl-friend's apartment whether to testify, a knock at the door interrupted her thinking. Mr. and Mrs. Pirrie had found Carole.

According to Carole, the pair asked her "not to take the stand because if no one in the group did, 'the state won't have a case.'" Carole also claimed that the three defendants and their attorneys met after jury selection ended and decided to have the Pirries talk to Carole because the attorneys could not legally talk to her, a claim Melvina Pirrie disputed during her testimony which came later the same day. Carole claimed, under oath, that she sat in the middle of the front seat of Patrick Pirrie's brother's car, between Mr. and Mrs. Pirrie, ironically the same spot Ziemer sat in his own car between Pirrie and William Thompson. As they sat in the car, the Pirries tried to convince Carole not to testify.

Mrs. Pirrie, in her testimony, claimed she told Carole, "We would be prosecuted if we didn't testify."

Roberts followed up Mrs. Pirrie's answer with the question, "Who told you that?"

To that question, Mrs. Pirrie replied, "You did."

"When did I tell you that, Melvina?" Roberts asked.

"When we were arrested."

"Was I there? Did I arrest you?" an exasperated Roberts asked.

Melvina Pirrie claimed that Roberts himself was present the night the two girls were detained as material witnesses, to which Roberts replied, "You know better than that, Melvina."

Roberts's line of questioning was cut off when defense attorneys successfully argued that Roberts was "using himself as a witness."

The next day, the prosecution called their last witness, Detective Joe Molinet. Molinet took the stand to provide details regarding the confession William Thompson signed while being interrogated at Fort Campbell. Judge Beavers did not allow the actual statement to be introduced as evidence because it only pertained to Thompson and, if introduced to the jury, would unfairly taint the defense of Pirrie and Greymont, who had not signed confessions.

The prosecution's line of questioning was routine but allowed the defense an opening they gladly took. Greymont's attorney, Howard Sandusky, cross-examined Molinet.

"Did you ever hear of Rudolph Ziemer before you investigated his death?" Sandusky asked.

"Yes, I did," replied Molinet.

"What did you investigate him for?"

"You asked me if I knew him. I didn't investigate him."

"Oh, that's right, you are investigating this murder. Did you ever investigate him?"

"No, sir."

"Has a member of the Evansville Police Department for the past seventeen and half years, or have you ever heard of any of your fellow officers ever investigated any of his activities?" Howard Sandusky asked awkwardly.

"Yes."

"What type of activities?"

At this point, prosecutors objected to the questioning, which Judge Addison Beavers sustained.

"How well did you know Mister Ziemer?"

"Oh, I know him pretty well. I've known him all my life," Molinet replied.

"Did you ever see him in the jailhouse?"

"No."

"You are aware of the fact that he's had sodomy charges filed against him in various courts in Southern Indiana during his lifetime?"

"Do I know it?"

"Are you acquainted with that fact?"

"Nope."

"I just want to ask you if you don't know that he had a reputation for being a homosexual pervert, a queer, in other words, you know?" Sandusky asked in another confusing manner.

"Yes."

"And he had a pretty widespread reputation for that activity, didn't he?"

"That's correct."

"Matter of fact, he was one of Evansville's best-known queers, wasn't he?"

"Oh, we object to that counsel. How do we know what 'best-known queer' means, your honor?" O. H. Roberts interjected.

Judge Beavers sustained the objection forcing Sandusky to conclude, "He was well known as a queer."

"I would guess so."

Howard Sandusky's Friday afternoon cross-examination of Detective Joe Molinet ended the prosecution's presentation of witnesses. During a brief recess, two women spectators gave defendant William Thompson a matching set of cufflinks, tie clasp, tie pin, and money clip in celebration of his twenty-second birthday. Mr. and Mrs. Pirrie had wrapped a few children's toys and given them to Thompson as a joke.

Later that day, defense attorneys Sandusky, Wever, and Lopp motioned for direct acquittal of all charges, a motion Judge Beavers denied. At the end of the day's proceedings, the juror James J. Wathen, Alcoa employee and farmer, went to The Old Kentucky BBQ to have a few beers. While Wathen went to the bar where the troopers first met Rudy Ziemer, the three defense attorneys debated whether to call any defense witnesses.

On Sunday, the funeral business continued as usual when Rudy Ziemer's sisters prepared to handle the funeral arrangements for a ninety-one-year-old former Evansville resident who died in Sonoma, California, about four hundred miles north of the home of Mr. and Mrs. Patrick Pirrie.

THE VERDICT

● ● ● ●

"From a thousand pulpits, his name was spoke in prayer," read the *Associated Press* article on the front page of the *Evansville Courier* on Monday, November 23, 1964. Because Judge Beavers rarely held court on Saturday and did not plan to change that custom, the three defense attorneys had a chance to confer over the weekend. As Howard Sandusky, Paul Wever, and James Lopp discussed their strategy for defending the three paratroopers accused of killing Rudy Ziemer, America and the world mourned the one-year anniversary of JFK's assassination.

The front-page article continued:

> *Respectful crowds thronged in places intimate to him. They filled the churches where he worshipped, stood in small groups in the cold at the spot where he was felled and bowed their heads where he laid buried.*
>
> *At Kennedy Airport in New York, 10,000 travelers and workers stood in silent prayer for one minute at noon.*

Automobiles and aircraft on the ground were stopped.

World leaders issued renewed declarations of sorrow—French President Charles de Gaulle, Mexican President Adolfo Lopez Mateos, West Berlin Mayor Willy Brandt, and Spanish Gen. Francisco Franco among them.

Flowers, fragile and beautiful as life is fragile and beautiful were offered to the memory of the nation's 35th president. They were placed on the assassination site in Dallas and on a bridge named for Kennedy over the Rhine River in Bonn.

German students sent red carnations to his widow in New York. Two teen-aged girls in Tokyo, fulfilling a private commitment as they have each month since his death put carnations, lilies and chrysanthemums on a Kennedy Memorial at Yokota Air Base.

Addressing one of the many public ceremonies here and abroad, Rep. Richard Boiling, D-Mo., told a Kansas City audience that the enduring memorial to Kennedy will not be built of stone and steel.

"They will be found in the face of the Negro child who goes to school without fear. In the serenity of our parents who enter old age with dignity and in the laughter of our children who play in a world at peace."

As spectators filed into the courtroom for the beginning of Monday's proceedings, defense and prosecution attorneys huddled with Judge Beavers while Alvie Brogan, the owner of The Old Kentucky BBQ, and several of his employees stood by as potential witnesses. As the owner and his employees waited, a bailiff escorted juror James J. Wathen from a waiting room that separated Wathen from the other jurors.

Prosecutor O. H. Roberts learned over the weekend of Wathen's night out at The Old Kentucky and heard that, while in a drunken state, he had a conversation with defendant William Thompson and witness Kay Goble, who were also at The Old Kentucky. Upon learning this, Roberts asked that bail for Thompson be revoked. He also asked that Patrick Pirrie's bail be revoked because of his attempt to dissuade Carole Sue Gentry from testifying.

Judge Beavers immediately dismissed Wathen and replaced him with an alternate juror, a telephone worker from Boonville. Beavers charged Wathen with indirect contempt of court, meaning his actions had occurred outside of the courtroom, and admonished him for potentially causing a mistrial, wasting tax-payer money, and perhaps requiring all future juries in Warrick County to be sequestered. Judge Beavers did not revoke bail for either Thompson or Pirrie.

With the early drama out of the way, the trial continued, albeit briefly, as the defense attorneys informed the court that they would not be calling any witnesses. And with that, the closing arguments began.

The three prosecutors all participated in the closing statements, as did the three defense attorneys. Prosecutor Terry Dietsch began the summation by reminding the jury that the coroner had ruled that Rudy had drowned, and investigators determined that the car, when found, was in drive and that the emergency brake was not engaged, insinuating that the car was intentionally and willfully driven into the flood waters.

Defense attorney Paul Wever followed with an argument that the prosecution did not show "beyond a reasonable doubt" that the car would roll into the water while also disputing other findings of the investigation.

James Lopp then followed with an hour-long speech highlighted by the statement that he was proud of Patrick Pirrie and that "he hit him. There's no doubt in my mind he hit him. He should have hit him. They had a right to defend themselves from a drunken pervert." Throughout his summation, Lopp continuously referred to Rudy Ziemer as a "drunken pervert."

Burley Scales followed Lopp and told the jurors, "We're not on trial here," referring to the prosecutors, but also said, quite confusingly, "Neither am I going to defend Rudolph Ziemer. He is dead by the acts of these three men."

Howard Sandusky, the most vocal of all of the attorneys and the one with a heavy drawl, provided the most blistering attack on the prosecutors and Rudy Ziemer by criticizing O. H. Roberts for not "rounding up all the old perverts" in Evansville. He also told jurors, "The only thing poor Bob Greymont is guilty of is taking a ride in a car driven by Carole Gentry, who should have been indicted if anyone was indicted because she drove the car that led them around."

Roberts then completed the summation by telling jurors, "The three defendants should pay the ultimate penalty." He concluded, "I knew Rudy Ziemer as an unfortunate homosexual, but if these defendants killed him because he was a homosexual, next it could be because they don't like men with curly grey hair or because they were Jews or Negroes. The defendants want you to accept their right to play God."

The day began to draw to a close, with the jury commencing deliberations around 7:00 p.m. While the defendants waited and wondered if the jury might deliberate late into the night, word came the jury had reached verdicts for all three defendants.

As spectators gathered as the defendants entered the courtroom, the jurors filled the jury box like students ready to take a test. As tension filled the room, Judge

Addison Beavers read the verdicts one by one from three sheets of paper.

"In the case of Robert Greymont: not guilty. So say you all, gentlemen?"

"We do," replied the twelve farmers and workers.

"In the case of Patrick Pirrie: not guilty. So say you all, gentlemen?"

"We do."

Pirrie turned to his wife, Melvina Pirrie, a witness for the prosecution, and gave her a hug.

And then came the final defendant, William Thompson, who had signed a confession stating he beat Rudy Ziemer unconscious and then drove his car into the Ohio River floodwaters. He told police he could hear Rudy breathing as he drove his car into the waters. He told them that he had taken his wallet. Jurors never got to see that written statement because Pirrie's and Greymont's attorneys successfully argued it would prejudice the jury because the men were not being tried separately.

"In the case of William Thompson: not guilty. So say you all, gentlemen?"

"We do."

Stunned, Thompson stood and stared straight ahead for almost a minute. He then turned to his parents. Prosecutor O. H. Roberts angrily left the courtroom.

When asked by reporters what was next for him, William Thompson responded, "Just live for a little while."

The three paratroopers did it. They lived to brave another day.

Mom, Dad, Grandma Mil, Grandpa George, and Great-Uncle Bud fumed when they heard the verdict on the news and read about it the next day in both the morning and afternoon editions of the newspaper.

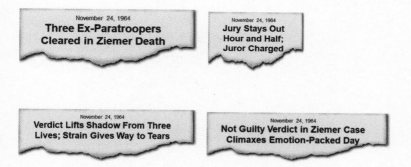

November 24, 1964
Three Ex-Paratroopers Cleared in Ziemer Death

November 24, 1964
Jury Stays Out Hour and Half; Juror Charged

November 24, 1964
Verdict Lifts Shadow From Three Lives; Strain Gives Way to Tears

November 24, 1964
Not Guilty Verdict in Ziemer Case Climaxes Emotion-Packed Day

Mom's side of the family felt the jury got it right. While the Melchior and Evans families disagreed about the "whole Rudy Ziemer thing," they did agree about Mom and Dad's kids. "Dan and Dots have a nice little family."

After the verdict, Mom spent more and more time with Dad's side of the family than her own. She did, however, agree with the jury foreman who told the families of each of the defendants, "Be sure he goes to church now and makes something out of his life."

Mom, but not always Dad, made sure to take Sam, Amy, and even five-month-old Andrew George to church every Sunday. As the defendants went back to their families and their lives, Mom wondered what was in store for her family in a world that she viewed as too violent and full of hate, a word she loathed.

"You don't hate anyone," she often said, "No matter what."

Rudolph Severin Ziemer. Senior picture. (Courtesy of Reitz Memorial High School, Evansville, Indiana)

Ziemer Funeral Home. The former home of Evansville mayor Benjamin Bosse.

Mom looking quite determined at a young age.

Mom's First Communion.

Abraham Elmer (Bud) Carr. United States Army portrait.

Dad's grade school picture.

Grandpa George's portrait in a Rainbow Cleaners advertisement.

Rudy Ziemer and his mom on the Ohio River in Rudy's Truscotteer speedboat. Evansville Courier and Press — USA TODAY NETWORK

Mom and Dad's wedding party. L - R Ronald "Ronnie" Campbell, Uncle Charlie, Jack Gruebel, Dad, Mom, Norma Jean Kissell, Aunt Kate, Aunt Mary.

Mom at the stove in Grandma Mil's kitchen. "That Dots is a hell of a cook."

Daniel Carr Melchior. United States Army portrait.

Dad and Mom in Williston, South Carolina. On the back of the picture, Mom wrote, "How do you like the hats?"

Rudy's Dodge station wagon being pulled from the Ohio River floodwaters. His body is still inside. Evansville Courier and Press — USA TODAY NETWORK

The Evansville Press

Served by United Press International, Scripps-Howard Leased Wire, NEA Service, Science Service and United Press International Telephoto

97TH YEAR, NO. 232   EVANSVILLE, IND., SATURDAY, MARCH 16, 1963   12 PAGES

FINAL HOME
EDITION
★ ★ ★ ★ ★
PRICE SEVEN CENTS

Jets Chase 2 Red Planes Over Alaska

U.S. Envoy Hands Formal Protest To Soviet Ministry

Bosse Trounces Ireland, 61 to 36

Riggs Paces Bulldogs

Only One Point Difference at Half

Rains Total Over an Inch

3 GIs Held in Jail On Murder Charges

Paratrooper defendants. L-R William Thompson, Robert Greymont, Patrick Pirrie. Evansville Courier and Press – USA TODAY NETWORK

PART II

LAST COMMUNION

● ● ● ● ● ●

Dad's right hand shook the dice box with a gentle vigor, his preferred technique. The box sounded like popcorn popping in a car driving over gravel—or a broken maraca. He laid the light brown leather round box on the table and slid it to the right....

After working at Rainbow Cleaners all day, Dad drove to the Colony Cocktail Lounge on Weinbach Avenue. Ed Klenk, a friend of Dad and Grandpa George, owned the Colony and ran a neat little game for his customers.

At the back of the bar sat a dice box containing five dice. If a customer chose to, they could give Ed a quarter to roll the dice box one time. If the dice came up five of a kind, the customer received the jackpot, which, according to Ed, included all the quarters that had been surrendered since the last five of a kind. He turned the quarters into foldable money, so whether Ed took a cut or vig is not certain, but one night in 1965, Dad gambled a quarter.

Dad had a brown leather dice box at home. We sometimes played Ship, Captain & Crew while Dad drank a few or more beers, so I knew his shake well. Dad preferred the one-handed, hold-it-by-the-bottom casual shake, but every now and then, he shook it more vigorously, albeit still with one hand. For the vigorous shake, he placed his palm over the opening of the box and shook as hard as he desired. He usually did this if he needed a specific roll. I suspect, though, that knowing five of a kind was a rarity, and he wasn't known for his luck—"the only one in the family to get drafted, for Christ's sake," he used to say—he probably handed Ed his quarter, gave the box his preferred shake, and lo and behold—*five of a kind.*

That's how we got the house on Audubon. Dad rolled five of a kind and came home with almost $1,500, or so the story goes. He never said what number (one, two, three, four, five, or six) delivered the win, perhaps because he forgot in the drunken celebration, but all Mom remembered was Dad coming home with the money. He threw it on the bed and said, "We're buying a house." I'd heard that story enough times to believe it, but I also thought about the odds of rolling five of a kind and Dad scoring a jackpot a little early according to the math. "What are the odds?"

Mom believed him, so I believed him when he told that story many times over the years. If that's where he said he got the money, that's where he got the money.

In September 1965, Mom and Dad bought our house on Audubon Drive for around $13,000 and used the $1,500 jackpot as the down payment. The split-level brick home sat on a horseshoe-shaped street with about thirty or so other houses, the most idyllic neighborhood a kid could imagine.

Awaiting her thirty-second birthday, preparing for the first Christmas in their brand-new home and three months pregnant with me, Mom stood at the brown stove, fixing breakfast for Dad, Sam, Amy, and Andy. Mom's rotation of breakfast meals included homemade waffles or pancakes, scrambled eggs, and bacon or on Sunday, fried eggs and bacon, French toast, deep-fried donuts, biscuits, and sausage gravy and one day a week, cereal from a box and the new sensation, Pop-Tarts.

While she cooked or poured cereal and milk in bowls, Dad, wearing a pair of khakis and a T-shirt, his usual attire, sat at the solid wood table, which was rectangular when the leaves were up, and read the newspaper.

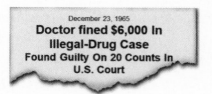

December 23, 1965
**Doctor fined $6,000 In
Illegal-Drug Case
Found Guilty On 20 Counts In
U.S. Court**

An Evansville doctor was fined a total of $6,000 Wednesday in U.S. District Court in Indianapolis after entering a nolo con-

tendere (no contest) plea to 20 counts of illegally dispensing drugs.

Dr. Charles E. Moehlenkamp, 56, who has offices at 614 N. Governor St., originally pleaded innocent to the charges.

It continued:

The charges related to prescription purchases on five separate occasions by the FDA inspectors, with the 20 counts arising from the fact that several times an inspector received more than one prescription, the agent reported.

He said the first inspector went to the doctor's office on July 2, 1964 and claimed to be a truck driver. He asked for "bennies" (Benzedrine) and received a prescription, the agent said.

He added the inspector returned on Aug 5, noted he'd been there previously and asked for another prescription.

This time, however, the agent said the inspector told the doctor he had several friends who were truck drivers and "were having trouble getting them (pills)." He received six prescriptions, his own and five others in names he supplied the doctor.

Dr. Moehlenkamp told the court he had sold the drugs to truck drivers "only because I felt sorry for them."

The article continued:

Dr. Moehlenkamp had been investigated in 1963 after two men arrested for contributing to the delinquency of a minor said they had bought barbiturates from him.

"This is the threat that hasn't caught up with Congress yet," Judge (S. Hugh) Dillin told the doctor.

"There are more violent crimes associated with users of barbiturates than with persons addicted to heroin."

As he ate his breakfast and sipped hot coffee, while Mom made sure Sam, Amy and Andy ate everything, Dad continued reading the paper, unaware that Uncle Bill regularly visited Dr. Moehlenkamp.

"Poor Danny looked like a little plucked chicken," Mom liked to say.

I arrived at 10:25 a.m. on Wednesday, June 15, 1966, weighing in at a slight five pounds, ten ounces and measuring eighteen inches long. I was an easy birth, she said, although I must believe no birth is "easy." Apparently, that morning, Mom got up, took a shower, and told Dad, "I think we need to go to the hospital." Being her fourth pregnancy, Mom, always efficient, knew the drill and most likely wanted to get it over with and get back home to continue cleaning, pressing, cooking, and doing all the things she felt made for a good wife but, more importantly, a good mom.

Mom and Dad arrived at the hospital around nine o'clock. I didn't disappoint her and certainly didn't tarry. Just as soon as the hospital got her in a room and ready to deliver, I showed up just like that. A little plucked chicken. My birth certificate reads: Daniel Carr Melchior II. Traditionally it should have been Jr. but Dad didn't want anyone calling me Junior. That sounded too country for Dad, who hated country music.

A few weeks after Mom gave birth to me, the spitting image of Uncle Bill, Fred Gresser, the former soldier who survived the 1918 Spanish Flu and now a retired farmer, donned overalls and a painter's cap as he followed behind an old-fashioned grain-harvesting twine binder. Officials at the Vanderburgh County Fair planned to demonstrate a steam-operated thresher during 150-year observances of Indiana becoming the nineteenth state. In preparation for the demonstration, the grain could not be harvested with a modern combine because it harvests, threshes, and even winnows the grain in one combined operation; hence the name *combine*. Gresser had to pick up the bundles of wheat and put them into a shock to keep the wheat dry and to prevent it from sun bleaching. Fred was accustomed to hard times and trying circumstances, so he had no problem at age seventy-four keeping up with the twine binder, especially in the very pleasant mid-sixties, low-humidity afternoon.

As a retiree, Gresser got up at 4:00 a.m. to go to Helen's Drive-In for breakfast. The owners let him in the back door when "Front Doors Not Open Yet" hung in the entrance. He ate breakfast, went to work on a family farm, and then returned for lunch. Five days a week, he got home around eight and went to bed by ten.

"Before I retired, I used to get up early, at 3:00 a.m. Now, I sleep late. Until 4:00 a.m.," Gresser told reporters when they interviewed him about surviving the Spanish flu.

Fred Gresser typified Evansville's west siders.

I looked a little less like that "little plucked chicken" Mom described upon first seeing me by the time I was baptized at Holy Rosary Catholic Church. My godparents were Forrest Arvin, Great-Uncle Bud's best friend, and Mary Jo Basham, a next-door neighbor of Grandpa George and Grandma Mil.

Mary Jo's dad, Mr. Basham, contributed to Grandpa George's souring on the Catholic Church. When Mr. Basham fell gravely ill and wanted to see the parish priest, the priest refused because of Mr. Basham's spotty or non-existent Mass attendance. Mr. Basham died without ever getting to talk to a priest. Grandpa George never forgave the Catholic Church and, specifically, the priest for refusing to see Mr. Basham.

Later that year, in October, my oldest brother Sam had his First Communion, memorialized with the only picture of most of the Evans and Melchior families in the same room. Standing in the middle of the black-and-white picture, Sam, knife in hand, wearing a white shirt, black pants, bow tie, and a faint grin, stood ready to cut the quarter-sheet cake. A small statue adorned the cake's left, a sugar bowl on its right. Candles burned on either side. Paper plates, forks, three ashtrays, and a book of matches completed the tabletop décor.

In the picture, starting on the right, Forrest Arvin, whom I don't ever remember meeting, looks on, standing next to Mom as she holds Andy, probably the same way she held Uncle Dave when he was that age. Uncle Dave, in horn-rimmed glasses and a cardigan, stands next to Mom, whose hair hasn't yet turned grey, the only color I remember it being. Grandma Bessie, smiling and wearing a long coat, stands next to Grandma Mil, whose arms are folded. She is also smiling. Grandpa Al, almost scowling, lurks in the back. Great-Uncle Bud stands next to Al, a wide smile beneath his thick, somewhat receding hairline. Grandpa George, the patriarch, holds Amy, his belly a pillow for her hands. Thin Uncle Tom, wearing a cardigan and smiling broadly at someone or something out of the frame, rounds out the group. Among the nine adults in that picture, seven believed Rudy Ziemer didn't deserve what happened to him, while two didn't necessarily believe he deserved to be killed but also didn't care that he was. Flanked on both sides, Grandma Bessie and Grandpa Al were outnumbered.

Great-Uncle Bud, always the instigator, surely brought up Rudy's case, or maybe the Vietnam War or Civil Rights, just to get things going with Grandpa Al. That's how Great-Uncle Bud operated. He enjoyed getting under your skin like a burrowing tick. Playing poker, he used to tell Uncle Tom, his nephew and perhaps the most competitive guy in the family, especially when it came to cards and board games, "I'm gonna beat you this hand without looking at my cards. Open for a dime." A dime was a huge bet in the family poker games in 1966. When Great-Uncle Bud won, which was often, Tom fumed, sometimes storming away from the table after throwing his cards. Sometimes he came back; other times, he didn't.

While there were many more poker games throughout the years, especially on Thanksgiving, Christmas Day, Easter, and Fourth of July, the First Communions stopped with Sam. The crowd in the basement of the home on Audubon dispersed that October evening smelling of beer and cigarettes. Like Uncle Tom, that group of nine got up and left. They never came together again.

FEARS

● ●

Fred Gresser and Dr. Moehlenkamp, despite the lat-
ter's pleading guilty to illegally providing drugs, personified two different versions of success in Evansville:
hard work and faith versus scheming and money. Uncle
Bill typified the many who struggled with addiction to
alcohol or worse. The electroshock treatments didn't
have the desired (or any) impact at all on Uncle Bill,
while Grandma Bessie's overcompensation for their
mistreatment of Uncle Bill during this childhood did
not sit well with Grandpa Al. The father and son, living
under the same roof in the two-bedroom cracker box,
hated each other and didn't have room to separate. Like
boxers in a phone booth, inevitable fights repeated,
round after round. In one, Grandpa Al, attempting to
throw a flowerpot at Uncle Bill, grabbed the pot with
so much force that it broke in his hand, causing a large
cut across his palm like a stigmata.

As Uncle Bill's alcohol-induced joblessness, laziness,
and surliness continued, guilt, according to relatives,
crept into Grandma Bessie's mind. "Did our mistreat-

ment of Bill cause these troubles? Am I to blame?" she thought.

Grandma Bessie never mentioned her first son, John Jenne Jr., when talking about guilt, but surely, she must have felt it like a rock in her pillow.

Grandma Bessie paid Uncle Bill's bail money, lied to people about his whereabouts, paid his rent, and even supported him financially when he got married at age twenty-six. He had told his eighteen-year-old bride, Mary Louise, that he was twenty-four when the couple married after she became pregnant. Uncle Bill never showed any interest in being a father. He simply wanted to spend time drinking, either at home or in bars. Eighteen months after Mary Louise gave birth to my cousin Chuck, another son, Mike, came along. Again, Uncle Bill showed zero interest in the boys, but that didn't stop Grandma Bessie from supporting Uncle Bill, including buying him more beer when he ran out.

One day, he came home after drinking to watch Chuck and Mike while Mary Louise worked at Helen's Drive-In. He ran out of beer at home, so Grandma Bessie brought him some more. By the time Mary Louise returned from work, Uncle Bill had passed out, Chuck had fallen asleep on the floor, and Mike cried incessantly in a soaked and soiled diaper. That night, Mary Louise had seen enough. She filed for divorce, paying the court fees with her wages earned at the diner where Fred Gresser ate breakfast.

Alcohol no longer soothed Uncle Bill's troubled mind, so he sought "help" from Dr. Moehlenkamp. Uncle Bill and his barstool friends, hard laborers, factory workers, or unemployed like himself, frequented "the poor man's doctor" as addicted customers, not patients, for everything from stimulants Dospan, Ionamin, and Fastin to depressants Placidyl, Doriden, Noludar, Carbrital, and Parest.

Uncle Bill visited Dr. Moehlenkamp's Governor Street office frequently. Wayne Ellison, the owner of Wayne's Pharmacy, readily filled the prescriptions Dr. Moehlenkamp wrote. Whether Grandma Bessie knew the money she gave Uncle Bill supplied him with uppers and downers remained a mystery until Monday, November 27, 1967.

As B-52s bombed North Vietnam and fighting raged in the Mekong Delta, temperatures in the mid-twenties and partly cloudy skies opened the work week for Evansville residents, including Fred Gresser. Gresser often used his beat-up dump truck to haul coal, gravel, grain, or anything else that could earn him a few dollars. Like many in Evansville, "retirement" didn't mean retirement. It only meant working fewer hours. That day, he spent a few hours delivering coal, perhaps to places like Rainbow Cleaners, for the coal-fired boiler that burned the color of my auburn hair.

As temperatures rose to comfortable low forties, Grandpa Al dropped Grandma Bessie at Deaconess hospital before making his way north on Highway 41 toward Whirlpool in his red 1963 Ford Galaxy. Uncle Bill slept in until the house was his alone.

He got up, dressed, walked outside, and got into his own car, making his way toward Dr. Moehlenkamp's office for more prescriptions to get more pills. After the morning rush hour north toward factories like Whirlpool, the three-and-a-half-mile drive usually took less than ten minutes, especially via Highway 41. With Grandma Bessie's money in his pocket and probably a few morning beers in his belly, Uncle Bill found a parking spot along the curb of Governor Street, a one-way road, as Fred Gresser drove his truck, full of coal, south.

Without looking, Uncle Bill started across the street toward Dr. Moehlenkamp's.

Like the little boy that Dr. Moehlenkamp didn't see before hitting and killing him, Fred Gresser didn't see Uncle Bill as he stepped into the path of Gresser's large truck carrying enough coal to fill a thousand Christmas stockings. The large mirror on the truck, or the bed, or both struck Uncle Bill on the head. He crumpled in a heap on the blacktop road.

News traveled fast on that partly cloudy, typical fall day that both the Evans and Melchior families loved. Uncle Bill had been hit by a truck and was in the hospital. Some on both sides of the family viewed the tragedy as a blessing from God if he survived. Given his toughness, everyone felt he surely would. If so, maybe the accident would slow down fast-walking, hard-living Uncle Bill.

When he regained consciousness in the hospital and could open his eyes, Uncle Bill couldn't see. Perhaps his retinas detached or swelling in his head was putting pressure on his optic nerves. Maybe his sight would return, doctors initially told him. But, after a series of tests and time spent in a St. Louis hospital that specialized in such cases, doctors determined that Uncle Bill's encounter with Fred Gresser had totally and permanently blinded him.

He wouldn't see his sons, who he'd never really seen anyway. He wouldn't see the horses that he loved to bet on but rarely ever won. He wouldn't see me, his spitting image, his favorite sister's son. He couldn't see... she couldn't see; Uncle Bill and Mrs. Mamie Duncan, both permanently blinded, one by a coal truck and one by a gun.

While Uncle Bill spent time in and out of hospitals, institutions, and the Evansville Blind Association, learning to live as one who couldn't see, I went to Dr. Walters to get vaccinations for smallpox and polio. Dr. Walters scared me to death. I came out of the womb scared, especially of water, to hear Mom tell it. I screamed, cried, wriggled, and writhed anytime she tried to wash my hair. I didn't mind water on my body, but water on my head sent me into a spiral of fear and rage that she couldn't understand. She bathed me just as she bathed Sam, Amy, and Andy, but for some reason, I threw a fit when she put my head under the faucet of the sink or the tub.

Other things that scared me were dogs, strange kids bigger than me, the dark, heights—perhaps even more than water—the UFOs that people talked about but never saw. Things I couldn't see scared me, and now that Uncle Bill couldn't see, going blind scared me.

In Dr. Walter's office, what I could see was a needle and syringe in his hand, waiting to jab me with the polio vaccine. I hated being jabbed but, like all kids, endured it and eventually forgot about it until I saw Dr. Walter a few weeks after being vaccinated. I saw him at the ABC department store at the corner of Washington Avenue and Green River Road, where Mom and Dad shopped for everything from clothes and curtains to cat food and coffee. We didn't need kitty litter because our cat, Sidney, was mostly an outdoor cat except for the few times Mom would let him in the house, but only in the kitchen. Somehow, she trained or scared that cat to death because even Sidney knew to only go where Mom let him go.

Sidney was a tabby, so we looked a bit alike, me with my flaming red or orange or auburn hair and him with his yellow and orange fur. We made a small house for him that sat beneath the big maple tree right outside the backdoor. Dad once put a small screen as a door on the cathouse and put a concrete block in front of it to keep Sidney in at night. Dad must've thought he was somehow protecting Sidney, but it didn't work. Sidney pushed open that screen door with ease.

The ABC store sold shorts for $1.66 and boys' jackets for $1.97. Maybe that's what we went to purchase that day. I saw Dr. Walters standing in line. The second I saw him, I started to bawl, scream, and cry as Dad held me near his shoulder. At first, he couldn't understand why I went so ballistic, and then he saw Dr. Walters. They laughed as Dad carried me out of the store to avoid any more embarrassment. "Well, if nothing else, the kid has a good memory."

With the needle jabs behind me, I started kindergarten, which consisted of half-days at Plaza Park Grade School. Because Mom didn't drive, I attended with Laura Miller, daughter of Helen Miller, one of our neighbors and Mom's best friend. Helen and Mom were the types of friends that didn't knock on each other's doors. They simply opened the door and shouted, "Yoo-hoo."

Each day of kindergarten that I attended—according to my report card, I missed sixteen days my first year of school—Laura and I either rode with Helen or Laura's dad, Robert, or Bob, as some called him. On the days we rode with him, he would turn around, look at me and say, "Gonna getcha." Like the dogs, the strange kids bigger than me... Bob Miller scared the hell out of me. He knew it too. Everyone knew it. I feared everything.

About my memory, though, according to my report card, I recognized my name, could print it, knew my address, my telephone number, the basic colors, could tie a bow, knew how to use scissors and crayons well, and understood numbers one to ten. I scored satisfactory in all "Social Growth" categories, so I was off to a good start.

Mom periodically took Sam, Amy, and Andy to church. Me and Dad never went; instead we'd go the store, after dropping them off at Holy Rosary, and buy a dozen or so donuts. Dad read the paper while I watched TV.

Later that year, and four years into his now-even-darker journey, Uncle Bill spent four weeks in Rochester, Michigan. When he returned home to his house on 1005½ Mary Street, one day before Mom's thirty-eighth birthday, Dollie, a one-and-a-half-year-old German Shephard guide dog, accompanied him. Finally, a Christmas gift other than coal for Uncle Bill and both a birthday and Christmas gift Mom could enjoy.

January 9, 1972
Leader Dog Provides 'A World of Difference'
Dollar-wise, William J. Evans' Christmas gift is worth approximately $2,000. But Evans blinded three years ago when struck by a coal truck.

A few weeks later, for a newspaper article, Uncle Bill told a reporter he could walk "with complete confidence."

"I go to the grocery store, shopping, and visiting with my friends with Dollie by my side."

"Most of all, Dollie gives me speed again. Before I was blinded, I was a very fast walker."

Mom's uncle, Uncle John, John Wilkerson, also walked fast until he broke his leg somehow and had to spend a couple of months or so in a wheelchair while it healed. I don't call him Great-Uncle John because I never met him, or if I did, I don't remember meeting him. I'm not the only one. My aunts and uncles said they mostly just heard about him but didn't remember much of anything about him other than him sitting in the wheelchair one Christmas with his leg in a cast. Uncle John was Grandma Bessie's brother, the one who, like another Hoosier, James Dean, moved to Hollywood, California. Less than a year later, he died by suicide, some believed. His short obituary read:

JOHN KEITH WILKERSON, 49, formerly of Evansville, died yesterday in Hollywood, Calif.

Mr. Wilkerson was a former employee of Deaconess Hospital, Double Cola and Cedars of Lebanon Hospital in Los Angeles. He left Evansville last spring.

In March 1972, my teacher Miss Beth Casper wrote this on my report card: *Dan is well-behaved. He is very serious about his work. He listens carefully. B.C.*

By June 1972, she wrote this: *Dan is very polite and dependable. It has been an asset to have him in the room. He seems sensitive at times. I wish more were like him. It has been a pleasure knowing him and having him. Good luck. B.C.*

"Polite and dependable," close kin to "hell of a worker."

"Polite" might have been my demeanor in school but often not at home. Once, in our shared basement room, I hit Andy over the head with a Coke bottle. It didn't break, but it must've hurt like hell. When I hit him, he screamed, Dad came running, and I screamed louder.

"What happened?" Dad yelled.

Before Andy could utter a word, I screamed, "Andy hit me with a Coke bottle."

Dad took off his slipper and whipped Andy several times with it as I sat back beneath my Captain Crunch poster and smiled. After the storm passed, Andy locked me in the closet. I can't remember how long I was there, but I think he did it on a Saturday when Mom and Dad were both working, so it wasn't a short sentence.

Amy and Andy spent more time together than they did with me, which is maybe why Amy asked me to walk in front of her one day while she rode her bicycle. Not questioning why, I walked ahead toward the basketball goal at the end of the street. I loved playing basketball even though I struggled to get the ball near the rim, much less in the basket.

Unlike Dr. Moehlenkamp on Stringtown Road or Fred Gresser on Governor, Amy on Audubon did see me when she ran me over with her bicycle. I scraped my hands, knees, and my forehead on the concrete street. Unlike the slipper to Andy's backside, Dad didn't hit Amy for that one. Instead, he let me go into her room and pick out any toys or things I wanted. I chose her microscope. I can't recall if scraped hands and knees and a banged-up forehead were worth it, but I did enjoy taking her microscope. If she was paying me back for hitting Andy, at least I got a microscope out of my pain and could see the bugs up close, and oddly enough they didn't scare me.

When Mom showed up at school, my classmates confused her for my grandma. I moronically told her that once. I can never forget the look on her face. She had to realize she looked older than the other mothers, but that couldn't have made it any easier. I later learned that she didn't want to color her hair because, for one, it took too much time to maintain, something she didn't have because not only was she taking care of us, but when we were in school, she pressed clothes at Rainbow in exchange for grocery money. She also cleaned Grandma Mil and Grandpa George's house when there weren't any clothes to press. With the business at Rainbow slowing and choking due to the recession and joblessness in Rainbow's neighborhood—by the 1970s, virtually all of Rainbow's customers were African American and were significantly impacted by the recession—there were fewer and fewer clothes to press, so she did whatever else needed doing. Cooking, cleaning, cutting grass, cutting Grandma Bessie's toenails, cutting coupons—literally anything but tarrying.

I remember the summer of 1972 as one filled with laughter and fun, including an attempt at building a clubhouse out of old scrap wood full of rusty nails. Amy and Andy, three and two years older than me, did most of the work. I think Sam might have helped a bit, but he also spent time building model destroyers, battleships, and cruisers only to then blow them up with firecrackers. We'd all gather with the neighborhood kids to watch the explosions.

The Melchior family, including Uncle Tom, came out nearly every Sunday that summer. Tom had gotten interested in model rocketry and would often launch rockets high above the cornfield. After watching the launch, our job was to find the rocket and parachute, which wasn't always easy but still fun.

One Sunday evening, around dusk, when the insects began their evening chorus and fireflies danced, Dad and Uncle Tom came up with an even better way to have some fun. They decided to experiment with one of those homemade hot-air balloons made of a flimsy plastic bag, straws, and a few birthday candles. Dry-cleaning bags from Rainbow Cleaners provided excellent material, and we had plenty of straws and birthday candles. The experiment worked, and a few of them drifted into the night sky. Years later, Dad claimed some people had seen them and called to report seeing UFOs. I never believed that story, but we saw them close up, so maybe from far away, that's what they appeared to be.

I did find one article from October 1973 that said there had been a rash of UFO sightings in the Midwest but that some of those sightings were military helicopters flying from Fort Campbell, Kentucky, where the paratroopers who killed Rudy Ziemer once trained.

Another afternoon that summer, we went over to Grandma Bessie and Grandpa Al's house. I had heard about Dollie and seen her picture in the paper, but because dogs still scared me, I'd never seen her in real life. A large Doberman lived just down the street from us in a fenced-in yard. Some of the older boys would throw rocks at the dog to make him bark and growl anytime someone walked by. That dog scared the life out of me, so my imagination ran wild about what a dog like Dollie could do to me.

Grandma Bessie and Grandpa Al knew about my fear, so they kept Dollie in the house as we played in the backyard. The back door to the house was open, but the screen door was closed. I looked at the door and saw Dolly looking out at all of us kids playing. Somehow, she opened the door, or perhaps Grandma Bessie forgot to latch it. Either way, Dollie came out barking. I ran as fast as I could and climbed over the chain-link fence that surrounded the yard. Everyone but me laughed.

Eventually, they carried me into the house and let Dollie play with my siblings and cousins while I sat at the kitchen table with Uncle Bill, listening to the radio. After being blinded by the coal truck, Uncle Bill's slumped posture as he sat, smoked, and drank, never really changed. His eyes, broken cameras, pointed near open spaces where no one sat or stood. No eye contact ever, but also no dark glasses to hide where his eyes might be trying to find a bit of light.

As I drank a Double Cola from a brightly colored aluminum glass, Uncle Bill asked me to stand up and come next to him. He never scared me, so I readily did as he asked. He spun around in his chair, almost knocking his beer over. He put his hands out and grabbed me under my armpits. Still sitting, he easily picked me up about six inches off the floor. My legs dangled as radio announcers called a horse race from nearby Ellis Park.

He smiled and chuckled, "Still light enough to be a jockey."

I returned to my chair as we listened to the races.

That day was the one and only time I saw Dollie in the flesh instead of a picture. From then on, every time I went to Grandma Bessie's, Grandpa Al's, and Uncle Bill's house, they put her in Bill's bedroom and shut the door. I hated that she scared me and envied my siblings and cousins who loved her.

THE SIGN

● ● ●

Mom worried less about Uncle Bill because he had Dollie, but the recession and Rainbow Cleaners' declining business caused Mom to have new worries. As 1972 meandered along and I worried about going back to school in the fall, Dad had started to look for another job because, apparently, Rainbow Cleaners couldn't support two families. He still worked at "the plant" cleaning and sometimes delivering clothes but knew the end for him and Rainbow approached like a speeding car. That summer, he started driving a "new" car. A loud green beater of some type that had mismatched tires and looked like it had been driven long and hard. Smoke billowed out of the exhaust when Dad turned the ignition and gunned the gas. The whole neighborhood heard the rumble when he came and went.

One day, while playing basketball at the goal near the end of the street where Amy ran me over, I heard the rumble of Dad starting the car. I turned around and saw him backing out of the driveway and heading back to work. I sprinted toward him as fast as my short six-year-old legs would allow and yelled, "*Dad...*

Dad...Dad!" Mom, Amy, and Andy, all standing in the driveway, stared at me, as did a few neighborhood kids, while Mom smiled. Dad stopped the car as I ran to the rolled-down driver's window. He had a cigarette dangling from his lip and sweat on his brow.

"I wanna run the route with you," I said. He laughed and rubbed my auburn head.

"I'm not running the route; I've got a new job. I'll be back," Dad replied.

I walked onto the driveway. Mom rubbed my shoulders.

"It's okay, hon, it's okay."

Mom and Dad had taken a second mortgage on the house to help fund Rainbow Cleaners and our growing family. Grandma Mil and Grandpa George did the same with the house on Reis. Four mortgages on two houses for one business in a deteriorating part of town and a recession didn't add up. Unlike William Cantrell's boat *Why Worry?*, Mom and Dad had plenty to worry about.

One day a woman, whose name I remember as Joyce, but I could be mistaken, stopped by the house. She drove a newer car and wore nice clothes. She parked her car along the curb, not in the driveway. She went inside and sat at the kitchen table with Mom and Dad, but not before we were told, "Go outside and play, and don't come in until we tell you so." I could tell they meant it.

As we played in the front yard with a few friends, Mom, Dad, and Joyce walked out of the house. Dad led the way. The woman walked to her car and opened the trunk lid. She pulled out a metal black-and-white sign.

FOR SALE.

"What? Are we leaving? Why?"

"We might just want to live somewhere else," or something like that, was the response.

I smelled the sixty-four-count crayon box with the built-in sharpener that meant the start of a new school year. Unwrinkled stacks of paper, clean folders without scribbles, tears, and bends, sat neatly on the homemade hanging desk Dad had fashioned out of a piece of plywood and decorative chains used for hanging swag lamps. He painted the plywood fire-engine red. The desk hung on Andy's side of the room in the basement. Captain Crunch posters—I begged for Captain Crunch and got him, while Andy had Seadog—hung over our parallel twin beds.

Andy and I didn't always share a basement room in the "house on Audubon." At one point, I had my own room, but Dad decided to take correspondence art and drafting classes and needed a room with a drawing table, so Mom and Dad moved me down to Andy's room.

Just like Great-Uncle Bud, Dad had always viewed himself as a bit of an artist, at least as far back as his high-school years. At thirty-eight years old, Dad had yet to find his place, while his middle brother Uncle Tom, twenty-three, had avoided the Vietnam draft, although his asthma might have disqualified him anyway, lived at home, went to the University of Evansville, and earned a degree in Electrical Engineering before going to work for an engineering firm. Tom bought a brand-new Chevy Vega, similar in style, not color, to the one Robert Miller drove Laura and me to kindergarten in. Dad envied Tom and his new car. Hell, he envied Robert Miller and his car, but at least Dad had his own room.

Dad had his own room, and we had a "new" color TV. Sometime in the early '70s, Great-Uncle Bud gave us a color console he no longer needed. It sat in the living room where we watched shows like *Dark Shadows*, *Bewitched*, and *The Flip Wilson Show*. I often did a pretty good impression of Flip Wilson's character Geraldine. The adults thought it was funny and often asked me to do it, especially when they were drinking.

When Mom turned off the TV, and we went to bed, I no longer headed down the hall to my old room, now Dad's drawing room; I headed downstairs. Two years less three days older, Andy not only had to share a room, but he also had to share birthday parties. For one of those birthdays, I got a bug catcher that resembled a plastic lantern. "Bug catcher" was a misnomer as it didn't catch bugs but rather housed bugs I had to catch with my hands. I caught red and black ants, red and black bees, and spiders of all types and watched them fight, which they did with reckless abandon, always to the death of one or both.

Other than the smells and crispness of new school supplies, nothing marked the end of summer more than the Jerry Lewis Labor Day Telethon. The show stayed on in the background as we came in and out of the house. Amy loved that show because she loved seeing people help each other, and because of that, Labor Day marked the one day she didn't spend as much time outside as possible. While I came in and out, in and out, Mom would invariably yell at me, "Make up your mind. Either stay outside or stay inside." I had trouble making up my mind, so she yelled that a lot.

My first-grade teacher, Mrs. Smith, was much older than Miss Casper, my kindergarten teacher. That wasn't the only difference. Kindergarten only lasted the afternoon. For first grade, I had to get up early, ride the school bus, and spend most of the day in school. I didn't want to go and told both Mom and Dad. Given my stubbornness, they most likely sensed it was going to be a tough year.

My first day certainly didn't go as planned. Mom walked me to the school bus that stopped at the corner of Audubon and Pollack. Amy and Andy walked ahead while Mom held my hand as she talked to Helen Miller, who walked with Laura. Sam, an eighth grader, either walked by cutting through cornfields and neighborhoods or got a ride with the parents of his eighth-grade friends.

As we waited for the yellow-and-black school bus, something I had seen but never been on, I almost shook with fear, like when Mom shook and shivered like a chihuahua when anyone argued or fought. The bus arrived, the door opened with that swooshing sound that all school buses make, and kids eagerly stepped on. Mom led me to the line, a few kids in front, a few behind. I held my Scooby-Doo lunchbox in my right hand and got on. As I got to the stop step, the latch on the lunchbox came open, and my sandwich and thermos fell on the floor of the bus. A kid behind me accidentally stepped on my sandwich. Luckily, it was neatly folded into a plastic baggie, so at least it didn't get dirty, just a little smashed. I bent down, picked everything up, and put it back. My first-grade year started off with me whimpering as I sat in my seat.

Nowadays, this is how I tell the rest of the story:

> *I find a seat, sit down, open my lunchbox, look at my squished sandwich and then open my thermos. Oh great, the inside broke, and there's glass in my milk. This is great. No wonder I hated school.*

That story never fails to get lots of good laughs. And yes, when I got to school, I had to tell Mrs. Smith that I didn't have anything to drink for lunch because my thermos broke and there was glass in my milk. What a start. By the way, Mrs. Smith did make sure I had a carton of milk to drink.

One day in Mrs. Smith's class, we had to write a few simple words and sentences on lined paper. Finishing early, I decided to make the period at the end of one of the sentences a bit larger. As other kids continued writing, I made the period bigger and bigger until it became the size of a dime.

Mrs. Smith came down my aisle to collect my paper. I handed it to her. She looked at the paper and then the period. She looked at me and shook her head. She went up to her desk, got a pen, wrote something on my paper, and handed it back to me.

"Take this home and give it to your parents and bring it back tomorrow. Do you understand?"

"Yes."

My heart raced. What was going to happen? I couldn't read her cursive handwriting. I folded the paper and put it in my back pocket. Like a pebble in my shoe, I couldn't help but feel it all day long as I worried about what Mom and Dad would think or do.

The bus ride home felt longer than most days. When I got home, I came in the back door and walked up the stairs. I don't know why we used the back door more than the front, but we did. Both Mom and Dad were home. I handed Dad the paper. He looked at it, laughed a bit, and handed it to Mom. She looked at Dad and then at me.

"Why'd you do that?"

"I don't know. I was bored."

"Okay, don't do it again, alright?"

I shook my head.

Dad took the letter into his drafting and drawing room and quickly came back into the kitchen. He folded the paper back up and handed it to me.

"Give this to Mrs. Smith."

I took the letter and went downstairs. I couldn't read what Dad wrote, although I tried. How do you read scribbles? I thought.

The next day, I gave the letter to Mrs. Smith as soon as I walked into our classroom. She unfolded it, read it, and put it on her desk.

"Thank you."

I stood there looking at her.

"Go on, sit down," she said.

I turned around and walked to my desk.

That's it?

Why worry?

Although Mrs. Smith treated me well, and I enjoyed some aspects of school, I hated going to school that year. I preferred spending time with Mom because it was just her and I. Sam, Amy, and Andy were in school, and Dad was usually at work. I didn't want to leave her, so much so that I would feign stomachaches or headaches or lock myself in the bathroom to stay home. It became so bad that in the mornings, Mom and Dad wouldn't let me go to the bathroom by myself because they knew I would lock myself in. Our bedroom in the basement didn't have a door, so I couldn't lock myself in my room. On many occasions, Dad had to get me out of the bathroom, carry me out of the front door, and forcefully walk me to the bus stop. He made damn sure I got on that bus, although a few times, I did manage to delay long enough that I missed it. One day I did miss the bus is a day my brother Andy will never forget, and he makes sure I don't forget it, although I've tried.

I missed the bus, and because Dad had to get to his new job at Big G Lumber, Mom had to ask Helen Miller if she could take me to school. Mom didn't drive, and besides, we only had one car. Helen, being the friend she was, didn't mind at all. Mom rode in the passenger seat, with me sitting in the middle of the back seat. I cried the entire way, and the closer we got, the louder I screamed, cried, and yelled.

As I squirmed and screamed, Mom got me out of the car and insisted that I walk with her.

"Don't make me carry you into this school," Mom said.

Mom rarely got mad like that, but I could see it in her face, although that didn't stop me from crying. When we got to the doors, I must've dropped to the floor. According to Andy, he could hear me yelling and screaming as Mom dragged me down the hallway toward Mrs. Smith's class. I caused enough of a commotion that teachers poked their heads out of doors. From his seat, Andy caught a glimpse of the dragging.

"What is that?" some kid in Andy's class asked.

"That's just my little brother being drug down the hallway."

That was the only time I had to be dragged down the hallway, kicking and screaming, but my insistence that I didn't want to go to school, like blows to the body, wore Mom and Dad down my first-grade year. According to my report card, I missed a total of fifty-one days that year.

On the back of my final report card, Mrs. Smith wrote this:

> *Dear Dan,*
>
> *As smart as you are, you shouldn't be such a "worrywart." I'd like to take some of your over-conscientious worrying and inject it into a couple of others.*
>
> *I hope your second year will be as successful as your first—minus the worrying. Mrs. Smith*

She wrote that in cursive, so Mom or Dad must have read it to me.

We didn't have air-conditioning in the "house on Audubon" when the For Sale sign went up, and perhaps that's why it stayed up for so long. Summers in

Evansville can be stifling. Hot, humid, stagnant air often hangs in the Ohio River Valley without even a suggestion of a breeze. In 1972, the house was only seven years old, and many houses the same age had central air-conditioning. By comparison, the Benjamin Bosse home that Rudy and Ted Ziemer renovated to turn into their funeral home in 1935 had air-conditioning.

Sometime during the Fall of 1972, Dad managed to get his hands on a central air-conditioning unit. Perhaps he paid for it with one of four Evansville Morris Plan Company second mortgages Mom and Dad took out on the house. The first of those mortgages carried an 8 percent interest rate and the last 17. Dad insisted on managing the finances but obviously wasn't very good at it.

The summer of '73, like a merry-go-round, looked the same as the summer of '72. Fun with friends, stifling heat, but now we had air-conditioning. Because of that, Mom added, "You're letting all of the air-conditioning out," to her "make up your mind..." rant when we came in and out too often.

As Labor Day and Jerry Lewis approached, Mom and Dad sat us all down at the kitchen table.

"We sold the house. We're moving."

Apparently, the air-conditioning had done the trick. They told us we were moving to an apartment, whatever that meant.

"It's brand new and very nice. You'll like it."

"We like it here."

Because I was seven, Sam was fourteen, Amy was ten, and Andy was nine, any answer Mom and Dad would've given to "But why?" would not have sufficed. None of us wanted to leave the brick split-level house with four large white columns. The cornfield behind the backyard stretched for miles. Orange-and-red late-summer sunsets bathed the green stalks and golden tassels in a fiery glow. All spring and summer, Andy sat on the picnic table that Dad and Grandpa had built and watched every time they tilled, plowed, or harvested the field. Mr. Quisenberry, a black man who worked the field with a large tractor, would sometimes stop by our yard, step off the tractor, and give us pieces of candy. My siblings and I all remember Mr. Quisenberry, but we only knew him as the man with the candy who drove a tractor. When the sun disappeared, and the fields grew quiet except for rustling leaf blades, fireflies flashed on and off, creating tiny glows among the stalks.

Sidney continued his nighttime escape act, but his and Dad's luck had finally run out. After escaping his house one hot summer morning, Sidney didn't return. Me, Amy, Andy, and our friends called his name and looked into the cornfield and down by the ditch where Sidney could catch and kill frogs, bugs, or anything else that moved at night. We couldn't find him, so we headed back home to see if maybe he had slipped past us. That's when someone yelled, "I think I found him."

We ran toward Pollack Avenue, and there lay Sidney, sprawled in the street, his eyes bulging out, blood-spattered about his head, his mouth agape making him look angry and terrifying. Sidney never terrified anyone, including me, but looks often deceive.

Dad walked down the street with a shovel. He scooped Sidney onto the shovel and walked him back to the house. That afternoon, Dad buried him in the backyard near the rusted-out trash barrel that smelled like a dump until Dad set the trash on fire about once a month. Then it smelled like burning trash: not as distinct or weirdly pleasant as burning coal.

Before we left the house on Audubon, the Watergate hearings started to air on television. For some reason, my family taped those hearings on a small tabletop tape recorder. They would play them back and tape their own conversations as they sat around the table, eating, drinking, and smoking. One night, when Grandpa George, Grandma Mil, and Great-Uncle Bud came over and conversations were being taped, I asked, "Can I say something into the recorder?"

They all looked at me. "Sure," Dad answered.

I leaned toward the cassette player. "Richard Nixon's an asshole."

Dad, Grandpa George, and Great-Uncle Bud laughed out loud. Mom and Grandma Mil seemed pissed as they shook their heads. I didn't get in trouble for that, probably because I was right and simply mimicked what I heard them say over and over. I remember speaking into that microphone as much as anything that ever happened on Audubon Drive, including our last night.

During that last summer night in the house on Audubon, I said goodbye to friends that were as much a part of the thirty or so homes in the horseshoe-shaped neighborhood as the greenness of the trees and the grass or the oxygen we gasped after games of Kick the Can. We all said goodbye to Sidney, who rested in the ground near the trash barrel.

I shot a basket or two at the goal at the end of the street. I brought out my bug catcher and caught a few fireflies with my hands. I put one in my bug catcher and watched it try to escape over and over again, climbing and slipping, climbing and slipping.

Mom woke me up early the next morning and said I was going to Grandma Mil and Grandpa George's house for the day and needed to hurry. I looked in my bug catcher as the exhausted firefly crawled in circles along the bottom. I put on a pair of shorts and a shirt and climbed the stairs for the last time.

At the end of that day, pulling up to our new apartment, the sound of tires on gravel echoed throughout the car. Mom assured us we would like our new "house." We stopped in front of two green metal doors, both with gold knockers, gold address numbers, and black mailboxes.

"The one on the left, that's ours."

Walking in the front door, I noticed peel-and-stick tile instead of hardwood; I noticed three stairs directly opposite the door instead of nine; I noticed metal closet doors instead of grainy wood doors; I noticed a sliding back door leading to a yard smaller than the basement room Andy and I had shared. What I didn't notice was the console color TV that Great-Uncle Bud had given us. For some reason, it hadn't made it out of the house on Audubon. I headed back toward the stairs and climbed three, turned left, and climbed eight more. At the top of the stairs sat a bathroom and two rooms to the right and two rooms to the left.

"This is your and Andy's room."

Not big enough to accommodate parallel beds, the beds were arranged head-to-head in an L-shape with a table in the middle. Sam's room was next to ours, and Amy's was next to Mom and Dad's. I sat down on my bed and looked around. I already hated it.

The next morning, I walked out of the green metal door, looked to my right, and noticed a kid, a strange kid, bigger than me. He probably walked our way because he noticed a car in front of the building. I later learned that a strange car usually meant someone new had moved in. He walked toward me and said, "I'm James."

Other than Mr. Quisenberry and Rainbow Cleaners' customers, James was the first black person I ever remember meeting in my life. For some reason, he didn't scare me, the strange kid bigger, not that much bigger, but bigger than me. We became instant friends.

He showed me around. He pointed out a large steel electrical box painted the same color as our new front door. That electrical box would serve as third base and any other thing our imagination needed it to be. He showed me how short our walk to McGary grade school would be. A new school for me.

While James and I never shared homeroom or even one class, we became "after-school" friends. We usually walked home together, agreeing to meet back up as soon as we dropped our books or whatever else we carried home from McGary. We played either football, basketball, or baseball nearly every day. I sucked at baseball and preferred it least of the three. Too much standing around for a fast walker like me.

McGary Grade School and Plaza Park Grade School could not have been more different. Large brick homes with even larger yards surrounded Plaza Park, while large brick apartments with even larger asphalt parking lots surrounded McGary. Plaza Park had a shiny wooden basketball floor. At McGary, ours was peel-and-stick like the tile in our apartment. Coming from a short family, at least on Mom's side, and being a summer baby, meant I was very often the smallest kid in class. Being new and the smallest gave me something else to worry about. Luckily, I made friends fast and could play football and tag very well, so some of the boys took to me immediately. I also started to play lots of basketball at the outdoor goals on McGary's playground.

Like the overly large period I drew on my paper containing a few simple sentences, I had a bit of trouble with a two-page story we had to write in Mrs. Russ's second-grade class. She gave us the assignment on Tuesday, and we had until Friday to turn it in. Friday came and I did not turn it in. I told Mrs. Russ, "I'm still writing it."

She gave me until Monday. By Monday, I told her, "I'm not done yet."

I turned the story in a week late after she had sent a note home to Mom and Dad. She didn't believe what I had been telling her, but I did write more than ten pages about a man who went to live by himself in the woods. He built a cabin before winter came. At night, as I fell asleep with the night-light on, the one Andy hated and hated me for needing, I pretended to be him, the man sleeping in the woods. What I pretended at night, I wrote during the day. The man survived the winter, but when spring came, a bear came out of hibernation and killed him. End of story. I turned it in but didn't stop pretending to be him.

Trying to alleviate the sting of leaving our old neighborhood, Mom and Dad took us to the Fall Festival on the west side. I remember riding a carousel and eating a brain sandwich. I also won a goldfish, the color of my hair or a marigold, which I took home in a small fishbowl. We didn't have any fish food, so Dad crumbled a cracker into the bowl. He or she gobbled it up, well, like a starving catfish. The next morning, I crumbled another cracker and said goodbye before heading out the back sliding door on my way to McGary.

Like every school day, James and I walked home after school.

"I have to feed my goldfish, but I'll be back."

When I rushed through the sliding glass door, I found my goldfish floating on the water like a leaf. I bawled.

I adapted well to my new school, although I missed twenty-four days that first year. On the very last day of second grade, as I looked forward to summer break, I got the news that no McGary second grader ever wanted to hear. I'd been assigned to Room Six for the third grade: Mrs. Hansing's class. She was the oldest teacher in the school, and according to legend, horns came out of her head when she got mad, which she did very often, they said. My summertime joy faded immediately to worry, a worry I carried for three months. I couldn't believe I'd been so unlucky. A chip off the old block.

The summer of '74 faded like the long-stagnant air sunsets in Evansville as ads for the Jerry Lewis Labor Day Telethon began to air. As we played in the heat, which often caused me headaches so severe I had to go inside and lay down with a washcloth on my forehead and neck, Mom prepared to tell Amy that she would have to babysit us the rest of the summer as Rainbow Cleaners needed her full-time. Mom also had some disturbing news to convey.

Sitting on Amy's bed, Mom told her, "Hon, there was a little girl murdered last night in Savannah Gardens." Mom got up from the bed, went to Amy's window, and pointed to the building where the murder took place.

"I'm sorry to have to tell you this, but you need to know."

Police had arrested Bennie Daniels, a thirty-five-year-old man who lived just a hundred or so yards from our backdoor. He coaxed five-year-old Dawn Cosby into his empty apartment and smashed her face in with a brick. Police caught him only hours after she had gone missing, but the murder was done. Although only three miles away as the crow flies, Monroe Avenue felt light years away from our horseshoe-shaped neighborhood on Audubon Drive.

During my first day in Mrs. Hansing's class, as I sat near the front in my assigned seat, she confirmed the rumors.

"If you make me mad, horns will grow out of my head, and you don't want to see that." She looked right at me through her cat-eye spectacles, probably because I might have been the only kid in class that believed it. I don't remember ever believing in Santa Claus or the Easter Bunny, but horns growing out of Mrs. Hansing's head, sure, that could be real.

I never saw those horns grow, but they scared me. Scared me enough to miss ten days of the first grading period. One day, however, things began to look up when she told us we could pick any story out of the school library, and whatever we chose, she would read to the class. Me and a classmate asked her to read Edgar Allan Poe's "Tell-Tale Heart". She asked us if we were sure about that, and we insisted. Dogs, heights, the dark, and needles scared me, but not Edgar Allan Poe stories. Dad had a book of Edgar Allan Poe stories, and "The Tell-Tale Heart" was one of them. True to her word, Mrs. Hansing read the story to the class.

After that reading, my days absent fell from ten in the first grading period to eight in the second period, to four in the third, and eventually only two in the fourth. During that fourth period, Mrs. Hansing let us know that she planned to retire and move to Indianapolis. We were her last class. The day she told us that, she gave me a note to give my parents.

Mrs. Hansing asked my parents to bring me to her house so that she could give me some of her books. Being that both Mom and Dad loved to read, they happily accepted her invitation. Me and Dad drove to Mrs. Hansing's house. I don't remember too much about it, except that it was small and had a basement. That's where she kept the books.

At the beginning of the year, as Mrs. Hansing told us about the horns that would grow out of her head, I would never have imagined that I would be in her basement at night. I also could not have imagined that my days absent would creep down from ten to two. Mrs. Hansing, the woman I worried about and feared, had proven to be someone so different, so kind, so nice to me. Me and Dad picked out several books, including a three-book set of Edgar Allan Poe stories and a ten-volume set on the history of World War I. That night, when we got home, Dad wrote a note in each and every book, *"Daniel C. Melchior From Frances Hansing 3/11/75."*

On the last day of class, the worry and fear I felt had turned to sadness. I knew I was going to miss Mrs. Hansing. I learned that Miss Connor would be my fourth-grade teacher. I didn't know her, but Mom and Dad did.

When we weren't playing football or basketball, James and I liked to laugh. He introduced me, via cassette tape, to a dirty rapper named Blowfly. We played that tape over and over, laughing at the R-rated lyrics and catchy beats. One day, after listening to Blowfly, James handed me another cassette tape.

"You ever heard of Richard Pryor?" he asked.

"No, I don't think so."

"I'll let you borrow it but bring it back tomorrow. It's my dad's. He'll kill me if I lose it."

I listened that night on the "Richard Nixon's an asshole" tape recorder.

Assuming Richard Pryor was going to be dirty and not wanting to get in trouble if he was, I played the cassette low with my ear to the speaker, trying not to laugh. That night I realized that Wendell, our older friend who liked basketball and was considered the funniest guy in the neighborhood, simply copied Richard Pryor. The next day, I asked James if I could keep the tape for another day or so. I ended up keeping it for weeks. Soon, like Wendell, some of our friends considered me funny. They also considered me a hell of a basketball player. In the span of a few years, I'd become quite good. Most of the guys I played with were bigger than me and once strange to me because they were African American, and I, with my flaming red hair and freckles, obviously was not. I had adapted to living in Covert Village and rarely thought about our life back on Audubon Drive. I considered James, Wendell, Junie, and Eric friends, but to some, including my Grandpa Al, they were n*****s.

"See this ashtray; I made this ashtray. We make them as giveaways," Grandpa Al said as he held up a white steel ashtray with a Whirlpool logo stamped in the middle of it.

Grandpa Al gave everyone in the family, including Grandma Mil, Grandpa George, and Great-Uncle Bud, his ideological opposites, a white steel Whirlpool ashtray.

I knew Grandpa Al as a loving grandfather who liked to tease us and regale us with tales of fishing and frog gigging. He'd hold up his right hand and point his index, middle, and ring fingers to show us what a frog gig, which is something like a small trident-shaped "hunting" spear, looked like. He mimicked gigging a frog over and over until the story faded with a gulp of beer from a frosty mug. Like my dad, he also had a penchant for exaggeration, such as telling us one of his friends who had served in the army once sat on what he thought was a fallen jungle tree but instead turned out to be a Burmese python as big around as a barrel. He once caught a four-plus-pound bass that he had stuffed and mounted. He couldn't tell us that one was any bigger than it was because it hung on the wall where we could see it.

Unlike my dad, he practiced his Catholic faith loosely, yet tight enough to give him the belief he might be going to a better place than a spot at the small round kitchen table across from Uncle Bill.

Grandpa Al didn't have much use for or trust non-Catholics or non-whites, and that's where the divide between him and Mom really started. She loved him but didn't understand that part of him, nor did Dad, who seemed to like everyone and didn't see the need to write, etch, scratch, or paint his name and address, or sometimes his social security number, on damn near everything he owned. Grandpa Al did that and told everyone they would be idiots if they didn't do the same.

Regardless of the dynamic between Grandpa Al and my parents, to us grandkids, he was simply Grandpa Al, who drove the red Ford Galaxy, like the one Sheriff Andy Taylor drove in *The Andy Griffith Show*. Short and heavy with a horseshoe strip of blinding white hair and a corn tassel amount on top, just enough to comb over, Grandpa Al wore black browline eyeglasses like those worn by Malcolm X and LBJ when LBJ wore glasses. He also had a gut the size of a watermelon.

Working at Whirlpool meant Grandpa Al owned the finest refrigerator in the family, a side-by-side model with an ice maker. During our visits, Grandma Bessie filled bright-colored aluminum glasses, like the one I drank from as I listened to horse races with Uncle Bill, to the rim with half-moon-shaped ice and Double Cola.

Grandpa Al and Grandma Bessie's house, a shoebox two-bedroom, one-bath model with aluminum siding, the same material as those brightly colored glasses, gleamed like an operating room. It kind of smelled like one, too. They took great pride in their white-sided house. A row of hedges ran parallel along the gravel driveway, a driveway that contained enough fool's gold to keep my cousins and me searching for it for hours. The first color picture of my siblings and I came one Easter Sunday from the front and back yards of that tidy house.

While Grandma Bessie kept the inside spotless, Grandpa Al mowed the lawn, trimmed the hedges and the cedar trees, and swept the sidewalk. My brother Andy loved cutting grass and landscaping as much as he loved watching Mr. Quisenberry plow a field, so he often helped Grandpa Al during the summer. I did too, but not very often because Grandpa Al, who coined my nickname, would tell me, "Go pick the bagworms off the bushes, Big Red." That was his version of me helping to cut the grass. I never once got a chance to push his precious lawnmower. The one with his name etched on it.

During the summer of '75, I spent much of my time in Covert Village with more "after-school" friends, including Andre and Bakey, Channing, Tracy and Bennie, Junie, Eric, Gary, Chris, and of course, James and Stacey, his brother. All boys, all black.

Two days are seared into my brain from that scorching summer. The first is the day one of the older guys, and a very tall one at that, decided to set one of the large blue dumpsters on fire. The dumpsters sat inside a partial wooden fence to hide them from view. The tall friend went inside the fence with a roll of newspapers and some matches. We watched and waited, and then we smelled it. Burning trash, just like the trash Dad burned on Audubon.

We peeked in as the smoke thickened. And then, just like that: *crackle*, *crackle*, *pop*, *pop*, *pop*. An orange flicker, like my hair, leaped up. My first dumpster fire. We ran when we heard sirens. The flames lurched higher than the fence, fighting to get out. A firetruck pulled up. We watched as firemen quickly doused the flames.

The other searing day burned deeper and longer than the brief dumpster fire. The sun heated the pavement to the point that bicycle kickstands sank into the blacktop. I'm sure we could have fried eggs on that tar-colored surface, as some claim you can on scorching days. Channing decided to take a break from whatever game we were playing.

A few months prior, Aunt Mary had gotten divorced and had to also move into Covert Village, a destination for the downtrodden but hopeful. In her apartment, which was two buildings down from ours, Grandpa Al sat drinking beer and occasionally looking out the window, his version of babysitting. Unfortunately for Channing and the rest of us, Grandpa Al decided to look out the window as Channing took his break on the hood of Grandpa Al's Galaxy, a car he purposefully drove over any new blacktop he could find because he claimed, it "undercoated" the car.

The green steel front door of Aunt Mary's apartment swung open as Grandpa Al, in trousers and a button-down short-sleeve shirt, glared at Channing through his black brow line glasses like the ones....

"Get off my car, you fat-ass n*****."

Channing looked at us and then back at Grandpa Al. He didn't say a word as he eased himself off the hood. Grandpa Al slammed the door shut, and we went back to playing as if those words were never spoken.

A word that Mom and Dad did speak in the house got me in a good bit of hot water with my new teacher, Miss Connor. Apparently, Mom and Dad were about the same age as Miss Connor and had known her when they were in high school before Grandpa Al forced Mom to drop out. Mom and Dad knew Miss Connor as "Punkin," and I overheard them talking about her.

"Danny has Punkin as his teacher this year."

"Really; Punkin? That's great. He'll like her."

I did like her. She reminded me of the mom on the Waltons, who Dad thought was pretty. We watched the show every week. We sat around a table about the size of the one the Waltons sat around, except when we ate, Dad always wanted the small black-and-white TV turned on. We didn't always pay attention to it, but it was always on.

Several weeks into the new school year and wanting to test out whether I was funny and trying to tease my pretty teacher, I walked into the classroom last so that everyone would be there when I strolled past as she stood behind her desk.

"Hi, Danny, take your seat," she said.

I looked right at her, smiled, and said, "Okay, Punkin."

She looked like Mom looked when I told her everyone thought she was my grandma. My smile vanished, and my heart pounded. This was worse than the dime-sized period, the too-long-and-turned-in-too-late story, or even being dragged down the hall. I'd finally done it. She sent me to the principal's office. I sat in a chair, shaking like Mom. They called home. The principal talked to me, but I can't remember a word he said. I did know to never utter that word again.

Later that year, we got to take swim lessons at an indoor pool on Evansville's north side. My fear of water made the chlorine in that enclosed building smell like death. On my first day in the pool, I stood in the shallow end with others who couldn't swim. Some of my friends jumped carefree into the deep end. I understood envy. Green, unending envy.

The afternoon after our first lesson, I began to rub my eyes with my shirt collar. Miss Connor walked over. "What's the matter, Danny?'

"My eyes won't stop burning. I can't see." I thought about my Uncle Bill.

She put her hand on my forehead, raised my face, and looked into my eyes.

"Let's get you to the nurse."

"It's probably the chlorine, hon," the nurse said.

That night Mom and Dad handed me a note and told me to give it to Miss Connor.

"It's probably the chlorine," I heard Mom tell Dad.

For the rest of those lessons, I sat alone on the bleachers and watched the other kids learn to swim or jump into the deep end.

One month later, an outbreak of St. Louis encephalitis gripped the Midwest. Despite warnings that mosquitos were most active during the early evening, to avoid the heat, Grandpa Al cut his hedges at that time and suffered numerous bites on both burly arms. While babysitting us again on a Saturday, he complained of a severe headache, like the ones I had or sometimes pretended to have. Mom and Dad took him to the hospital, where he was diagnosed with the flu and sent home.

"Your Grandpa has the flu, so he can't babysit you until he gets better," Mom told us.

A week or so later, Mom said Grandpa Al still wasn't feeling well and needed to go back to the hospital. Later that week, on Saturday, October 4, 1975, Mom came upstairs to put me to bed. She pulled back the sheet and red blanket so that I could crawl under them.

"Hon, I need to tell you something," she said.

My head on the pillow, I looked at her face.

"You know your Grandpa Al has been sick. Well, he went to heaven today."

Her words didn't register. I continued looking at her face.

"Hon, your Grandpa Al died today."

I flipped over and buried my head into the pillow. My body convulsed as I wailed. Mom rubbed my back.

"It's okay, hon, it's okay."

Other than Sidney and the goldfish Sidney gladly would have eaten had they ever met, Grandpa Al was my first death. His death was also Mom and Dad's first family death as adults. Dad called on his high school classmates, Ted and Jerry Ziemer, Rudy's nephews, to handle the arrangements. Jerry signed the death certificate. According to that death certificate, Grandpa Al died at 7:48 a.m. that morning. Mom must have worried all day about giving me the news, waiting until right before I went to bed. Maybe she was so busy caring for Grandma Bessie and making arrangements and processing her own grief that she didn't have time for everyone. For me, she let a cozy bed and warm blanket provide comfort. That night, I stopped pretending to be the man in the woods.

Alvin A. Evans

Alvin A. Evans of 1810 Waggoner Ave., died at 7:48 a.m. Saturday at Deaconess Hospital.

Mr. Evans retired from Whirlpool in 1971 and was a member of Whirlpool Local No. 808 and Holy Spirit Catholic Church.

Surviving are his wife Bessie; two sons, William of Evansville and Charles of Nashville, Tenn; two daughters Mary Alice Brinkmeyer and Mrs. Dan Melchoir,

Another misspelling. "Who's gonna notice?"

We went to the visitation that Sunday, but we kids only stayed for a bit. Grandpa Al had never scared me before that day, but he scared me then. While Sam, Amy, and Andy walked up to look into the casket, I only looked from a distance. I could see his distinct nose and a bit of his white hair. Like viewing the edge of a pool, I didn't dare get any closer than that.

After our brief stop at the visitation, Dad drove us to now just Grandma Bessie's house, which sat not even half a mile from Holy Spirit Catholic Church. Mom and Dad were kind enough to know we didn't want to spend hours and hours at a visitation, so instead, they let us play in the backyard, just as we always did before, with Dollie locked alone, like me on the pool bleachers, in Uncle Bill's bedroom.

A few hours later, Mom and Dad brought Grandma Bessie home. We kids gathered in the sterile living room while waiting to leave. Mom scattered about picking things up, putting things down, asking Grandma Bessie what she needed, and telling her we'd be back tomorrow morning. I watched Mom and then asked, "How come everybody cries but you?"

With that, she stopped, plopped into an empty chair, and bawled into her hands.

We missed school that Monday to attend the funeral, one of sixteen days I missed that year and the only one that might have been legitimate. I'm not sure why I slipped back into perpetual absenteeism, but I did. Like the dogs, strange kids bigger than me, the dark, Grandpa Al in a coffin, and those mythical horns, walking into Holy Spirit Catholic Church scared me. It was the first time I remember being in a church; the organ, the statues, the stained glass, the muffled whispers, coughs and sniffles, the creaking of doors. As Halloween lurked around the corner, God himself couldn't have built a more haunted house.

After his funeral, we went home to our Section 8 apartment and threw a white plastic drug-store football with blue and white stripes I'd received for Christmas. I'd written my name on it in large black block letters like those on Dad's army coat. DAN MELCHIOR 3525 MONROE AVE, just like Grandpa Al insisted.

I was nine when Grandpa Al died. I hated the name Big Red, and I hated picking the bagworms he claimed had only arrived "when those n*****s down the block showed up." I hated what he said to my friends, and I doubted his theories on undercoating and those bagworms. I also couldn't help but love and miss him. He was, after all, my Grandpa Al.

A GUN, A BOMB, AND A PLANE

● ● ● ● ● ● ● ●

Early in 1976, Dad had managed to find a good job as a buyer at Grimm Lumber, which allowed Mom and Dad to buy another house. They signed the papers a few days after America's Bicentennial Celebration. This one was smaller than the house on Audubon and was the one we referred to as kids and still today as "the house on Waggoner."

The house was full of fleas that had no choice but to bite us instead of the nowhere-to-be-found dogs of the former owners. Within weeks, we "bombed" the house with a pesticide canister. It did the trick.

Dad soon received a promotion and a raise and went about spending it. He worked on the house constantly and had new carpet installed. Mom's friend Helen came over and wallpapered the dining room. Dad turned a closet into an entertainment center, albeit with a small black-and-white TV, until he bought a nineteen-inch, color RCA model to replace the lost console.

Dad also took advantage of working at Grimm when he stripped the paint off our dining table, the one with the squeaky leaves, and then had mill workers dip it into a maple stain. That made all the difference. Layers of paint did nothing more than hide the natural beauty of the wood grain, knots, and all.

"Dan, somehow Bill got a gun," Mom said to Dad.

Someone sold Uncle Bill a cheap "Saturday night special" that sat on his table, fully loaded, next to his pack of filterless Camels and his always-filled beer mug. He smoked up to four packs a day of those Camels.

Bill scared people enough without a gun; now that he had one, a blind man, he terrified some, including Dad. Without Grandpa Al around, being blind made Bill feel extra vulnerable, and the gun gave him a sense of safety. I learned about the gun as I sat at the kitchen table one summer afternoon. Mom had just returned from work and stood at the stove getting ready to prepare supper, most likely Spanish rice. Mom had found a recipe for it, and everyone loved it, except I didn't want green peppers in mine. She always put some in a separate pot before adding the peppers.

"What?" Dad asked.

"Bill has a gun. Somebody sold it to him."

"What kind of gun is it?"

"I don't know, a pistol of some kind."

"How do you know?"

"I saw it," Mom explained. "He said with Daddy gone, he and Mother needed some protection. He said he could tell if someone was coming in the back door or front door. Either way, if he heard someone, he knew where to shoot."

"Is it loaded?" Dad asked.

"He has a box of bullets on the table, so I'm sure it is."

I saw a look of panic in Dad's darting eyes. He knew immediately where this conversation was headed. He looked toward the blue China cabinet that housed his Kessler whisky. He opened the bottom door and removed the Kessler and a shot glass. He poured a shot and started to sip it before turning up the glass and finishing the shot in one gulp. He repeated the process but did not attempt to sip the second one. He simply downed it.

Mom didn't watch but probably knew from the sound of the latch on the China cabinet door that Dad needed a bit of liquid courage.

"Dan, you need to go over there and take that gun from Bill. He's gonna kill someone with that thing."

The Kessler didn't seem to blunt Dad's panic. He paced in the small kitchen as his eyes darted from ceiling to floor to China cabinet and back again.

"Either way, if he heard someone, he knew where to shoot," Mom repeated.

As Dad paced about, thinking of Uncle Bill with a gun, I thought of stories about Uncle Bill. After Fred Gresser's truck blinded him, everyone in the family, including Dad, became less afraid of him. Before losing his sight, Uncle Bill was an "aginner," meaning if you're for it, he's "agin' it." He could start an argument over the color of the grass. "Bullshit, it ain't green; it's yellow, yellowish green like those pineapples Hawaiians eat. Pineapples that ain't been skinned yet, you know what I mean?" And from those types of debates, the fights began. Over and over and over. And no one, I mean no one, wanted to tangle with Bill. One story that Dad told many times became legend in our household. Whether it was true or not didn't really matter. Dad believed it, and I could see him recalling it as he thought about retrieving the gun.

As Dad told the story, wishing it were his, apparently, Uncle Bill, sitting in a bar, got into an argument, maybe about the color of grass, with an equally drunk man. The argument turned into a fight, and other patrons had to separate the two men. While Uncle Bill went back to the bar to continue drinking, the other man went home. He returned thirty minutes or so later with a shotgun. Knowing he couldn't beat up a shotgun, Uncle Bill jumped off the barstool and ran. The man chased him out of the back of the bar. As Uncle Bill ran down the alley, the man fired the single-barrel, break-action shotgun, hitting Uncle Bill in the back with a load of buckshot. Figuring the shotgun could fire only one shell without reloading, Uncle Bill turned back toward the man and chased him down the alley. He caught the man and nearly beat him to death, the shotgun laying harmlessly next to him. As the story goes, the man spent several days in the hospital. Uncle Bill did not.

"That's what your Uncle Bill did to a man with a gun, and now he has the gun," seemed to be swirling in Dad's head.

After the nineteen-inch RCA, our next step up the entertainment ladder was cable TV, including HBO. I watched *One Flew Over the Cuckoo's Nest* over and over and learned what Mom and Dad meant when they said Uncle Bill received electroshock therapy. Uncle Bill never got to see that film, but I'm sure if he had, he would have seen himself in Randle Patrick McMurphy.

"You know you're asking me to get a loaded handgun from a blind man with a German Shephard that already bit me once?" Dad implored.

"He's gonna hurt someone, or he's gonna hurt himself. He sits there all day listening to the radio, drinking beer and smoking. Do you think he's happy? Maybe that's why he got it. Dan, you gotta do something. Besides, Dollie only bit you because you were carrying that toolbox. She thought you were gonna hurt him."

Dad had a toolbox that was actually a .50 caliber M2 ammo box he had taken when he was in the army. As much as Dad hated the army, he loved that toolbox. "Indestructible," he liked to say. The only other thing besides his dog tags that he kept from the army was his duffle bag, his name in white block letters, spelled out and spelled right—"IOR"—and his olive-green jacket with his name spelled in black block letters.

"What if he doesn't want to give it to me?" Dad retorted.

"He ain't gonna hurt you. He likes you."

"I can't just take it. He knows how close you are."

What Dad meant is Uncle Bill could tell how close people were to him just by the sound and feel. He knew if you stood five feet away or two feet away. For that reason, Dad couldn't just sneak over and grab it. And besides, if Dad did do that and Bill got mad, what would Dollie do? She'd already bitten Dad once.

"Dan, you've got to go get that gun. He takes it to bed with him. He might shoot Mother in the middle of the night. Who knows?"

Dad got a pleasant look on his face when Mom said that, as I don't think he would've minded if Uncle Bill shot Grandma Bessie.

Dad exhaled loudly. "Alright, I'll be right back."

And with that, Dad opened the kitchen door. I usually wanted to go everywhere with Dad, but that day, I didn't ask. Dad walked out into the driveway and started the blue Chevy Malibu with the cracked engine block. The funny thing is it started right up—just Dad's luck.

Grandma Bessie and Uncle Bill lived only one and a half miles away on the same street. I sat at the kitchen table, listening for sirens. Surely if something terrible happened, Dad or Uncle Bill or Grandma Bessie would call the police or an ambulance.

Mom continued getting supper ready and doing laundry while I listened. About an hour later, I heard the familiar sound of tires on gravel and the rumble of the Malibu's engine. I stood up and opened the door. Dad got out of the car, pistol in hand, smiling. I could tell he'd had more to drink than just the two shots of Kessler he'd taken before leaving.

That night, the gun sat on our freshly stained table as we ate, just as it sat on Uncle Bill's table. I'm not sure what happened to the bullets. Eventually, it made its way to Dad's sock and underwear drawer. When I was the only one in the house, I used to reach under his socks and grab that gun. I played with it like it was mine until I heard someone, and then I would return it to its place beneath Dad's socks.

In October 1977, Mom added a blanket to our beds and took our sweaters to the cleaners. Dad especially enjoyed wearing sweaters and sweatshirts. He loved the coziness of wool and cotton but hated acrylic, which, as mentioned, he claimed could shoot a static electricity arc three feet long during dry winters.

At 1:20 p.m. on Tuesday, October 18, after the sun had burned off the morning chill and caused some to remove their sweaters, three miles from our drafty home with a leaky kitchen ceiling, local oilman and Hollywood "hang about" Ray Ryan slowly backed his brand-new dark blue Lincoln Continental Mark V out of a parking spot at Olympia Health and Beauty Resort.

The health club sat among low-rise retail buildings and apartments on the east side. Ryan had a home one mile away on Lombard Avenue and called Evansville home, although he spent considerable time in Kenya and Palm Springs, California.

As the Lincoln rolled out of the parking space, a bomb blew Ray Ryan and his car into thousands of pieces, vaulting the hood over the top of a two-story apartment building. The hood landed in a courtyard, like a falling leaf, more than 150 feet away.

Before his murder, Ryan and actor William Holden had become co-owners of the Mount Kenya Safari Club, which became a focal point of an IRS investigation. In 1970, courts convicted Ryan of altering club records after receiving a subpoena in order to hide memberships of known Mafia leaders. Authorities sentenced Ryan to three years, but the conviction was later overturned on appeal because it was determined that Ryan had altered the records before the subpoena had been issued. Ryan's attorneys also argued the records were changed to protect charter members in the club, including President Lyndon Johnson and actor John Wayne.

Before his troubles in Kenya, Ryan testified against two organized crime figures he claimed tried to extort $60,000 from him in 1963. During his testimony, Ryan told the court that Marshall Caifano, known as Johnny Marshall, told him that not even then-Attorney General Robert Kennedy could protect him if he didn't pay the $60,000. Perhaps Marshall was correct. Because of Ryan's known mob connections and Hollywood friendships, the story of his murder became international news. Investigators never solved it. Everyone on the east side, including Dad, although technically Dad resided on the southeast side, home to hillbillies and mongrels like us, claimed they heard the blast. Ziemer Funeral Home handled the arrangements, but residents wondered if there was anything left to bury.

In the house on Waggoner, my bedroom with Andy was originally a one-car garage. Dad put in a window where the garage door used to be in case the furnace, which sat in an adjacent closet, blew up and Andy needed to escape the room. Apparently, the window near my bed served as my escape hatch. That furnace clicked and clacked twenty-eight times before igniting. I used to lay in bed at night and listen to the furnace kick on every so often. I always counted the number of clicks and clacks and still remember twenty-eight.

I kept counting those clicks and clacks, even when Andy took Amy's bedroom after she married not long after turning eighteen.

Not quite two months after Ryan's murder, on a typical foggy, drizzly night in December, all of us except Mom sat around the kitchen table watching *Happy Days* and *Laverne & Shirley*. Dad sat at the head of the table, best for viewing the tiny black-and-white television. While he ate a piece of cake, I snacked on cheese and Oscar Mayer™ Braunschweiger, a liver sausage that pretty much looks like shit on a cracker. No one else, except Dad and me, liked Braunschweiger, so I didn't have to worry about my two brothers or sister eating any of it. I applied that same logic when I used to ask Mom for birthday cakes with shredded coconut. Even Dad didn't like that.

As Mom finished doing the dishes and checked on the laundry, a breaking news story interrupted the shows. A DC-3 twin-engine prop plane carrying the University of Evansville Purple Aces basketball team to a game against Middle Tennessee State crashed during takeoff. With that news, Mom put down the dishtowel and sat down with the rest of us. She stared at the television. Mom had never been to an Aces game and didn't know much of anything about basketball, yet she cried. Dad got up and made a pitcher of Manhattans and a highball for Mom. He drank the pitcher dry. After watching the news for twenty minutes or so, Mom wiped her eyes, got up, and finished the laundry as we continued watching.

Three people initially survived the crash, but two died en route to the hospital. The last survivor died at the hospital. Twenty-nine people died. Twenty-nine people involved in the game of basketball, one of Indiana's many religions. Twenty-nine people with families, stretching from Bethel Park, Pennsylvania, to Miami, Florida. Twenty-nine people, twenty-nine people, twenty-nine people rang like a bell.

Dollie, once a highly trained guide dog, had forgotten most of her training. Uncle Bill didn't need her to guide him from the kitchen table to the finest refrigerator in the family that Grandma Bessie kept stocked full of beer for her youngest son.

Sitting so much took a massive toll on him. He got fat, and his back killed him in ways he had a hard time describing. It got so bad that Mom and Dad took him to the doctor, who ordered an X-ray. The news wasn't good. Uncle Bill was being consumed by cancer. Doctors determined nothing could be done but keep him comfortable.

Mom and Dad celebrated their twenty-fourth wedding anniversary with a very rare dinner out, followed by a stop at Welborn Hospital to see Uncle Bill. He had been admitted a few days earlier and wasn't doing well. An anniversary and a hospital visit, a twenty-first birthday and a "homicidal maniac," any birthday and Christmas Eve; Mom always shared "her" days but never seemed to mind.

The next day, Uncle Bill died at the age of forty-three. Mom, Dad, Aunt Mary-Alice, Uncle Charlie, and Grandma Bessie were with him when he died. Mom had worried about Uncle Bill her entire life; now, she could finally stop. "Surely, poor Bill's in heaven," Mom used to say, "because his life was pure hell right from the get-go."

Dad again called his former classmate Ted Ziemer and made the arrangements. Uncle Bill had requested that he be buried in a mausoleum.

"If you're buried in the ground, it's forever gonna be dark, but if you're buried above ground, you might someday see the light again," he said after going blind.

Mom and Dad made sure to respect his wishes. Grandpa Al's small marker on the ground in Parklawn Cemetery is near Uncle Bill's spot along the mausoleum wall. The distance between them is just enough.

A few days after Uncle Bill's funeral, Amy and Aunt Mary went to get Dollie. No one in the family either could or would take Dollie as a pet. Dollie greeted them with a smile and a wag when they walked into the house. They grabbed Dollie's leash as she looked forward to a walk. When they headed for the car, Dollie sensed trouble. They struggled to get her in the back seat. Once they did and had managed to shut the door, Dollie paced, twirled, spun and twisted, all while defecating and urinating all over the back seat. The car smelled like a baking outhouse. Amy recalled she had never seen an animal so nervous. "Poor Bill," had become "Poor Dollie."

At the end of the ride, they removed Dollie from the car and walked her toward a building. Dollie stopped resisting. They handed Dollie's leash to an attendant who walked her in. Dollie didn't bother to look back. She had accepted her fate. The door to Animal Control closed behind her.

WANTED

● ● ●

Although Grandpa Al said "n*****" many times, it was never uttered in any of our homes, not even by Grandpa Al, because Mom and Dad, but especially Mom, wouldn't allow it. That changed on Christmas Eve 1978 or maybe 1979, Mom's forty-fifth or forty-sixth birthday.

In the late 1970s, there were no explicit labels to stop parents from buying material not suited for children. For Christmas, I wanted Richard Pryor's *Wanted* album. "Hey Old Dude, I want Richard Pryor's new album...." That's what I would have written had I believed in St. Nick, but I didn't. If he was real, he seemed a bit of a jerk because he gave things like bicycles and real footballs, not the plastic ones, to rich kids while giving us drug-store imitations and always some article of cheap clothing. Like Nixon, Santa seemed a bit of an asshole.

Our Christmas tree resembled Grandma Mil's with tinsel, a nativity set, and a sheet playing the part of snow-covered rolling hills. We had small white lights instead of the C5s Grandma Mil preferred, but other than the color and size of those lights, the trees were at least cousins, if not siblings. The flesh of our three ceramic wise men ranged from tan to oak. Mom and Dad always said that Melchior, being Persian, was the oaken one who brought the gold. When we questioned why we were descended from "the black one," we heard something like, "Skin color is like hair color or eye color, it doesn't really matter." We didn't think much about it except that it seemed cool to have the name of a wise man even though no one, including Mom, went to church anymore.

Mom and Dad delivered on my ask. The white album cover featured a sketch of Richard Pryor scowling. Being a two-record set, the album opened like a book. Inside were pictures of Richard walking, talking, smoking, and performing. He looked so cool and had the same mustache Dad wore, which is why, to me, Dad looked like a white Richard Pryor, especially when Dad donned a sport coat, which he always did on Christmas Eve, Mom's birthday.

That night, before we got ready to head to Grandma Mil and Grandpa George's for Christmas Eve dinner, I put on the track "Heart Attacks." In that eight-minute bit, Pryor said, "bullshit," "fuck," "ass," "shit," "motherfucker," "piss," and more multiple times. He also talked about not being able to swim, an embarrassment I shared with him, my hero. During the next track, "Ali," Pryor said "n*****" multiple times.

At some point, Mom walked into the living room and didn't like what she heard.

"What in the world is that?" she yelled.

"It's the album you got me."

"That's what we got you for Christmas?"

Mom scowled while Dad laughed, which didn't surprise me, given he liked all kinds of humor. He told the same Confucius jokes Redd Foxx did on his *Burlesque Humor* album that Dad kept in his small collection of jazz and comedy records. Mom and Dad argued as I continued to listen. Despite the vulgarity and "n*****," they let me keep the album. I got the gold I wanted that day but hated that the gift caused an argument on Mom's birthday. It should have been her day, but it never was.

As one decade ended and another began, Theresa Gilligan, a name everyone in Evansville would soon know more than the name Ray Ryan or Richard Pryor, told her mother and sister, "There's really so few people who ever find the kind of love we have." She made those comments on a shopping trip as she bought a brass plate to hang in her kitchen. On the plate were inscribed the words "One Love Forever."

Theresa met Patrick Gilligan when they were both students at St. Theresa's Elementary School; Patrick and Theresa's first date was on a grade-school hayride. The young couple separated during their sophomore year of high school when Patrick moved with his family to

Chicago. Patrick ran track and became a member of the rifle club. When Theresa learned that Patrick's father, a former corporate executive, had died, she sent Patrick a sympathy card. That card rekindled their relationship. Patrick went on to graduate from Lake Forest High School in 1967.

Theresa attended Rex Mundi High School, where she participated in drama and the pep club. She also became a member of the Catholic Students Mission Crusade. When Patrick returned to Evansville, the young couple married. Theresa became active in Right to Life.

Theresa and Patrick started a family when Lisa Lynn was born. Gregory Patrick arrived one year later. The family of four lived a life of love, devotion, togetherness, strength, joy, hope, compassion, and conviction of faith, like many in Evansville.

Perhaps Theresa thought about hanging the plate after they had just completed a new addition to their fashionable northside home. The renovation included a family room and laundry area. Patrick, extremely security conscious, had installed triple-bolt locks throughout the entire house, although he had not yet done so for the new addition that had an outside door leading to the laundry area.

On Monday, January 14, 1980, Indiana State Police checking a neighboring home, discovered Gilligan's house had a broken window and decided to investigate. The officers discovered the home had been burglarized via the newly installed laundry area door. Upon entering the house, police found the bound bodies of Theresa, Lisa Lynn, and young Gregory Patrick. Each had been shot execution-style in the head. The police found Patrick, who had broken free but had been beaten about the face several times with a blunt instrument, perhaps a gun, before also being shot in the head. Police discovered a stack of guns by the back door. Whoever broke into the home had planned to take Patrick's guns but, for some reason, left them behind.

Police informed neighbors of the slaying and told them to lock their doors and remain alert. In the wee Tuesday morning hours, a team of more than twenty assembled to process the scene and begin a manhunt. State police alerted the media, and by the time most residents prepared morning coffee, Evansville was on edge. Another mad-dog killer remained at large.

Amy, who had just turned seventeen and stood about the same five feet or so as Mom and with a similar athletic build, also worried like Mom. But she felt safe during the day and prayed police would capture whoever had killed the Gilligan family.

Around 9:00 a.m., a citizen found a library card belonging to Patrick Gilligan and several shell casings in a Kmart parking lot near Highway 41. In the afternoon, during a press conference, police named an at-large suspect, Donald Ray Wallace.

Wallace, a troubled kid whose IQ was a reported 147, had attempted suicide several times while in the Indiana Boys' School, a juvenile correction facility in

Pendleton. At age sixteen, officials at the Evansville State Hospital found Wallace to be "homicidal with possible suicidal tendencies."

Fathers in Evansville checked their locks over and over while mothers held their little ones tighter and closer. Families prayed while peeking out of windows and listening for anything out of the ordinary. Owners put their dogs in the yard, and every bark became an alarm.

We didn't have a dog, and the only gun we had was Uncle Bill's .38 special. I'd never seen any bullets and Dad didn't get it out from under his socks that night, so it served no purpose. That night dragged on as we sat around the kitchen table with more lights on in the house than usual. Mom and Dad didn't complain about wasting electricity. We watched TV and waited for news that Donald Ray Wallace had been captured.

About twenty-four hours after police discovered the Gilligan family, Donald Ray Wallace climbed a wrought-iron fence, scaled a westside home, and entered the attic through a window. Inside the attic, he listened to a police scanner as officers continued their search. Downstairs, an elderly woman watched television, unaware the man suspected of killing the Gilligan family hid just above her like any spider in an attic.

Acting on a tip from a man who, while walking his dog, had seen Wallace climb into the attic of the woman's home, police surrounded the house. They knocked on the door, told the woman they needed to check her attic, and subsequently arrested Wallace without incident. He was unarmed and did not resist. Television stations broke the news of his 11:30 p.m. capture. Residents, used to turning in early, could finally get some rest. As Dad finished his last Manhattan, he turned the lights out, and everyone, including Amy, went to bed.

As a relieved city relaxed, Grandpa George and Grandma Mil contemplated closing Rainbow Cleaners, "the plant," after thirty-three years in business. They had been robbed at gunpoint twice over the years, including by a man wearing a red wig. That man had jumped the counter, grabbed Mom, and put a gun to her head. I don't think that had anything to do with the decision to close Rainbow Cleaners as Mom still pressed clothes while Dad barely went near the place except for the day that me, Grandpa George, and Dad slopped hot tar, another cousin to burning coal, on certain parts of the flat roof that Grandpa George suspected of causing the leaks that dripped on newly cleaned clothes. The plant that Grandpa George had envisioned as Dad's future was just about as big a dump as the Savannah River Defense Site, to hear Dad tell it.

Just over two months after Wallace's heinous crime, as Mom and Dad drove past 3204 Washington Avenue around six forty-five in the morning on the way to Rainbow Cleaners for Mom's work shift, former Republican Evansville Mayor Russell Lloyd, just awake and still wearing pajamas and a T-shirt, walked into the kitchen in his home at that address to get a cup of coffee. The doorbell rang, and Lloyd answered. Upon opening the door, he asked, "Who are you?" A loud argument followed. "You don't know what you've put me through. I want you to get this Joe Freeman off my back," the intruder implored. "What gives you the right to barge into my house at this time of the morning?" Lloyd asked.

Instead of answering, the intruder fired four gunshots from a .38 caliber handgun, similar to Uncle Bill's, striking Lloyd in the neck. The intruder fled in a beat-up, medium blue 1967 GMC pickup with a dented fender and missing tailgate. The truck had oversized tires and a California license plate on the front, and an Indiana license plate on the back. Witnesses had recalled seeing the eyesore truck in a driveway next to Lloyd's home.

Just over an hour after the shooting, police arrived at 2425 South Norman Avenue on Evansville's southeast side. The pickup was parked, headlights toward the street, near a decrepit shotgun house with a leaning, crumbling porch.

The home had been purchased on contract from an Evansville Fire Department captain, even though it did not have complete plumbing facilities at the time of the contract. The housing commission's office advised that the home should not be sold, leased, rented, or otherwise occupied until it was brought into compliance with Evansville's building codes. Apparently, the buyers of the Fire Department captain's home did not know the house had been condemned.

Upon entry into the southside home, Evansville police arrested Julie Van Orden, a commercial artist who was born in Indiana and raised in San Diego, California, before she returned with her mother to Indiana and the condemned house that she and her mother bought from the Fire Department captain.

The day after Julie Van Orden's arrest in the killing of Russell Lloyd, Van Orden's mother told reporters it was her daughter's idea to move back to Indiana, where she had spent so much of her childhood. "She loves the trees, and she loves the grass, you don't see much of that in California."

Mom and Dad remembered the day of the shooting well but never claimed to have seen anything out of the ordinary near the Lloyd home that morning.

Van Orden had been active in Republican politics and attended several local functions with Joe Freeman, the city housing inspector who had befriended Van Orden after meeting her while serving notices on the condemned home. Freeman, according to Van Orden's mother, began bringing her gifts, including earrings, a necklace, and a coat. He also loaned her $3,000 to help repair the home. Van Orden's relationship with Freeman eventually soured as he continued serving notices while also offering to help her with repairs. He often visited at night, according to Van Orden's mother, who believed their relationship was platonic and said she should know "because I live here."

On the fateful morning, Van Orden told her mother she was going out to look for Joe Freeman's car because she had thrown a brick through its window when Freeman had visited the night before. She wanted to take a picture to document that all she had done was break the window and nothing else. She wanted evidence in case she had to pay for it.

After Van Orden couldn't find Freeman's car, she drove to Lloyd's house and parked in a neighboring driveway before peering into the former mayor's house and then ringing the doorbell. Three days after that ring, doctors turned off the respirator that had kept Russell Lloyd breathing. The father of six was only forty-seven years old. Lloyd's funeral was held at Ziemer funeral home. Ted Ziemer Jr. was a close political associate and friend of the late mayor.

The violent crime in Evansville seemed normal to me; Benny Daniels, Donald Ray Wallace, Julie Van Orden, and a man in a red wig I heard about, seemed like characters in a story, nothing more. So normal, in fact, that I didn't blink or budge when a white kid with long hair that I didn't recognize, wearing blue jeans and a white T-shirt, walking with a girl, pointed a gun at me as I dribbled a soccer ball in the front yard. The gun looked like a .45, but so did the BB gun that the manager of Covert Village gave me one summer. The kid, older and bigger than me, laughed when he pointed it at me, so perhaps it was just a BB gun. Either way, by then, I wasn't scared.

Around the time of the Gilligan family tragedy and the murder of Mayor Lloyd, my collection of Richard Pryor albums expanded when I started shoveling snow, cutting grass, or selling stolen *Playboy* magazines to my buddies for money to buy Richard's albums. My collection eventually included *That N*****'s Crazy*, ...*Is It Something I Said?*, and *Richard Pryor's Greatest Hits*. *That N*****'s Crazy*, which was released in 1974, is considered one of the most groundbreaking comedy albums ever recorded. Richard Pryor exposed white audiences to places most had never been, but not me; I had seen some of the things, people, and places Richard described.

I listened to those albums over and over and over and memorized my favorite routines such as "Ali," "Have Your Ass Home by 11:00," "Wino & Junkie," and "Flying Saucers." Unlike Wendell, I didn't pretend the jokes were mine. I started them with, "Have you heard...." I practiced in a whisper at home and in my head on the bus. "Be home by eleven; you understand eleven, don't you, n*****? You can tell time can't you...."

I rehearsed those routines as I drifted off to sleep, pretending to be Richard Pryor. I wanted to be funny, not eaten by a bear.

My fourteenth birthday hovered a week or so out on the horizon when I read in the Evansville Press that Richard Pryor had suffered severe burns in an accident while freebasing cocaine. According to the short blurb, the burns were life threatening.

"Richard Pryor's gonna die," I remember telling Dad and all of my friends.

Whirlpool washer, Kenmore dryer, gas stove, broiler oven, kitchenette set...read the ad in the newspaper. No mention of the Whirlpool refrigerator because Amy's boyfriend bought the house, and he wanted the refrigerator to stay.

A few weeks before I prepared to start playing freshman football, real football, with helmets and shoulder pads, Mom, Dad, Uncle Charlie, and Aunt Mary had decided to put Grandma Bessie in a nursing home after she had been diagnosed with breast cancer. Grandma Bessie fumed when they told her, but no one had the time nor the money for her to remain at home. Although Mom and Aunt Mary went to visit her often in that nursing home, they had to take Andy or my cousin Julie with them to appease Grandma Bessie. She had told the staff at the nursing home that she didn't want to see her daughters.

After getting off the bus in the morning, my friends and I, including a few new ones who also played freshman football had about thirty minutes to kill before homeroom started. On game day, we were told to wear our football jerseys. My new friends walked the halls with me and James. Most of the guys were black, with a few other white boys in the group. To preppies, we were a mix of mongrels and mutts.

"Danny, do 'Wino and Junkie,'" James often said with a grin that had become wider after short updates in the newspaper hinted that Richard would recover from the burns.

With confidence, I launched into the routine.

"Winos don't get drunk like everybody else, though, right? Wino be directin' traffic on Sunday morning. That was my favorite thing about the winos 'cause I used to, I didn't want to go to church so I would hang with them. "Wino be standin' there, Hey fool, you better slow that car down. Goddamn, don't come drivin' down through here like you're crazy. This a neighborhood, this ain't no residential district. "[Singing] L...O...R...D...Jesus on my mind....

"Yeah, N*****, I know Jesus."

Suddenly we froze.

"Good morning, B-O-Y-S."

"Good morning, Miss Cupp," we replied.

I finished the routine once Miss Cupp, the speech teacher my siblings warned me about, ambled out of sight.

Quoting Richard Pryor verbatim was the only way to do it, and because of that, I said "n*****" a lot, but I never once said it in anger and never once directed it toward anyone, especially James or any of my other friends. If I had, I'm sure they would have beaten my ass, which they could have because they were bigger than me.

One late fall day, after my football season had ended, Mom and Dad invited Grandma Mil, Grandpa George, Uncle Tom, and Great-Uncle Bud over for Sunday dinner. Mom fixed steak and onions and, for Grandpa George, liver and onions. Grandma Mil had stopped making it for him many years ago, ever since that time when he came home, and he told her he wasn't hungry even though she had kept it warm for him while he sat in a bar getting drunk. Immediately after she put the liver and onions away, Grandpa George made a sandwich.

With that, Grandma Mil opened the fridge, took out the iron skillet, walked to the back door, and threw the liver and onions, skillet, and all into the backyard, all while Grandpa George silently watched.

"I'll never make liver and onions for you again as long as you live."

Mom and Grandma Mil both put up with similar men and became extremely close, but I'm guessing that Mom making Grandpa George liver and onions didn't sit that well with Grandma Mil. Mom, never one to hold a grudge, knew the story and why Grandma Mil stopped fixing it, but Mom made it for him anyway.

Great-Uncle Bud liked liver and onions, too, but didn't eat any that day, which was unusual for him. He usually drank martinis from a water glass and ate heaping plates of food, but he had been diagnosed with leukemia a few months back and had red scars all over his neck. I don't remember him eating anything that day. Cancer and radiation apparently ate any appetite he once had.

What I do remember about that Sunday is, as I watched an NFL football game, he handed me a 35mm Kodak camera with German writing on it. He told me he won it in a poker game during WWII.

"I want you to have this," he said.

With that, he took a nap on the couch. That day, his best friend and fellow WWII veteran, the godfather I don't remember, Forrest Arvin, who never married and never had any children, died of lung cancer.

Exactly four weeks later, on another Sunday, Great-Uncle Bud died. He didn't want a funeral or any visitation, so we simply went to Miller & Miller funeral home, looked at his body, carried the casket to the hearse, drove behind it in two cars, dropped it off at Oak Hill Cemetery, and left. I've been told by Uncle Dave that after we dropped off the casket, I said something like, "Well, that was like taking out the garbage." Perhaps I remembered Dad shoveling Sidney into the ground next to the trash barrel. Regardless of my intention or lack of consideration, my comment upset

Grandma Mil, who had given me Bud's veteran flag at the funeral home.

Apparently, many of Bud's friends felt the same way I did because when they found out he had died and that there was not a ceremony, they laid into Grandma Mil. Bud had far more friends than anyone had known, but his best friend had been Forrest Arvin, so at least Grandma Mil didn't have to worry about Forrest being upset.

That winter, as bleak as the leafless trees, grew colder and darker when Grandma Bessie died of breast cancer just thirteen days after Great-Uncle Bud's death.

During those long winter nights, Dad, often wearing a hideous creamsicle-orange sweatshirt, sat at the maple-stained dining room table completing paperwork for his latest job, selling life insurance. He sipped his Kessler Manhattans and took an occasional drag off a More cigarette. While he worked, Mom wiped, scrubbed, and tidied the kitchen. I usually sat at the table, watching whatever channel Dad wanted on, even though he didn't watch; he just listened. While he listened, I listened to Mom and Dad trade jabs.

"Did you pay SIGECO?" Mom asked.

"*Yes*…I paid SIGECO," Dad replied.

"What about the water?"

"Yes, goddammit, I paid the water. Jesus Christ. How many questions can you ask?"

"I'm just worried…."

"I know, I know, you're worried. You're always worried. Worried, worried, worried.... I know. Goddammit."

At that point, Dad usually got up, opened the bottom door of the China cabinet, and mixed another Manhattan. Once or twice a week, depending on how long the arguments lasted, Dad would realize he needed more Kessler whisky, and with that, I'd go to the malodorous closet and get his army jacket and my coat. I rode with Dad as we made our way two miles down Covert Avenue to Shamrock Liquor Store. I would sit in the cold car, watch Dad walk deep into the brightly lit store, disappear, and then emerge, standing at the counter exchanging cash for a bottle of whisky and often a laugh with the clerk. When he got in the car, he would hand me the bottle.

"Hold this," usually the only words spoken during our trips to the Shamrock.

A year later, in December, Julie Van Orden's trial began in Columbus, Indiana. Witnesses included Genna Lloyd, Russell's widow, and police officer Farrell Hodgkins, who testified that Van Orden "had a hatred for Lloyd, Freeman, and all city officials." He told the jury that the day before the shooting, Van Orden expressed to him and his partner Bobby Hollis that when she waitressed at the East Quarter nightclub in the Washington Square Mall, Lloyd, Freeman, and other city officials would come in there and try to date her. When she refused, they encouraged her to prostitute herself. She also told the officers that the two men spread dirty lies about her and had stories about her placed on television.

The jury also heard testimony from Caroline Freeman, widow of Joseph Freeman, who had died of a heart attack one year before the trial. Mrs. Freeman testified that the night before Van Orden shot Lloyd, Van Orden came to her home looking for her husband, who was not at home. Van Orden became agitated and told Mrs. Freeman she had filed two police reports against her husband and did not want him on her property.

"She said, 'He's crazy. He's crazy. Why do you stay with him? Is it for the movies and books?'" Mrs. Freeman testified. She said she did not know what Van Orden meant by movies and books. Van Orden also claimed Freeman had pinched her breasts and buttocks. Mrs. Freeman retreated into the house and then heard a tapping on the front door glass. When Mrs. Freeman turned around, Van Orden pointed a gun at her.

"She looked very grim when she was pointing that gun at me, very serious."

After Van Orden left, Mrs. Freeman called the police, who advised her to talk to her husband before deciding whether to press charges. She told the police operator, "It isn't easy to talk anything over with my husband. What should I do?" Again, she was advised to talk to her husband.

Earlier testimony had revealed that Freeman had, in fact, loaned Van Orden three thousand dollars to repair her home and that he had helped her do some of the work. Mrs. Freeman was asked if her husband had loaned Van Orden the money.

"I guess he did. I didn't have anything to do with it."

A jury of seven men and five women found Van Orden guilty of murder. The judge sentenced her to forty years in prison. Mom felt bad for Mrs. Freeman. She couldn't imagine being married to a man like Joe Freeman.

After my sophomore year of football, I stopped playing high school sports because I had my first real job, a job I got because Rainbow Cleaners closed forever. The same year, Richard Pryor released *Here and Now*, in which he spoke of his travels to Africa and his epiphany that he had been wrong all along. He vowed never to use "n******" again, and as far as we know, he never did, at least not on stage. Emulating my hero, I did the same thing when quoting his routines by changing that word to man, boy, fucker, motherfucker, or anything else less offensive but not entirely clean because that would dull the razor's edge that needed to remain. For using the word, even in imitation and admiration, I am profoundly sorry, especially to James, Clarence, Nick, Don, Tim, Mose, and all my other friends who walked the halls with me. And to Channing, I apologize on behalf of my Grandpa Al, who, unlike Mom, carried a hatred I could not understand.

"Never hate anyone, no matter what," is what Mom always said.

RICK-A-JAY

● ● ● ●

With Rainbow Cleaners shuttered for good, Mom went to work for Rick-A-Jay Cleaners as a presser, which is a step down from a silk finisher. To Mom, it didn't matter; the owners, Ron and Dorothy, seemed like nice people, and their plant was much cleaner and more well-run than Grandpa George's establishment, although it did sit among the seedy hotels with the musty drapes on Fares Avenue or "Old" Highway 41, as some called it.

"New" Highway 41 had just as many stop lights as Old Highway 41, but it was two lanes wider. Old Highway 41 and New Highway 41 ran as parallel as rails on a train track, both working to divide the Cake Eaters from the West Siders.

Rick-A-Jay had multiple outlets around town, including one on First Avenue a few miles north of Ziemer Funeral Home, one further east on South Weinbach Avenue near the levee where Rudy Ziemer died, one on Diamond Avenue in the back of a Busler's gas station, and even one as far east as Newburgh in another Busler's gas station. The clothes came to Rick-

A-Jay literally from east, west, north, and south. Unlike Rainbow Cleaners, Rick-A-Jay's work proved so steady that Mom could press clothes for eight, nine, or sometimes ten hours a day and not have any downtime, which she didn't crave anyway. Rick-A-Jay's steady business fit Mom to a *T*.

It didn't take Ron and Dorothy long to realize they had a keeper in Mom. She could press clothes faster and better than anyone they'd ever seen. If she pressed them faster than they could be cleaned and dried, she'd help bag clothes or wait on the customers. A five-foot, hundred-pound dynamo. "That Dots is a hell of a worker."

At first, Mom just pressed the basic trousers as well as sports and suit jackets, but once Ron and Dorothy saw her speed and mastery of removing wrinkles so quickly, they let her work on the more difficult items like drapes, curtains, dresses, and gowns. She had most likely told them she knew how to press anything, but they wanted to try her out first before trusting her with the more delicate and expensive weaves. Rick-A-Jay had a gas-fired boiler, so there was no fire to see in a firebox, but they had Mom and the fire in her belly.

The steady work at Rick-A-Jay comforted Mom and eased her worries. "We're always busy," she said with a smile when asked, "How was work?" After a couple of years at Rick-A-Jay, Mom grew so comfortable that she suggested to Ron that I would be a good choice to replace a delivery driver who had decided to quit. I was only sixteen and hadn't been driving very long, so I had my doubts, or rather my fears, about this opportunity. Also, football didn't excite me as much as it once had. Usually one of the smallest guys on the field, I had to play harder than I wanted and still took a beating and also suffered from many headaches. Between the headaches, I thought about the job.

I've never driven a van in my life.

What if I lose someone's clothes?

What if I get in a wreck?

Do I have to drive all the way to Newburgh?

Like the dogs, and the strange kids bigger than me, this idea of a job, a job where I drive in traffic all over town—and customers, and Mom, and Ron and Dorothy depended on me—scared me. Scared me to death.

"Why worry? You'll be fine. You're a good driver, according to your dad," Mom said. I thought to myself, you don't drive.

I'm not sure Mom's words comforted me, but I stamped down my fears and took the job. In order to learn the route, I rode around for a couple of days with the guy who quit. When we got to Newburgh, he told me he wanted to get a stromboli. When I went into the gas station and asked for the dry cleaning, he walked down to Pizza King, which was at the far end of the strip mall.

I got back to the goldenrod-colored van and threw two bags of clothes into the back while he strolled toward the van with a stromboli in hand. He got into the truck and unwrapped the stromboli, which, by the way, in Evansville, is a sandwich, not the type of stromboli that the rest of the world knows. He took a bite, then another and then another before getting out of the van.

"I'll be right back," he said.

I sat in the van and waited for him to return. He came back carrying a brand new, uneaten stromboli. He got in the van and laughed.

"I told 'em the first one was too burnt to eat. I got one and a half strombolis for the price of one."

"It didn't look burnt to me."

"It wasn't."

I rode with him for one more day. I didn't want Russell to teach me anything. On the other hand, I didn't have a choice when it came to Lenora Cupp.

Miss Cupp, who I loathed for interrupting my Richard Pryor imitations, taught my first and only high school speech class. Every time I saw her, I dreaded the thought of taking her class just like I spent a summer dreading Mrs. Hansing's class. Sam, Amy, and Andy, who all had her, told me she made students lie on the floor and mimic frying bacon. "Sink or swim," some told me at the time, an attempt, I suppose to get me to confront fear head-on, but which provided zero comfort because I hadn't been in a pool since the chlorine burned my eyes in the fourth grade. Like Richard Pryor, I still couldn't swim.

In high school, I talked a lot, but only to my friends I had known for years. When lumped in with college preparatory students, I stood out for not standing out. I didn't raise my hand and, despite being nearsighted, sat in the back, usually near a wall. The boy preppies wore neon Polo and Lacoste shirts with turned up collars, while I wore terrycloth imitations that, for some reason, were sold in those days. A kid I won't name once called me "dishtowel" and earned lots of laughs from the class before getting a right hook from me. I knocked him out cold, and to this day, I don't regret it, although his insult was clever.

Because speech was a required class, I thought at least some of my not-so-preppy grade school friends would be in Miss Cupp's class with me. I was wrong. The odds didn't work out in my favor. I walked in and saw twenty or so preppies, including many pretty girls, who liked the boys that wore neon shirts. I looked at the tile floor as I ambled toward an empty seat. I sat down and stared at the desk and thought about those horror stories my siblings told me about Miss Cupp and about her interrupting my Richard Pryor routines a year earlier. I was a determined little shit, and if Sam, Amy, and Andy could endure it, so could I.

That very first day, we had to get up in front of the class and state our name, grade school, and an interesting fact about ourselves. Miss Cupp started on the right and went down the row, motioning each student to come up front. Because I had been the last student to come into class, I had taken the only open desk, a middle chair in the middle row that didn't provide the back-of-the-room-near-the-wall comfort I craved. Although it would take a bit to get to me, my heart pounded, and I could feel the sweat beginning to drip from my armpits. A kid named Danny talking about working as a dishwasher that summer is the only thing that I remember hearing from any of my classmates.

As I stared at the Formica desk, I heard Miss Cupp call my name. Still staring at the desk and then the floor, I stood up and slowly walked forward. I moved past her desk and backed up until I felt the chalk tray against my ass. Raising my head, I realized, unlike me, no one else felt the need to stare at their desk. Forty eyes, like arrows, daggers, and spears, pointed directly at me. I glanced at the neon-framed faces but stopped on none and avoided eye contact altogether.

"Well...," Miss Cupp said.

Her eyes, beneath a grey-and-white beehive hairdo, pierced like two more daggers.

"Are you going to say anything?"

I looked from the corners of my eyes at her and the floor. I wanted to run home and never come back. Her black shoes shined as if freshly polished, something Mom would appreciate. Her pantyhose glistened. I noticed that she was taller than me. Her tied-at-the-waist dress, which accentuated her bloated midsection, reminded me she wasn't perfect. She continued staring while I tried to remember what I was supposed to say.

Still trying to remember, "name, grade school, interesting fact," I closed my eyes and tilted my head back, hitting the chalkboard. My classmates giggled. Like a frightened squirrel, I retreated to the safety of my desk. At first, I wanted to cry. But because I was muscular for a small guy, some kids thought I was tough, and I did not want to shatter that image.

While watching the rest of the class state their "name, grade school, interesting fact," *easy to remember when sitting down*, I looked at Miss Cupp as she looked at them. I stared at her as she had stared at me. One student walked away as another walked toward the front, and that is when Miss Cupp tilted her head and looked at me with the faintest grin as if to say, "Don't worry, you'll get through this."

That semester, I gave a speech on basketball and another on Muhammad Ali. I learned to outline my thoughts and slip in a funny comment and an impression of Ali's "I am the greatest." I could imitate Ali almost as well as Richard Pryor. And yes, I did lie on the floor vibrating, pretending to be frying bacon. Miss Cupp must have graded on improvement because I passed with a B despite getting a zero on "name, grade school, interesting fact."

Summer came, which meant I could run both the morning and afternoon routes. Twice the work, but twice the money. I rode my bike to Rick-A-Jay in the mornings, arriving by nine-thirty. My job was to get to each of the morning outlets after ten and then get the clothes back to the main plant on Fares as quickly as possible, so they could meet the "In by Ten Out by Two" service that most dry cleaners adhered to.

Each morning I stood outside to cool off from my bike ride in the warm breeze. The yellow concrete block building with the green awning and trim sat between a transmission shop and a seedy motel that advertised "daytime napper" rates. A sad, dilapidated strip club named The Busy Body sat on a nearby corner, within walking distance to the motel. I'm sure the strippers and customers inside The Busy Body made up the whole of the motel's "daytime nappers."

A large two-lane canopy attached to the front of the building allowed customers to load or unload their clothes without getting wet should it happen to rain. On top of the canopy was a large white, two-sided sign with "Rick-A-Jay" spelled out in green cursive letters. Even someone with poor eyesight could read it from more than a block away.

When my sweat slowed, I walked in the front door. Mom always stood off to the right, pressing a pair of trousers. Because the front door was open, she didn't always hear me come in. Air conditioning is not effective or efficient in a dry-cleaning plant because of the steam. During summer, all the doors and any windows that can open are always open.

"There he is," Ron yelled nearly every day. "Dan, the man."

Mom would turn around. "Hi, hon."

"Hey," I said to Mom while waving to Ron.

Early on, we had a routine.

Waiting for just the right time to leave so that I wouldn't get to Weinbach before ten, I sat on a bench next to Mom's station. Her oblong press was gunmetal grey with a goldenrod pad, practically the same color as the van. Plastic bags swirled in ninety-degree flashes of breeze. The smell of perchloroethylene (PERC, a dry-cleaning solvent), steam, and plastic swirled about as my sweat returned.

A standard dry-cleaning press is a bit over four feet wide and four feet tall and looks like an open hot dog bun waiting for a frankfurter. With the top pad open, Mom had to reach as high as her head to pull the pad down onto the clothes. She worked her press like a master. Smoothing trousers with her right hand before lowering the pad and engaging a burst of steam with the pedal at her feet. She opened the press, flipped the trousers, and finished the other leg.

Once, just for fun, I timed her. She could press two pairs, including putting them on a hanger and getting the next pair from the tote, in less than a minute. Two pairs of trousers in less than a minute. And not just any two trousers, two once-wrinkled, now perfectly pressed trousers.

One day, during the afternoon shift, Mom stopped her work and walked a pair of trousers back to Ron. I could see them talking, but the bags, steam bursts, and fans muffled their voices. Ron shook his head, took the trousers, and threw them in a tote. Mom had found a spot Ron hadn't removed. Spots and stains never got past Mom. She walked back toward her press, shaking her head and raising her eyebrows while looking at me in a "How did he miss that spot?" sort of way.

Later, Mom asked Ron, "Is there more that needs pressing today?" There was not, so we were released. Free to go.

I had loaded the truck with all the finished clothes that needed to be delivered east, west, north, and south.

Because Mom didn't drive, I took her with me to Weinbach before dropping her at the house on Waggoner. With Mom in the passenger seat, the clothes loaded in the back, and both windows open, we headed toward South Weinbach Avenue near the levee. The wind whipped through the van, causing the plastic bags to whistle and whine and forcing us to almost shout.

"Are you playing basketball today?" Mom asked loudly.

"Yeah, if it doesn't rain."

"Well, be careful and drink lots of water."

"Mom, I'll be fine," I shot back.

"Who do you play with?" she asked.

"A bunch of guys...Bushrod; why do you care?"

"Just asking."

"Have you seen Bushrod's mom lately?" I asked.

"I did see Bonnie. I saw her the other day at Great Scot; the woman never ages."

"You smell that?" I asked.

"You mean the brewery?" Mom replied.

"Yeah, I was thinking about that the other day. You know what that reminds me of?"

"What?"

"Tomato soup. That smells like Campbell's tomato soup."

"Hmmm," she thought. I haven't made you tomato soup in a while. Do you want some?"

"I don't like it in the summer. Too hot. Do you remember when I walked home from second grade at McGary for lunch that day, and you made me tomato soup? I think you turned the burner off so it wouldn't burn, and by the time I got home, it was cold. I didn't want to say anything, but I remembered Dad once saying that Tabasco made things hot, so I put a bunch in the soup. It didn't make it hot, but it sure made it spicy!"

Mom shook her head. "I'm sorry, hon, I don't remember that. I shouldn't have served you cold soup. Was it wintertime?"

"I don't remember. It doesn't matter. I think it's funny."

"Well, anyway, I'm sorry about that. That's horrible."

"It's not horrible, Mom. It was one lunch. Who cares? Anyway, I really like spicy food. Maybe that's why!"

When we arrived at Rick-A-Jay's Weinbach outlet, a small brick building painted Rick-A-Jay yellow and green, the smell from the brewery had faded, replaced by nothing, really.

Mary Sievers worked in the store. She was in her sixties or seventies, had severe acne scars and had an obvious but nice chestnut brown wig of perfectly straight hair. I heard someone, maybe Ron, once describe her as "hard to look at."

Me and Mom walked into the store, both carrying cleaned and bagged clothes.

"There they are!" Mary said, smiling. "How's my new favorite driver?"

"I'm good. You say that to all the drivers?" I asked.

"No, just the redheads. I was one, you know?"

"I didn't know that." We all chuckled.

After we unloaded the finished clothes at "Mary's," I dropped Mom off at the house on Waggoner.

"Bye, hon. Be careful," Mom said.

Mary was easy to talk to, even for a shy kid like me. She was sweet and funny. I liked her, and Mom liked her too. At some point, Mary retired and was rarely seen or heard from. I had heard someone found her dead, sitting alone in a chair, eaten alive by some sort of cancer, or so they said. Every time I think of Mary, I still get pissed at "hard to look at."

Banter with Mary and discussion about food and basketball and anything else was our routine the summer of '82 and the summer of '83, at least until late August, when things changed like they always did.

TWO CHAIRS AND A TABLE

● ● ● ● ● ● ● ●

Mom started cleaning at 4:00 a.m. She rose especially early that Saturday in August 1983. Our house always glistened, but it needed a bit more polish for the visitors—more accurately, the bidders—coming to look at everything we owned. These were people that we didn't know, who were likely to judge us as they determined the worth of our spoils. While Mom vacuumed the burnt-orange living room carpet and wiped down the already-spotless shiny paneled walls, I hid things. My things. Mostly football and basketball cards, a few favorite books, and the Kodak camera Great-Uncle Bud gave me before he died. I hid them in pockets of jackets that the bidders wouldn't touch. I hid them in the backseat of the blue '74 Chevy Malibu with the cracked engine block. I usually drove the Malibu while Dad and Andy drove a Ford Fairmont that Dad had purchased a few years back. It was Dad's first ever brand-new car purchase.

I hid things because, at age seventeen, I'd seen enough and knew enough that sometimes you just need to hide things. Earlier in the week, I had asked James to hold onto my Richard Pryor albums until after the auction.

After taking Mom to work, Dad returned home with a box of donuts, including cinnamon twists, my favorite. He took inventory of things he thought might bring a few dollars by writing them down on a yellow notepad, things like Mom's antique dented, patinated, copper tea kettle, which adorned the antique library table that someone, I don't know who, had given Mom and Dad. Dad's optimistic list indicated we could have a really good day, multiple thousands of dollars perhaps. One item on his list caught my eye: "Wooden lawn chairs and table - $100."

I built those chairs and that table out of scrap, framing two-by-fours, furring strips, and faded plywood. Over two steamy summer days when I was twelve, I measured, sawed, and hammered, measured, sawed, and hammered. I painted them white with leftover paint and a crusted brush Dad had failed to clean. I labored over those two chairs and a table but knew for certain they weren't worth anywhere near one hundred dollars.

Dad went to pick up Mom and returned before noon.

"Hi, hon," Mom said, walking in the door. "Is everything ready?"

"I guess. It's as clean as it can be," I said.

"Hey, Dots, look at this list I put together. I think we might do okay today."

Dad handed Mom the yellow notepad. She glanced at it and flipped a few pages.

"We're losing the house. How is that okay?" she asked, handing it back.

Dad's shoulders wilted.

"Do we really have to do this?" I asked.

"We don't have a choice. I'm sorry," Dad snapped.

Dad opened the fridge and grabbed a beer. He didn't mention why he was sorry. Was he sorry we were losing another house or for losing the job at Grimm Lumber or the job at Kentucky-Indiana Lumber or the others that I've forgotten that cascaded into us losing another house? Was he sorry for the affair that likely was the cause of him losing his job at Kentucky-Indiana Lumber? Dad's decisions had consequences that affected us all. What was he sorry for? Those decisions? I wondered.

A loud knock reverberated through the house. Dad walked into the living room with the burnt-orange carpet and opened the door. A man in a suit stood on the porch. He was taller than Dad and close to his age, but the man didn't have a full head of hair like Dad. He walked in and immediately started to look around. He had a notepad, too, only his pages were white.

The man explained that everything for sale needed to be on his notepad and that we should indicate a minimum starting bid.

"What if we don't get the minimum?" Dad asked.

"We'll adjust."

"What if we don't get any bids?"

The man explained there are usually buyers who will take the miscellaneous items that don't sell. They buy them for a lump-sum amount. He said not to worry; most things sell, although they might be at a price lower than we want. He also explained that as the auctioneer, he gets a percentage, so he was incented to get the highest possible price.

Dad and the auctioneer sat at the kitchen table and wrote down all the items that we wanted to auction. I noticed the auctioneer's white pages were pre-printed forms used especially for auctions. He seemed to know what he was doing.

Potential bidders started showing up at 1:30 p.m. Mom's hands shook as she paced around with a dus-trag and towel. Cars lined the curb as curious neighbors milled about and chatted with the bidders, whispering and faintly pointing at us standing in the driveway while trying to avoid eye contact. Soon the small yard resembled a ranch's pen, the herd ready to stampede our one-story home.

I waited for the auctioneer to begin. I looked forward to hearing him talk fast and drive prices up, as I'd seen on TV. Perhaps I could learn something by watching someone who wasn't too shy to speak in public. I stood in the driveway as nothing of that sort happened. He didn't talk fast, he didn't drive up prices, and he simply told people to walk through the house as he handed them copies of the list. They spent what seemed like an eternity inside the house. When they emerged again, most of the energy had evaporated.

"This one's a dud," I heard someone say.

Some people stayed and listened as the auctioneer went down the list. A few people asked if they could see certain things again, which was okay by the auctioneer, so some ventured back into the house. A few items, including the library table, sold quickly and for a decent price.

After that, a few other items sold—a decorative wood-burning stove, sconces, iron trivets, and iron ice tongs—before the herd continued to thin. Silence from the remaining few prompted the auctioneer to stop and walk over to Mom and Dad. They whispered. Mom and Dad looked at each other and shook their heads.

"For all remaining items, the minimum bid will be one dollar," the auctioneer told the bidders.

Like a storm approaching a cornfield, a buzz returned. Items moved quickly, with most going for the minimum.

"The antique copper kettle. Do I have a bid for this beautiful decorative piece?"

"One dollar."

"Any other bids, two dollars, do I hear two dollars?"

Mom stared blankly at the house's white siding.

"Sold, one dollar."

Mom's head drooped as she turned and walked toward the backyard.

Buyers grinned and whispered about their buys. Cheer and gloom became neighbors in the same yard.

"We have a few more items on the list," the auctioneer said to fewer and fewer people.

"The lawn chairs and table. Any bid on the lawn chairs and table?"

"The ones in the backyard?" someone asked.

"Yes."

The questioner smirked. "Those homemade things? No bid here."

A few other buyers chuckled.

"So, we have no bids. Okay."

After everyone left, Dad, his shirt hanging on him like a limp rag, and the auctioneer went into the house, sat at the kitchen table, and tabulated the results.

"Eight hundred dollars," the auctioneer declared.

After the auctioneer left, I went into the house and retrieved the Bob Griese football cards and Jerry Sloan and Moses Malone basketball cards, along with those of lesser talented players. I rescued the Edgar Allan Poe books given to me by Mrs. Hansing from above the ceiling panels in my bedroom, the place I normally hid Playboys and Penthouses. I took *Pudd'nhead Wilson*, the book Grandma Mil and Grandpa George gave me for Christmas and the one that had $142 hidden in its pages, from beneath my mattress. Finally, I went outside to the Chevy Malibu and reached under the seat for the WWII-era German camera. I thought about Great-Uncle Bud.

On Sunday, we started to load things that hadn't been sold into a U-Haul. I walked into the backyard and moved a pot of marigolds off the white table before picking it up and carrying it on top of my head. Mom and Dad walked through the house while I went through the shed and backyard, looking for anything we might have forgotten. Mom and Dad were standing in the gravel driveway as I came around the corner. Mom grinned when she saw me carrying the pot of marigolds.

"What about the chairs?" I asked Dad. "The ones I made. Are we taking those?"

"Yeah, let's get 'em."

As Dad and I carried one of the homemade wooden lawn chairs up the ramp and into the truck, he grunted. "Damn, these are heavy," he said. "You did a hell of a job on these. They'll probably last forever."

I smiled.

INDIAN WOODS

● ● ● ● ●

A few days after the auction, Mom and Dad filed for bankruptcy. Other than the mortgages on the house and car payments, Mom and Dad also owed $2,500 for Mom's hysterectomy. Apparently, we didn't have health insurance. A blow that was perhaps crueler than even the bankruptcy and auction was the fact that the guy who repossessed Dad's car was in Uncle Dave's wedding and one of Uncle Dave's best friends. He remembered Dad and was embarrassed when he showed up in a suit, exchanged pleasantries, and then drove away in the silver Ford Fairmont.

After all of that, we moved into a townhome in an apartment complex named Indian Woods. We kept the living room set, four beds, pots, pans, dishes, forks, knives, spoons, placemats, pictures, books, clothes, and, of course, the maple-stained kitchen table, with fold-down leaves on either end. We also kept the matching chairs that frequently caused Mom to yell, "Stop leaning back in the chairs; they're going to break," which they never did. The chairs did, however, need to be repaired more times than I care to remember. The legs became loose and groaned like an old man getting out of bed due to our leaning back in them in defiance of Mom's pleas. The squeaky leaves on the opposite ends of the table were like Andy and me: two brothers who had shared the same place for too long.

While looking for a place to live, Dad had discovered Indian Woods, a new development of rental townhomes that had a "luxury" façade, which, in part, meant a four-by-eight wooden deck off one of the bedrooms. In exchange for cheap rent and a paycheck, Dad became the manager. Yet another job, but with his handsome looks, parted hair, tasteful mustache, and propensity to wear a sportscoat, Dad cut the figure of a man well qualified to manage a luxury apartment complex. A fresh start at forty-nine.

The day we moved in was his first day on the job. Dad oversaw an operation that included a swimming pool, community room, tennis courts, and luxury grounds. The luxury grounds just meant there were grassy areas between buildings and a small playground house in the middle of a parking lot. The playground consisted of that playhouse and a swing, nothing more.

The bedroom with the deck, intended as a master bedroom, should have been Mom and Dad's; instead, Mom gave it to me and Andy, presumably because it would provide us with a bit of room, like the space Grandpa Al and Uncle Bill needed.

The room was more Andy's than mine because he had a record player and a black-and-white TV and didn't want me using either. Perhaps that was his pay-back for me insisting that Mom and Dad hang the Captain Crunch poster over my bed in the basement of the house on Audubon. Captain Crunch was my ver-sion of Aunt Mary's crinoline. Andy also hated Richard Pryor and Prince more than I hated Michael Jackson, his favorite singer and dancer, and didn't want their albums playing on his record player.

At the house on Audubon, we had our own rooms, and then we didn't. At the house on Waggoner, we shared a room, and then we didn't. At Indian Woods, we shared a room and then…I doubt Andy ever thought he would have to, at nineteen, share a bedroom with his little brother.

When we moved into Indian Woods, Mom didn't plead with Andy and me to get along. She knew we were much too old for that. She simply told us, "I'm sorry, but you two will need to share a bedroom again." She told us that as we sat, leaning on the squeaky leaves at opposite ends of the kitchen table, never bothering to look at each other.

Andy and I had to share a room because Sam, still trying to figure out what to do after graduating with a business degree from Indiana State University of Evansville (ISUE before becoming USI), moved back in with us after a short stint living with a buddy of his, who also happened to work at Grimm Lumber where Dad once worked. Sam's roommate married the own-er's daughter and took Dad's job. Losing that job at

Grimm Lumber sent Dad into a job vortex he would never recover from. Every other job paid less than the one before, and as Dad's pay plummeted, his trips to the Shamrock became more and more frequent.

Still "running the route," as we called it, Mom and I continued our routine of me showing up in the afternoon at Rick-A-Jay, waiting for all of the clothes to be cleaned and pressed, and then driving to Mary Sievers on Weinbach to drop off the first load. After that, instead of heading to the "House on Waggoner," we headed to Indian Woods. During our drives, we talked more than we ever had up to that point. Twenty, thirty, or forty minutes a day in the van, just me and Mom. In my earlier years, I grunted, groaned, snapped, yelled, or simply ignored Mom, but ever since I took the job at Rick-A-Jay, I learned how to talk to her. In 1984 I was eighteen and wasn't certain what I wanted to do, but I knew I wanted to go to college.

"Maybe I should just go to ISUE, like Sam," I told Mom.

She listened.

"I could live at home and keep running the route. The only thing is, I've looked at class schedules and won't be able to run the morning route. I want to take all my classes in the morning, right in a row, so I can get in and get out, kind of like "In by Ten, Out by Two."

She laughed. We are, after all, a practical bunch.

I did choose to go to ISUE, at least for the first year or so, to see how it went, but because all my classes would be in the morning, Ron would need someone to run the morning route. I had an idea, but I didn't tell Mom, and I didn't tell Ron. I wanted to see for myself.

Sitting at the small round table in Grandpa George and Grandma Mil's kitchen, where they sat after Bud's fiancée died while he was in the army, where they sat after Rudy Ziemer was killed, and where they sat after JFK was killed, and where they sat after the three paratroopers accused of murdering Rudy Ziemer were acquitted, and where they sat when they told Dad Rainbow Cleaners couldn't continue to support two families is where me and Grandpa George and Grandma Mil sat as I waited to run the afternoon route.

"Grandpa," I said, "I have a question."

"Okay."

"You know I'm going to ISUE in the fall, right?"

"Yeah, I heard that."

"All my classes are going to be in the morning, and Ron's looking for someone to run the morning route."

Grandpa George's eyes opened a bit wider. He looked at Grandma Mil, as did I. I saw her grin that signaled her thoughts: *We've been retired for three years; please help me get him out of the house.*

"You wanna do it?"

"Sure thing, I'd love to," he said before I finished asking him.

Dry cleaning was the only business Grandpa George had ever known, and at seventy-one, he went back to work. Within a few days of that conversation, I taught Grandpa George the morning route, but more importantly, I taught him to wear a seat belt. "Ron told me when I started that sitting up this high in a van, if you hit someone and you're not wearing your seatbelt, you're gonna go right through the windshield. I don't know if he's right, but I don't wanna find out." Grandpa wore his seatbelt, which was easier for him to do than to stop searching for the clutch.

In his life, Grandpa George had rarely driven an automatic. Every time we got in the van during the training rides, his left foot beat the floorboard like a Clydesdale. We laughed our asses off every time, but not as much as we did when he'd forget to take his seatbelt off and try to get out of the van.

"Goddammit," he'd say, laughing.

We laughed a lot.

Speaking of laughing, I figured I might as well show Grandpa George the afternoon route, which included the trip to Newburgh, in case he needed to fill in for some reason. One afternoon, I drove while Grandpa sat among the clothes on a horizontal bench seat in the back, and Mom sat in the front passenger seat. That day was particularly busy, and the van was stuffed with clothes so tight that the bags barely moved in the wind coming through the wide-open windows. I could barely see Grandpa George amongst the clothes. Ron had helped us load the van and watched as we headed out of the parking lot, three generations: a son, a mom, and a grandpa. I gave Ron a quick salute, and him looking every bit like the character Henry Blake from *M*A*S*H*, yelled at the top of his lungs as we drove away, "Grapes of Wrath!"

The clothes swayed a bit as I turned onto Old Highway 41. Me, Mom, and Grandpa George laughing our asses off.

PUEBLO PASS

● ● ● ●

"*What?*" Mom screamed at Dad.

My elbows rested on the squeaky leaf of the maple-stained kitchen table. My chin topped my overlapping fingers and thumbs. I stayed calm as Mom frantically rushed upstairs to use the phone that sat on a bookshelf in the small hallway between the three bedrooms.

"What?" reverberates in my head to this day. The year was 1984 or 1985. I cannot remember exactly which, but I remember the yell.

The Indian Woods apartments we lived in were only the first phase of construction in a complex that would also include small, single-family patio homes ideal for new families or retirees. Charlie Braun, Dad's boss, and his partners planned to build a whole mess of them, and that's where Mom's scream came in. Charlie explained to Dad that he needed someone to clean the new houses as they were being built so prospective buyers would see nice, clean, well-maintained homes. When Charlie asked Dad if he knew of anyone who could do this, Dad immediately thought of Mom. She had cleaned

Grandpa George and Grandma Mil's house for years, and she had cleaned our house to the point that no one in the family even tried to imagine or say that their house was cleaner than ours. Mom was known by one and all as the cleanest woman they had ever known. Perfect for the job.

Dad came home one day and mentioned to Mom that Charlie was offering eleven dollars an hour to clean those houses. She didn't even make six an hour at Rick-A-Jay. "It's almost double the money, and it's right here. You can walk to the houses that need to be cleaned."

"They won't be building houses forever. The cleaners is steadier. I don't want to clean those houses," Mom countered.

Mom and Dad talked about it for more than two days. "It means a lot more money," Dad said over and over and over.

"It's not stable," Mom said over and over and over.

"Charlie's going to build houses all over Evansville when this is done. You'll have plenty of work." Mom didn't buy it, but Dad could be very convincing. Finally, he wore her down. She agreed to leave Rick-A-Jay and go to work for Charlie cleaning newly built houses. Dad could barely contain his excitement. His wife was finally getting paid real money, and for something she was better at than almost anyone.

Mom never walked to those houses. Dad proudly delivered her along with all her cleaning supplies. This could turn into something big. Maybe she could get more people to help. Maybe they could start a business. They could clean houses all over. Dad saw an opportunity.

One late afternoon, around five-thirty—I was back from the afternoon route because not having to drop Mom off saved me time—Mom arrived after cleaning the latest house. Dad seemed antsy, like when he had had to get the gun from Uncle Bill.

"Hey, Dots, I need to tell you something."

"What's up?" Mom asked as she looked in the refrigerator for what she planned to fix for supper after drinking a glass of iced tea.

"Charlie came to see me today."

"Okay," Mom said, not really paying attention.

"He found a company that will clean the houses for cheap."

The first "What?" Mom uttered was not so loud....

"He found a company that will clean the houses for cheap. He doesn't need you to clean the houses anymore."

That's when I heard it. Hyping and exaggerating like Dad, the "*What?*" that I heard, I swear, could be heard around the world.

"*What?*" Mom screamed.

"Maybe you can work for the company," Dad tried to reason.

The fire in Mom's belly, like Vesuvius, spewed lava all over the kitchen.

"Motherfucker. Goddammit. Goddammit. We just lost a fuckin' house, and I just lost a fuckin' job. You dumb son of a bitch. Goddammit...goddammit!"

Mom sounded like Richard Pryor, but unlike Richard, I wanted it to stop.

"I've gotta call Ron," she said before rushing up the stairs.

Dad didn't say a word. He stood in the kitchen, staring at the floor or briefly glancing at me like a dog that had pissed *and* shit on the floor.

"Hey, it's Dolores. Is Ron there?" I heard her say.

"Ron, I made a mistake. I need my job back. I'll never leave again, I promise. Just please give me my job back."

Dad stood at the foot of the stairs and listened. I heard everything fine from the kitchen table, but Dad's hearing had started to slip by then, something he blamed on being a riveter at Servel, an anti-aircraft gunner in the military and a dry cleaner.

"Are you sure? Thank you so much. Thank you. Thank you. Thank you so much. I promise. I promise. I'll never leave again. Okay, Ron, thank you so much. I'll see you tomorrow."

And that was it. In less than thirty seconds, Ron gave Mom her job back. Dad breathed a sigh of relief and took a long swig of beer.

Mom came down the steps and moved past Dad toward the refrigerator. She opened the door and took out a package of hamburger and set it on the counter. She got a packet of taco mix from the cabinet.

She didn't bother asking us if that's what we wanted for dinner.

She retrieved an iron skillet from the oven and put it on the stove. She opened another cabinet and took out a short highball glass. She walked to the blue China cabinet, opened the bottom door, and removed a bottle of Kessler. She walked back to the counter, opened the freezer, and put a few ice cubes in the glass. She poured about half an ounce of Kessler into the glass and followed that up with Coca-Cola from an already opened two-liter bottle.

"Did Ron give you your job back?" Dad asked sheepishly.

Mom took a sip of her drink and then lit a cigarette. She took one drag and put it down. She opened the package of ground beef as Dad and I watched. Her hands shook and trembled.

Never looking up, Mom said in a voice louder than her normal tone, but not as loud as the "*what*" heard around the world:

"You'll never make another fuckin' decision as long as we live."

And with that, Mom went back to fixing tacos and, the next morning, finishing silk.

FLORIDA

• • •

D ad lost his job at Indian Woods for whatever reason. It had become so commonplace for him to be working at a new job that I barely noticed. When he was helping Charlie Braun with the new houses and Indian Woods apartments, he met a man who ran an insulation company. Dad went to work for him as an estimator and salesman. He enjoyed the estimating part a great deal. It allowed him to use some of the drafting and drawing skills he had learned many years before at the homemade drafting table.

Because Dad no longer had the Indian Woods job, management, probably Charlie Braun, increased our rent, so me, Dad, and Mom were on the move again. Sam and Andy had moved out to be on their own, so it was just the three of us. This time we moved to a neighborhood of World War II–era duplexes. Our two-bed, one-bath townhome sat in the middle of Corregidor Circle, a name Dad loved because it was the Philippines island Douglas MacArthur recaptured. For a man who disliked the military, at least his experience with it, he sured loved the history of it. We had an unfinished basement full of spider crickets that jumped at me if I got too close. The washer and dryer sat in a dark corner of the basement that the insects found very inviting. I hated that duplex on Corregidor Circle, particularly the corner where Mom did the laundry.

While living with Mom and Dad, I continued at USI (formerly ISUE) in pursuit of an accounting degree. I never enjoyed accounting, but we are a practical bunch. Despite the spider crickets and one bathroom that Dad seemed to always be in because of mounting stomach problems, the three of us liked living together. Every now and then, Dad and I would play gin rummy, or we'd look at pictures like we did in the house on Waggoner. Also, like Grandpa Al and Uncle Bill, Mom, Dad, and I sometimes argued. Two arguments stand out; one involved a piece of cheesecake, and the other a newly purchased shirt.

Mom sometimes made cheesecake, the kind from a box. She also made homemade cheesecake, but again our practicality crept into everything we did. Dad and I loved those box cheesecakes, and being a college-aged boy, I sometimes would eat two or three pieces a day, but for whatever reason, one day, I ate four or five, including the last piece, before I went to bed. I forgot, or didn't care, that sometimes Dad liked to eat cheese-cake for breakfast. Lying in bed, I heard Mom and Dad moving about and Dad coughing relentlessly, pretty much like every morning my senior year. I'd told him numerous times that his coughing didn't sound normal and that he should go see a doctor, but he refused, so Dad continued to be my alarm clock, even though I always fell back asleep. They usually left the house at six forty, so Dad could drop Mom off at work. He would then come back home for a bit before going to his job at Builder's Specialties, yet another job after the insulation job faded away.

When Dad got back home that morning, I could hear him hustling up the steps, which usually meant his stomach bothered him, and he would be in the bathroom for a while. This time, however, I didn't hear the bathroom door close. I heard my bedroom door open.

"Dan, get up, goddammit."

"What?"

"You ate the last goddamn piece of cheesecake."

"What?" I mumbled.

"Goddammit, you ate the last fuckin' piece of cheesecake. You know I eat that for breakfast, and you ate it anyway."

"I forgot. Jesus, Mom, will make another one. No big deal."

"You selfish son of a bitch."

"Relax, I'll ask her to make another one. You can have it all. I don't give a shit."

Dad shook his head and walked out of my room. I stayed in bed until he left the house, unlike on other days, when I would get up and we would talk a bit before he left for work.

That afternoon, when taking Mom home from work in the delivery van, we talked about it.

"Don't tell Dad that I told you he yelled at me. Just tell him that I said it was so good, we wished you would make another one."

When I got home that evening from the delivery route, Dad watched *Andy Griffith* on the black-and-white kitchen TV. I looked at Dad and smiled but didn't say a word to him. I walked into the kitchen and looked at Mom. She looked back at me.

"Hi, hon," she said.

"Hey, Mom. What're you doing?"

"Making another cheesecake."

Months later, after graduating with my accounting degree, I landed a job as an insurance adjuster for Crawford & Company. I made good money and needed to wear a shirt and tie and sometimes a sport coat on most days. Because of that, I often went shopping for new clothes. Dad had always been a snappy dresser, and I wanted to dress like him. One day I bought a few shirts at Marshall's. When I got home that night, Dad again sat at the table watching *Andy Griffith* while Mom cooked dinner. I opened the shopping bag and started to unwrap the shirts. As I did, Dad looked at them and commented, "Nice, I like that one," and, "That one too."

The last shirt I opened turned out to have French cuffs. I didn't own any cufflinks and didn't particularly want any, so I figured I would have to take it back. "That's a shame; this is a nice shirt," Dad said.

"Do you want it?" I asked.

Dad smiled. "Yeah, I'll take it."

Mom, still cooking dinner, overheard our conversation.

"You're not keeping that shirt. Take it back."

"Why?" I asked. "If he wants it, he can have it."

"I said no. Take the shirt back," she shouted.

"Mom, it wasn't that much. It was on sale."

"I don't care if it was free. You're not giving that shirt to your dad, and that's that," she shouted even louder.

Mom rarely shouted, except for the "*what*?" heard around the world. Something made her mad, but I couldn't figure it out. I knew better than to press it, though, and just let it go. I took the shirt back the next day because if I'd kept it, Mom would have known.

I looked at Dad, shrugged my shoulders and furrowed my brow. He shook his head and went back to watching *Andy Griffith*. I wondered why Mom was being so tough on Dad.

A few months later, Dad and I found out how tough Mom really was. Early one morning, she got up and headed downstairs. Somehow, she slipped on the stairs and severely sprained her foot and ankle. She wrapped it in an ace bandage and had Dad take her to work like any other day. She stayed at work all day, standing up, pressing clothes, which included pressing the steam pedals over and over and over, all day long. By the time she got home her foot looked about twice as big and her ankle resembled a softball.

Dad insisted she go to the emergency room, which she did. Doctors confirmed she had broken her foot, but they could only put it in a walking boot. She just had to wait for her broken foot to heal. The next morning, she got up, put on the walking boot, made breakfast and went to work on-time like she always did. She repeated her same routine every day for two months while wearing that walking boot. She didn't miss one minute of work that required her to be on her feet all day long, due to that broken foot. I realized then, and I think Dad did too, that Mom was the toughest person in the family, and it wasn't even close.

After seven months of adjusting insurance claims for car crashes—some with injuries, others involving alcohol, and a few with both—house fires, burst pipes, hail-damaged roofs and broken-into businesses, I had seen enough. I hated that job even though it paid well and included a company car. As we sat eating dinner and watching *Andy Griffith*, I told Mom and Dad I wanted to move to Florida. I had watched every *Miami Vice* episode and knew for certain that Miami looked like a lot more fun than Evansville.

I don't think they thought I meant it, but I did mean it. My Dad drove a beat-up Chevy Chevette with a hundred-plus thousand miles on it. I drove a brand-new Ford Tempo, somewhat like the Fairmont Uncle Dave's friend repossessed, and didn't even have to pay for it; my first job, Dad's twentieth or so; I had a brand-new car, and he didn't.

They, especially Mom, thought I was crazy.

"It ain't about the money," I said. At first, I liked being an insurance adjuster, but then I realized I had to talk to people all day about horrible things like car wrecks, floods, house fires, and sometimes even deaths. Since I worked on behalf of the insurance companies, the goal was to try to hold down the claims payments as much as possible. I once got a car crash victim to settle for five thousand dollars. I got lots of praise for that one, but I felt guilty about it. Twenty-two thousand dollars a year and a company car full of free gas just weren't enough to make up for not enjoying my work.

I'd made up my mind and prepared to move to Florida. My high school buddy Chris and his girlfriend came to Evansville for a visit. They drove up in his new Acura Integra. Chris went to Purdue, got a degree in electrical engineering, like my Uncle Tom, and got a great job in Boynton Beach, Florida, working for Motorola. I'd told him I wanted to move to Florida, so we planned to drive back together after his visit.

On July 4, 1989, we headed out, but not before standing in the driveway of our duplex on Corregidor and saying goodbye to Mom and Dad. Chris knew them well, so they trusted that I was in good company, although they looked worried and sad. I hugged Mom and shook Dad's hand. I'd never hugged my dad in my life, or really, he'd never hugged me, at least not that I could remember, and we certainly wouldn't start with that form of goodbye in front of friends.

We drove fifteen hours straight, although Chris did all the driving. I mainly sat or lay in the back seat while watching fireworks in the distance. We arrived in Lantana, Florida, around midnight. Lantana sits about right in the middle of Palm Beach County, home to Lion Country Safari, the island of Palm Beach, and swanky Boca Raton: "Mouth of the Rat."

Chris had an old mattress set up for me on the floor of the small second bedroom in his two-bedroom apartment. It didn't have sheets, but I'd brought a pillow. In the middle of the night, I woke up to piercing bites. After turning on the light, I discovered I'd been sleeping with a bunch of fire ants.

After just a month, I had spent most of the $1,200 I had saved from my first job on a rent payment to Chris, food, and a few nights out. I walked daily to the gas station to get a newspaper so I could browse the Help Wanted ads.

After a few interviews for a copier salesman position and a week-long turn at selling Bose Acoustic Wave machines in people's houses, I knew I had to do something different. I only took the Bose job so they would verify I had a job and income, which in turn meant I could buy a car. As soon as I signed for the car, I drove to Bose and told them I quit. My first hustle.

The next day I read an ad for a loan collector at Barnett Bank: Florida's largest. I called, was told to come in, and promptly drove my "new" Honda Civic with seventy thousand miles on the odometer to Riviera Beach for an interview. They asked if I had any experience collecting loans; I told them, "No, but I have experience avoiding bill collectors. My dad didn't do so well financially, so I answered calls and knocks on the door."

I got the job. It paid eighteen thousand dollars per year and didn't come with a company car, a step back for sure, but I felt pretty good about being on my own at twenty-three and in Florida, home to the heat I loved so much. Lantana wasn't Miami, but it was close enough.

Because I was new and the bank needed to collect all the money it could before the end of the year, I did not get to go home for Christmas in 1989, but I did fly home in early January. Mom and Dad kept the tree up and Mom made her usual sugar cookies, Mexican wedding cakes, and snickerdoodles.

With a beer and some cookies sitting on a plate next to him, Dad unwrapped the box I handed him. The box resembled the one that sat on the shelf in the hall closet of the house on Waggoner. The one that contained the pictures that were not stored in the few family albums. Dad opened the box to find a pair of hunter-green Tommy Hilfiger corduroy trousers.

"Thank you," he said, holding up the trousers. "I love the color and how thick they are. They'll be plenty warm."

"I know you like green," I replied.

"Yep, nice, nice." Dad folded the trousers and put them back in the box big enough for that pair of trousers or perhaps twelve marigold seedlings.

I can't remember what I got Mom. It should have been her day, but it never was.

Eleven days after I returned to Palm Beach County, doctors admitted Dad to the hospital due to a severe blood clot in his leg. Mom called to tell me she didn't think it was anything to worry about, which seemed unusual for her. Just over two weeks later, doctors told Dad he had lung cancer. When I talked to him, he seemed upbeat, typical for a man whose favorite new song—he hated most new songs—was "Don't Worry, Be Happy" by Bobby McFerrin.

While collecting money for Barnett, I talked to the same customers virtually every month.

"Hi, Mister Williams; when can I expect your payment?"

"Hey, Mister Navarro, you're forty-five days late. I need a payment."

"Hey, Miss T., when can I expect a payment?"

Miss T. lived in Jacksonville. She had moved from Palm Beach County a couple of years back. I almost never spoke to her but left her many messages. She always paid. One day, she showed up in the office. She asked for me by name. Someone led her to my desk.

"Hi, I'm Rosa," she said.

"Hey, nice to meet you."

I must have looked surprised. On the phone, she sounded forty, but then again, I probably sounded fifty. She couldn't have been more than twenty-one, maybe twenty-two. I was twenty-three. I wound up going to Jacksonville to visit her. We quickly became close. When Chris' girlfriend decided she didn't want me living with him any longer, he asked me to move out. I couldn't afford my own place, so I asked Rosa to move in with me. She said yes, and just like that, we were living together. When money was tight, I thought of Mom and Dad eating popcorn and drinking tap water in Williston, South Carolina.

One collection phone call I made reminded me of Dad.

"Hi, son. Is your mom home?" I had asked.

"No, she's not here," said what sounded like a young boy.

"Are you sure? It's kind of late for you to be home by yourself."

I waited during a long pause.

"I'm sure," he said.

"Well, I just want to let you know that I'm close to your house, and I can see your mom through the window. I know she's there." Of course, I was lying.

I waited during a longer pause.

"Who is this?" a woman yelled.

"This is Dan from Barnett Bank."

She cussed me up one side and down the other. She also made her payment the next day and called to tell me so. I explained to her that I was on her side and didn't want to take her car.

"Do me a favor," I asked.

"What's that?"

"Don't put your son in the middle of this. It's not fair to him. He's just a kid."

From that day forward, she called me every month to let me know when she was going to pay. Her name was Beryl. I won't provide her last name, though I remember it well. I think of her and her son often.

In March 1990, after Dad's diagnosis and during his treatments with radiation, Amy and Andy decided to throw a thirty-fifth-anniversary party for Mom and Dad. I didn't have much vacation time built up—or money—but decided to go home after talking to Delta and learning I could fly home for about four hundred dollars. I planned to pay with my only credit card. Delta held the ticket for twenty-four hours while I confirmed dates and times with Amy.

I called Delta the next day to buy the ticket, and they explained that the hold had expired after twelve hours, not twenty-four. The ticket price more than doubled, which I didn't think I could afford. I didn't make it to Mom and Dad's anniversary party.

Mom and Dad called me every Sunday. We usually talked for ten minutes or so to keep the long-distance charges down. The Sunday after the party they told me how great it was to see all their friends and family. They thanked me for my $150 toward the cost of the party, which Amy or Andy had told them about. I told them I planned to take my vacation in August that year when Mom took hers, so the three of us could spend some time together. They liked that. About his cancer, Dad said, "The treatments are working. The doctor said the tumor is shrinking." We talked about me coming home in August. I wanted to go get brain sandwiches. Dad loved brain sandwiches as much as I did.

The one-bedroom apartment Rosa and I shared sat near two tennis courts and a field. I taught her tennis while she showed me a few things about softball and baseball. In El Salvador, Rosa had played lots of softball. She could hit, run, pitch, and catch very well.

One Sunday afternoon, while we were preparing food after a day of playing, the phone rang.

"Hello," I said.

"Hi, hon."

"Hey, Mom, we're—"

"Hon, your dad had to go back to the hospital. He's not feeling well."

"Okay, what is it?"

"His leg is bothering him again. They're looking at it."

That night Mom called to tell me the doctors released Dad from the hospital. I called Dad almost every day for the next couple of weeks. I didn't call him on July 4, exactly one year after we stood in the driveway on Corregidor and shook hands.

The next day, I called home, and no one answered. I assumed Dad was in the bathroom, so I waited a few minutes and called back. No answer. I tried again and again and again. No answer.

I made one more call.

"Saint Mary's Hospital," the woman said.

"Dan Melchior's [I pronounced it Melcher] room, please."

The operator connected me without speaking a word.

The phone rang three times.

"Hlllllo," Dad mumbled just enough that I recognized his voice.

"Dad, it's Danny."

"Hhhh...."

"Dad, what's going on? Why are you back in the hospital."

"Thhy...thnk...I...hd...a...strk."

"You had a stroke?"

"Mmmm-mhhhh."

"Dad, hang in there; I'm gonna call Amy."

"Kkkyy."

"I'll call you back."

"Kkkyy."

Amy confirmed Dad had a stroke, but the doctors felt he could recover with therapy.

Rosa had to work on Sunday, so I played golf with a few of my collector friends. I had an old bag and rag-tag mix of hand-me-down clubs. Everyone I played with was far better than me, but nonetheless, I enjoyed playing. I got home around three or four. Rosa planned to bring home bacon cheeseburgers from Wendy's, where she worked as a manager. When she got home, like always, she stripped out of her clothes that smelled like the sack of burgers and fries she carried with her. While Dad could get a sack of hamburgers for less than a quarter when he was a kid, I could get a sack of burgers and fries for free because Rosa worked for Wendy's. I need to tease him about that "deal of the century," I thought.

In the kitchen, Rosa took the burgers and fries out of the bag and put them on plates, while in the bedroom, I set up two TV tables at the end of the bed. As I sat on the end of the bed and pulled the TV table near me, the phone rang. I pushed the table away and walked to the nightstand.

"Hello."

"Hon, you gotta come home."

"*What?*" I asked.

"Hon, you gotta come home; your dad's not gonna make it."

"What are you talkin' about?"

"Hon, just come home; you gotta come home."

Unable to speak through tears and bawls, I listened.

I didn't hear Rosa come into the room, but I felt her embrace. I slumped as she hugged me.

I talked to Delta but didn't have them hold the ticket; I just bought it, a ticket to fly home on Monday, July 9, 1990.

Watching people walk through Palm Beach International Airport in everything from suits to shorts, dresses to dashikis, I asked myself, who presses all these clothes?

The gate announcement startled me. "For those passengers on Flight 1252 to Atlanta, we will begin boarding in about five minutes."

Sitting in a window seat, I looked down as we ascended.

Mar-a-Lago. Jesus, that's a big place. Right in the flight path, though. I'm sure Trump doesn't like that, I thought.

I hated rough landings, especially when they were turning at three thousand feet. What if they turn too much? Will it fall? Jesus! Always so fuckin' windy.

"Mommy, that man just stared out the window the whole time," said a little girl sitting next to me as we waited to deplane.

"Some people are that way, honey. Not everyone likes to talk," her mom tried to whisper. Unlike Dad, I had great hearing.

If I did talk to the little girl, I would have answered, "Talk? Do you want me to talk? Okay. Hey, kid, how were the pancakes? They looked yummy. Where you headed? I hope somewhere fun. Me? Oh, I'm headed home to see my family. Specifically, my dad. He's dying, or maybe he's already dead. Dad told my sister Amy that I needed to hurry. So, I'm trying to hurry, but West Palm to Atlanta to Evansville ain't the fastest trip."

"He's still staring out the window."

"Quiet, honey."

I forget who picked me up from Evansville's Dress Regional Airport. We arrived at St. Mary's Hospital: the same place I had been born twenty-four years ago, a little plucked chicken.

"Hi, hon."

"Hi, Mom."

"He's in here."

I walked into Dad's hospital room. His eyes were closed, and his arms rested neatly at his side. A corpse already, I thought.

"I'm sorry. I'm so fuckin' sorry," I whispered as he attempted a word or two.

"I didn't know. I swear to God; I didn't know it was so bad. I was coming home in August. Remember? We talked about it. We were gonna get brain sandwiches at The Hilltop. Hilltop brains. Remember? Fuckin' brains, Dad. We were gonna get brains."

Can he hear me? Do I just stand here? Where is everybody?

"Give Danny his space," someone said, probably Mom.

I walked out of Dad's room.

"Hey, Sam."

"Hey, man. How was the flight in?" he asked.

"Rough. Lots of wind. Where's Grandpa?"

"Said he had to run an errand," Sam told me. "Something about the car."

On Monday, July 9, 1990, at 1:42 p.m. Dad took his last breath.

Why did I just stand in the hall? Why wasn't I in the room? Was that intentional? Was I a coward? I don't know.

"You should go home, Mom. Get some rest. I'll wait for Grandpa," I said.

"Someone's gotta wait for your grandpa. He said he'd be back," Mom insisted.

"I said I'll wait. Go home. We'll be there in a bit,"

Mom seemed as worried about Grandpa George as she was herself.

I sat alone on a bench outside the elevators and waited for Grandpa George.

"Open. Open, goddamnit," I demanded of the elevator doors.

Finally. Fuckin' elevators.

Grandpa George walked out of the elevator. I told myself to stand up, which was harder than I thought it would be.

"Hey, Grandpa. He didn't make it. I'm sorry. Dad didn't make it."

In typical Grandpa George style, he didn't say a word. The ride home, a mere two miles, was the longest ride of my life.

It hit me that I had told a man his son died, and the son was my dad.

Mom went into Rick-A-Jay to press Dad's only suit, a Hickey Freeman he got when Great-Uncle Bud died.

The next day I unfolded the *Evansville Press*.

"At least they spelled his name right," I told Sam.

"Half the time, it's O-I-R."

"Yep, M-E-L-C-H-O-I-R," Sam replied.

"Let me see the rest of the paper," I said.

"World's Richest List Doesn't Include Trump"

by The Associated Press

New York—"A new list of the world's billionaires includes 62 Americans. None of them is named Donald Trump. The New York developer had an estimated net worth of $1.7 billion last year, but that dropped sharply as the value of his real estate and airline empire plummeted."

I don't remember much about Dad's visitation other than someone telling me how young Dad looked but also how much he smoked. I didn't comment on that but thought, *Damn near everyone in this family smokes.*

At Dad's funeral, Grandpa George and Mom sat in the front row of the "family room" of Ziemer's funeral home. We could see Dad's casket and where the priest would stand. As we prepared for the funeral to start, an elderly lady, at least in her eighties, approached Grandpa George.

"Are you George Melchior [pronounced Melcher]?" she asked.

Grandpa George, puzzled, looked up from his lap. "Yes."

"Did you grow up in Jasper?"

"Yeah, I did."

"You probably don't remember me; I was a teenager, and you were just a little boy. A cute little boy. I was your neighbor."

"Okay," Grandpa George said.

By that time, the priest had gotten behind the lectern. He looked in our direction as the woman continued.

"I often think back to those days. They were so nice. I loved Jasper as a kid."

Grandpa started to look around as the woman and her long-winded, go-nowhere story continued.

My shoulders started to shake, and my stomach tightened. As much as I tried, I could not contain my laughter. Soon Sam, Uncle Dave, Uncle Tom, and even Mom started to chuckle.

Grandpa George stood up.

"I appreciate you coming; this is my son's funeral. We need to get started."

"Oh, I'm sorry," the woman replied. "I'm here for another visitation. I just saw the name Melchior and thought I would see who it was. I can't believe it's you. You were such a cute—."

My laughter became loud enough that people not in the family room were looking at us, as was the priest. Everyone laughed as Grandpa gently escorted the kind but longwinded woman toward the door. And with that, Dad's funeral began.

"Of course, you can have them, but why do you want them?"

"I can use them; they fit perfectly," I said as I laced up Dad's work boots, the pair that contributed to the malodorous air of the closet in the house on Waggoner.

Mom smiled. She gave me a pack of undershirts that she bought Dad but he never even opened. Grandpa George took the Tommy Hilfiger trousers.

I took off the boot I had tried on and sat it underneath the desk, the desk that used to be mine when I studied accounting.

"There is something else I want you to have," Mom said before handing me a plastic six-inch by three-inch 1990 calendar notebook.

"It might bring you comfort someday to see his handwriting. He loved you and admired you for having the guts to leave Indiana. He knew you wanted more than what's here."

My shoulders shook as tears raced down my cheeks. "DAN MELCHIOR, SR." in all-cap block letters, like those on his army jacket and on my white, red, and blue plastic drugstore football, graced the identification page. Mom rubbed my back as I read.

> Monday, January 14, 1990.
> "DAN RETURNED TO
> FLORIDA TODAY"

> Thursday, January 25, 1990.
> "BLOOD CLOT. ADMITTED"

> Friday, February 2, 1990.
> "DR. SARTORE CONFIRMS
> CANCER IN R LUNG"

Mom continued rubbing my back as I flipped forward in Dad's plastic notebook.

> Saturday, April 21.
> "SURPRISE ANNIVERSARY AT HADI.
> GREAT PARTY, GOD BLESS THE
> KIDS, DAN COULDN'T MAKE IT"

"It's okay, hon. It's okay."

PROMOTED

● ● ● ●

A few weeks later, back in Florida, my manager at Barnett Bank called me into his fourth-floor office overlooking the Intracoastal. This is the kind of office I envisioned I'd have when watching *Miami Vice*, I thought.

"Dan, how's it going?" he asked.

My manager typified a South Florida "Southerner." He loved NASCAR, muscle cars, working on cars, and talking about cars.

"You're from Indiana, right?"

"Yep, Evansville."

"Indiana, home of the sprint car."

I furrowed my brow. "I don't watch much racing. I prefer basketball and football." I didn't tell him I'd never heard of a sprint car.

His smile lessened a tad. "Anyway, you've done a great job collectin' loans, you dress nice, you look good, and because of that, we'd like to put you in a branch as a loan officer. We think you'd be good with customers. What ya think?"

"Sure, that'd be great."

And with that, I got promoted to loan officer. I received a very small raise, but I didn't really care about the money; I just didn't want to sit in an office and collect money from those who couldn't pay. I'd rather help people buy cars and boats and home improvements.

Rosa and I celebrated that Saturday. I grilled burgers and dogs on a small tabletop charcoal grill while drinking a few beers. She made potatoes with adobo, a spice I'd never seen until moving to Florida.

It turned out my manager was right; customers liked me. I wrote lots of loans for cars, boats, and home improvements to all kinds of people, some rich, some famous, some poor, and some just regular Dans like me. We received bonuses for selling rip-off credit life and disability insurance and for cross-selling other bank products like checking, savings, and CD accounts, safe deposit boxes, credit and debit cards, and anything else banking leaders dreamed up.

While covering for a vacationing loan officer in Riviera Beach, I met a couple that needed a loan to fund a few home improvements. The African American couple had been married for more than thirty years, they told me. She worked as a Palm Beach County school teacher, and he drove a truck. Both had been in the same jobs for almost as long as they had been married. They had paid off their Riviera Beach home once before and had perfect credit and no debt to speak of. They wanted to borrow $35,000 on a house that would sell for at least $70,000. An easy decision.

I only had $25,000 signing authority, so I needed my manager's signature. I took the loan to his office for approval and signature on the check. I handed him the file. He looked through it for about a minute.

"Look where this house is. Have you been by it?"

"Yeah, I drove by it. It looks fine. It will appraise easily."

"I know, on paper, but we can't make a loan in this neighborhood. It's a shithole."

"I know it's a shithole, but that's illegal. We can't deny this loan. What reason am I gonna give 'em?"

"I don't know, that's your problem. I'm not signing it," he said as he handed the loan papers back to me.

"Are you out of your mind?" I asked.

"I'm not signing it."

"Okay, but I am. And when the check bounces because I don't have the authority, you're gonna explain it to 'em." I tidied up the file and walked out of his office.

By the time I got to my desk, my phone had apparently rung because my assistant said my manager had called and needed me to call him back. After talking to him, I went back to his office.

"Give me the file," he said.

He signed the check.

A few weeks later, my manager called and said he had left a file on his desk he wanted me to look at. The "file" was a fake menu for a Chinese restaurant with sexual-sounding dishes like "Cum of Sum Yung Gai and other perverted menu items. I left the menu and didn't call him back or acknowledge what I had seen. I learned from others that he had seen me with Rosa and thought she was Asian, hence the "joke." Perhaps he wanted to pay me back for forcing him to sign the check for a loan to an African American couple he thought about redlining.

Whatever my manager thought of me didn't stop him from moving me up the ladder to swanky North Palm Beach, swankier Jupiter, and then down to a large working-class branch on the corner of Congress and Hypoluxo in Boynton Beach.

I loved working in Boynton Beach, where the clientele consisted of hard workers, up-and-comers, and middle-of-the-road retired folk. I also liked my co-workers. The branch manager, a tall fellow named Mike, who regularly put his feet on the desk and easily related to the customers, reminded me of Ron Tindle, the Rick-A-Jay owner, if Ron Tindle had been a banker, not a dry cleaner.

Patti Garcia, our customer service manager, who stood, with heels on, a few inches taller than me, called me "Shorty" when not within earshot of customers. We talked about everything from basketball to children. She had two with her husband, Daniel, her high school sweetheart. I told her I didn't know if I wanted kids, but I was sure that Rosa did. Daniel came into the office a couple of times. He liked to talk about softball.

The more and more I talked with Patti, who spoke so often of her family, the more I felt like going home to Evansville. In Florida, it was just me and Rosa, and Rosa's family, whom I enjoyed spending time with, but it wasn't the same as being around my own family.

While considering leaving Florida, Mom called and told me her cousin's son had been killed in a plane crash. The bell that rang "twenty-nine lives" in 1977 rang again as residents relived the Purple Aces' tragedy when a C-130 military transport plane crashed into the Drury Inn and Jo Jo's restaurant, killing sixteen people. That same cousin had lost another son years earlier in a drowning accident.

"What are the odds?" Mom said.

When Mom and I talked, which became more and more often, she spoke almost exclusively about Dad. She missed him dearly. It seemed as if all his lost jobs, all his drinking, all his wearing French-cuffed shirts had vanished like the steam that surrounded her press. Mom seemed lost without Dad.

"The only thing I want in life is to have your dad back," she answered when I asked about what she wanted to do.

"I'm sorry Mom, life doesn't work that way." I didn't know what else to say.

Rosa and I weren't doing as well as we could have, and I struggled with Dad's death about as much as Mom did. I wanted him back. I gave Mike, my new boss at Barnett, two weeks' notice. On my last day, my co-workers gave me a mini basketball that they all had signed. Patti signed it, "To Shorty, Good luck, Patti."

Mom enjoyed having me home again. I wasn't Dad, but she had someone to cook, clean, and care for. While back in Evansville, I earned an MBA via a part-time evening program at my alma mater, the University of Southern Indiana, while helping a friend establish a business and working as a Graduate Assistant for the University. I had been accepted to Indiana University's prestigious MBA program but balked at the $50,000 price tag that would require taking out student loans. I'd seen enough of what debt could do to a person.

Most mornings, I took Mom to work rather than bring her home from work like I had done when delivering dry cleaning for Rick-A-Jay, which Grandpa George was still doing when I returned home that year. He was seventy-nine, even older than Fred Gresser when he hit Uncle Bill. As I said, men in Evansville retire, but they don't stop working.

Mom and I talked even more than we did when I ran the route for Rick-A-Jay, but those morning drives were about the only time we saw each other because, by the time I got home from school or work, Mom was in bed. But I did see the food she fixed for me. Chili, beef and noodles, chicken noodle soup, bacon sandwiches, grilled cheese, spaghetti, tomato soup (without Tabasco sauce), and, of course, tacos.

It was good to be home again although we both missed Dad.

THE SURF
● ● ●

After earning my MBA in 1995 and after Sam bought a house near Mom's rented duplex, I yearned for South Florida again and decided to give Chris, my hometown buddy still living in Boynton Beach, a call. He had married and divorced Heidi by the time I got back. A credit union in Evansville had offered me a job, but I didn't really want to stay in Evansville, so I told them I needed a couple of weeks to think about it. They were kind enough to give me that time.

I took Chris up on his suggestion to fly down, spend a week or so with him, and decide what I wanted to do. I brought a suit and a few resumes. I ended up interviewing with an international construction firm in their accounting department. The man who would be my boss had New York Yankee pictures all over his office. He told me they had an internal candidate but would like to interview at least one external candidate. His statement made me think I was not about to get that job, but then I had an idea.

"So, you must like the Yankees, yeah?"

"Yep, I love baseball and the Yankees."

"I know Don Mattingly. He's from my home-town. His brother, Randy, coached me when I played high school football. I also won a free-throw contest at Donnie's restaurant. We did a quick radio interview after I won. He autographed a picture of us that reads, 'Congrats Danny on HotShot '95, Don Mattingly."

My interviewer laughed. "Really?"

"Yep, he's from Evansville. A great guy. We used to go to his restaurant all the time. He sometimes tended bar like a regular dude. You'd never know he was one of the best baseball players on the planet."

My interviewer, whose name was Mick—I think his dad named him after Mickey Mantle—stood up. "I'll be right back."

I sat in his office and looked at his pictures. Everything I told him was true.

He came back after about ten minutes.

"I'm gonna take you upstairs to meet our CFO."

I had put Chris's address and phone number on my resume. Mick called me that night to tell me I got the job. My second hustle, although I didn't view it as a hustle since everything I said was true.

I flew home and rented a Penske truck. Sam helped me pack the furniture I had stored in the cricket-filled basement. I planned to leave first thing the next morn-ing. Sam had been taking Mom to work, so I didn't have to worry about that any longer. Like always, Mom got up around 4:30 a.m. I got up as soon as I heard her moving about.

She had purchased a box of Pop-Tarts for my road trip. She filled a cooler with Diet Cokes. Everything was ready and I was ready to leave once again.

"Thanks, Mom," I said as I started to pick up the cooler.

"By the way, I have to tell you that I couldn't have done any of...."

That's as far as I got. I cried harder than when Dad carried me down the steps toward the school bus, harder than when Grandpa Al, Uncle-Bill, Great Uncle-Bud, Grandma Mil, or Grandma Bessie had died. Harder than when Mom told me I needed to come home; harder than when I saw Dad and he couldn't speak, only mumble. I cried and wailed as she held me up. We hugged both knowing we'd never live under the same roof again.

My morning routine, again living with Chris, consisted of drinking orange juice, eating Pop-Tarts, and usually reading the *Palm Beach Post* while sitting in the sun-filled kitchen.

One morning, as I bit a corner of the brown-sugar cinnamon breakfast treat, I flipped to the local section and read "Woman Killed in Shooting."

I didn't make it past two or three sentences before tears dripped onto the white ceramic plate holding my breakfast.

Someone, perhaps in a drive-by, had shot Patti Garcia to death. Her husband Daniel had been shot in the leg. I wiped away my tears, folded the paper, and got ready to go to work. I had only been on the job six months and could not afford to be late.

Only three days later, Daniel Garcia confessed to the murder. He initially said he was trying to scare Patti when he fired his .357 Magnum into their car. Apparently, he was annoyed with her constantly nagging him to spend more time with her. Authorities sentenced him to thirty years for killing the mother of his two children. I imagined the sadness and outrage that Mom, Dad, Grandma Mil, Grandpa George, and Great-Uncle Bud had felt about Rudy Ziemer and the three paratroopers. I remembered Russell Lloyd and Dawn Cosby. I thought about Evansville, and I thought about Mom.

While living in a spare bedroom in Chris's new house, I thought about his plans to be out of town for a few weeks on a work assignment. Although Mom had never been on an airplane in her life, I planned to convince her to come to visit me in Florida.

I called her one night, knowing that being naturally nervous and inexperienced, she would never be able to navigate an airport on her own, especially Atlanta's Hartsfield-Jackson, one of the busiest in the nation, and the required layover coming from Evansville.

"What if someone came with you?" I asked her.

"Like who? I don't think Amy, Andy, or Sam can do it."

"What about Aunt Kate?" I asked.

Mom paused. She couldn't see my smile over the phone. Her pause meant I'd hit on the one person that Mom would trust with such an endeavor. Aunt Kate, Dad's sister, had flown before and lived in places as far away as Helena, Montana, Washington, DC, and Detroit. She and Mom had always been close but especially since Dad died.

"Seriously, think about it, Mom. You've never seen the ocean, you've never been to Florida, and I'll pay for it. Don't worry about that."

She balked about me paying for it but said she would call Aunt Kate that night. I could afford the tickets, unlike the one I hadn't bought for Mom and Dad's party: the one that still haunted me.

While August is one of the worst months to visit Florida, it was the month Mom usually took her one week of vacation time. Early August is a slow time in the dry-cleaning industry as kids are not in school, many people are on vacation and not wearing suits and dresses, and most importantly, the cumbersome and labor-intensive band uniforms had not yet marched across the counter.

Mom called one night and told me she had talked to Kate. Not only did Kate agree to accompany Mom, but she also looked forward to it. And with that, Mom decided to visit me in Florida.

I sat in a small windowless office as my heart beat a bit faster than normal. I came down to the title office during my lunch break. I didn't plan on spending more than an hour signing what seemed like hundreds of pages of documents. By the end of the signing session, a house would be mine.

The house was listed for $125,000 if I remember correctly. I'd originally offered less than $100,000 for the two-bedroom, two-bath ranch that had been sitting empty for a few months. Apparently, the owner had lost his job, so he and his wife relocated to South Carolina. Their relocation and lost job meant that no one tended the already-overgrown landscaping. An untended South Florida summer landscape can swallow a house, like a Venus flytrap swallowing a fly, in a matter of months, which is exactly what happened to the house at the end of the cul-de-sac that I hoped would be mine. I took advantage of the couple's plight—something I'm less proud of today than I was then—and the overgrowth when making my initial offer. It so insulted them they did not counter. I knew better than to relent and offer more. I told Janet, my realtor, the sister of Chris's new girlfriend, "I'm in no hurry, but they will be eventually."

The overgrowth around the house was so bad that most prospective buyers refused to get out of the car because the front door was barely visible, and half of the two-car garage was hidden behind a wild bougainvillea. Much of the house was covered in rust-colored stains from the well-water sprinkler system that fed the overgrowth. Uninformed buyers probably assumed the entire house needed to be painted. What they didn't know was that a rather cheap chemical available at all hardware stores, mixed with water, removed those stains in seconds.

As for the back of the house, it contained two orange trees and a lemon tree that produced so much fruit that most of it lay rotting on the ground. Rotting fruit draws rats, flies, and other insects, which in turn draws snakes, frogs, and lizards, which in turn draws carnivorous birds. The tiny jungle, a menagerie of species, was almost impossible to navigate. Any buyer that walked onto the back, foliage-encased patio immediately walked away, so I waited. I waited another month but drove by every so often to see how bad the growth had gotten. It had gotten significantly worse, so I asked Janet if I could take one more look at the house.

We met one day after work. After navigating the driveway and the bougainvillea, we entered the front door. Walking into the kitchen, I saw a custom kitchen with real wood cabinets, a feature Mom and Dad would have loved. I didn't love the seafoam-green carpet in the living room and bedrooms, but that could easily be ripped out. The inside of the house, built in 1973, ironically the same year we were forced to sell our "House on Audubon," was mostly original except for the kitchen but was also well cared for. I had read about what to look for in a house and remembered that adage: location, location, location. Being at the end of a cul-de-sac on a quarter-acre lot certainly had its advantages. The only immediate work requirement was ripping out or significantly trimming almost all the landscaping. Doing that alone would probably increase the value of the house immediately. I thought about sweat equity and remembered how much I liked to sweat.

After the third or fourth viewing, I decided to increase my offer to $113,000. Even at that price, the house had significant potential, or so I thought.

"That's my last and final offer," I told Janet.

The couple quickly countered with $113,500.

"Are you serious, five hundred dollars? That's ridiculous."

My competitive nature got the best of me. I made them wait for another few days. They didn't budge. I commended them for that. I eventually buckled and signed the offer for $113,500. It bothered me, but I soon forgot it when a day-before-the-closing walkthrough revealed a leaky AC unit that needed to be replaced. The owners had no choice but to replace it for a cost of more than $1,500. Sadly, I felt a bit of glee knowing that timing worked well for me and more than offset the ridiculous plus-$500 counteroffer.

With pen in hand, I signed the endless stack of papers and forms. The house and two keys were mine. After work, I went by Home Depot and bought a small tree saw. I drove to the house and pulled into the driveway in my 1995 Honda Civic, the first brand new car that was all mine and had cost $13,500, one hundred thousand less than the house.

I changed into shorts, a T-shirt, and Dad's work boots laced to the top. I started with the bougainvillea, cutting away enough to clear the two-door garage completely. I then moved on to the tree whose branches hung over the front door. By the time the sun set that night, the front door and garage were fully visible. I dragged the branches to the street as my neighbors looked on. One neighbor, John, who, like Ron Tindle and Mike, the branch manager, also resembled Henry Blake. What is it about tall, lanky, balding men being goofy? Are they all Henry Blakes? Regardless, he liked the fact that I had already started to cut away the horrendous eyesore at the end of the SW 13th Court. As I was putting away my tools, John yelled, "Hey, heads up!" I turned around to see John throw a beer like Ron had once thrown an apple core into the back of the seedy motel on Fares Avenue.

A few days before Mom and Kate were scheduled to arrive, I lied to Mom. I told her she would enjoy staying at Chris's house because Chris was out of town, and we would have the place to ourselves. She genuinely seemed excited, albeit very nervous. What she didn't know is we weren't going to stay at Chris's house; we were going to stay at my house, the house I closed on three days before Mom and Kate were scheduled to arrive.

The day before their visit, I washed and cleaned the inside of my car, went to the store, and filled up the fridge with orange juice. I purchased a Weber charcoal grill and a card table, as we needed a place to eat other than the same two TV trays me and Rosa used to eat on. Chris and a couple of his friends helped me move the few items I did own, including a queen bed, an armoire that my brother gave me, a couch and love seat left over from my previous time in Florida, and personal items, including a few of my dad's paintings, record albums, cassettes, VHS tapes, and clothes. I bought another queen-size bed and frame for Mom and Kate. After loading my belongings into the house, I stayed up until two or three in the morning, arranging everything and getting the house ready for the big day.

In the three days I'd owned the house, I hadn't had any time to cut down anything other than the bougain-villea and the tree I cut on the first night. The house, still barely visible, didn't look much better than when I first arrived.

I sat in the gate area, waiting for Mom and Kate's plane to arrive. I couldn't have imagined that someday, Mom would walk through the same airport, near the same gate area where I waited to fly home and see Dad on his deathbed. I promised myself I wouldn't mention that to Mom or Aunt Kate.

The gate doors opened, and passengers filed out, one by one, two by two. Mom and Kate arrived in the middle of the pack. I smiled immediately when I saw Mom. She was too nervous to see me. Her eyes darted around like water bugs.

"Hey, Mom."

She seemed startled. Kate smiled and talked first. "Hey, Dan. Good to see you."

"You too, Kate."

"Hey, Mom, how was the flight? You okay?"

"Yeah, hon, I'm okay."

We hugged. Mom looked as scared as I felt the day she walked me to the end of the street for my first-ever school bus ride.

"How do we get our luggage?" she asked.

"Don't worry, Mom…don't worry."

We went downstairs to baggage claim. Their bags arrived safe, sound, and on time.

"Where's your car? How do you know where you're going?"

"Don't worry, Mom…don't worry."

We got in the car, exited the parking lot, and headed east on Belvedere Road toward I-95. After noon and before rush hour, the traffic wasn't too bad but was more than Mom had ever seen. She and Kate argued about who would sit in the front seat.

Pulling into our Golfview Harbor neighborhood, which was nowhere near a golf course, I told Mom that I had a surprise for her.

"What's that?" she asked.

"Well," I said as I pulled onto SW 13th Street, "you're not going to be staying at Chris's house."

"What do you mean?"

We pulled into the driveway of the house, hidden by overgrown landscaping.

"We're going to stay at my house. This is my house, Mom. I just bought it."

"What?"

"This is my house. I just bought it. Wait until you see the inside."

Mom exited the car first. The amount of overgrowth shocked her. Kate followed and looked around.

"Well, congratulations," Kate said. I couldn't tell if she meant it.

"Come inside."

I unlocked the door, and we walked into the very clean but sparsely furnished house. The living room resembled a netless tennis court. The couch and loveseat that used to be mine and Rosa's were in the family room/dining room combination.

"See, the inside is great. I just need to tear out all the landscaping outside, and it will be perfect for me."

Mom perked up a bit when she saw how clean and nice the house was, other than the seafoam-green carpeting. I showed them the second bedroom where they would be sleeping. Being both just around five feet and one hundred pounds, Mom and Kate could easily share a queen bed, which they gladly did. After showing them the entire house, all fifteen hundred square feet, and the overgrown backyard, Mom, too, saw the potential and why I liked it. She worried it might be too much work for me to do alone, but she understood I wanted a home.

That week, Mom discovered that grout wasn't mud, sugar ants could find store-bought chocolate chips left on a plate on the counter in about three minutes, and that her son could make it on his own. That week I took Mom and Kate to Miami Beach and showed them Gianni Versace's house, where he'd been shot to death just one month earlier. I had planned to take them to Miami Beach anyway, but the Versace tragedy just made it that much more interesting. When I told Mom what had happened as we stood near the steps where he took his last breath, she commented, "Maybe we shouldn't be here."

I chuckled, but then thought about Patti Garcia, then Rudy Ziemer, Evansville's Gianni Versace who might have been Miami's or Reggio Calabria Italy's Rudy Ziemer if anyone outside of Evansville had ever heard of Rudy Ziemer—or Evansville, for that matter.

Madonna never compared Miami to Prague, and though she spent some time in Evansville certainly didn't know of Rudy Ziemer. Standing on the marble steps where Versace died, I couldn't help but think murder in Miami is murder in Boynton Beach is murder in Evansville—or Prague, for that matter.

The highlight of the week came a few days later, after we had been to the Everglades and were swarmed by a cloud of mosquitos probably like those that Grandpa Al or Dad experienced in the Okefenokee swamp, and after we'd been to dinner in Boca Raton and after I'd left Mom and Kate alone for one day because I didn't have enough vacation days to take the whole week off. That day, they stayed around the house, walked to Chris's and used the pool, and cleaned up my already-clean house. That's when Mom discovered the grout she tried to get out from between the tiles was, in fact, grout, not mud.

The next day, I decided to take them to Boynton Beach, not far from the house. Mom and Kate both put on their bathing suits. Mom had to buy one before coming to visit because she had no need for one in Evansville. She had never learned to swim, and water scared the daylights out of her just like it did me. She had purchased a navy-blue one-piece number that almost matched the one Kate had. Except for Mom's greyish-white hair and Kate's auburn brownish hair, the pair looked more like sisters than sisters-in-law.

We packed a bag with towels, sunscreen, and a few bottles of water. I didn't think we would stay long, but I didn't know how long it would take me to convince Mom to go into the water. She had warmed up by going into Chris's pool, a mighty step for someone so afraid of water. During the trip to Miami Beach, she had at least seen the ocean, so now, I should be able to convince her to go in, or so I thought.

Mom and Kate wore their bathing suits under shorts and shirts. We kicked off our shoes and let our toes dig into the sand as we walked. Mom had never seen this much sand in her life. If she had, she'd have tried to sweep it up, of that, I'm sure. Mom, the fastest walker in a family of fast walkers, walked slowly. She looked around. She looked up and down. She listened to seagulls chirping.

"Let's get in the water," I said.

I still didn't know how to swim, but I enjoyed walking into the ocean.

Mom looked nervous but happy.

"Look, you can just sit here and let it come to you," I said, pointing to the surf. With Kate's help, Mom seemed to think she could do that. They removed their shirts and shorts and stood in their one-piece navy-blue suits. I guided Mom toward the ocean, helped her sit down where the surf would eventually get her, and took out my camera. As I stood ankle-deep in the water, Mom and Kate sat on the dry sand. I heard a wave crash and felt the Atlantic Ocean rise to my calf. I knew Mom was about to get wet. The aqua blue water, clear, with a white foamy frothiness, rushed past me and made its way up her feet, ankles, knees, hips, and hands that held her up. The smile on her face when the water hit made the entire trip for me. Fortunately, I pressed the shutter at the right time and captured that smile forever. She sat there as wave after wave crept around her. She couldn't stop smiling.

Moments later, I convinced her to walk with me into the ocean. Having felt the water, her worry disappeared like the retreating surf. We walked until the water hid our knees. Kate took our picture. I retreated to shore and took a picture of Mom and Kate after Kate convinced her to walk out even further. I'm not sure I'd ever seen Mom smile so much. All the convincing, all the cajoling, all the coaxing had been worth it. That week Mom had taken her first plane ride and had seen, felt, and conquered, in her own way, the Atlantic Ocean. She saw mansions, pretty women, and sand; she felt the sun and the ocean breeze; she ate a grouper sandwich and relaxed in a pool. And for those moments in that week, Mom knew what it was to be me, someone who had moved away.

LENORA AND PATRICE

● ● ● ● ● ●

Convincing Mom to conquer some of her fears so she could visit me in Florida provided relief and almost indescribable motivation. While I had conquered my fear of leaving home years earlier by moving to Florida, I had not conquered my biggest fear. A fear so overwhelming that it compelled me to begin writing a story titled "Die Laughing" about a man who always wanted to be a standup comedian but never did it. The story began with him lying on his deathbed, enveloped in soul-crushing regret. Writing that story frightened me so much that I stopped writing the story and began writing jokes. I didn't commit to doing anything with them; I simply wrote and rehearsed, wrote and rehearsed. I took a speech class at Palm Beach Community College, hoping to improve my public speaking skills. My fellow students laughed at my speeches, so I kept writing and rehearsing, writing and rehearsing.

While exploring my humorous side, I had grown tired of working for the construction company and had learned via a news article in the *Palm Beach Post* that Universal Music and Studios had established a shared services center in Delray Beach, just a few miles from my now-perfectly manicured house. I wrote a letter to a man mentioned in the article, and just like that, I had a new job working for one of the largest media companies in the world.

Although more confident than ever, leaving what I thought was my last comfort zone became a slow, methodical journey. I wrote and rehearsed, wrote and rehearsed. I had written and rehearsed for five years. In those five years, not once did I step onto a comedy stage. That changed in August 2002.

I honed three minutes of material over the course of three months after learning that the West Palm Beach Improv, the best comedy club in town, held a weekly open mic night. Each aspiring comedian got three to five minutes of stage time. I chose the minimum amount of time to be in what I assumed would feel like a fishbowl. I rehearsed those three minutes more than one hundred times. I even rigged a light to shine directly into my face to simulate what it might feel like on a real stage.

On open mic night, the emcee scheduled me in the middle of the pack, so I drank a beer and watched a few comedians mostly bomb. I didn't tell anyone about the show in case I bombed also. After the comedian before me walked off stage, I shuffled into the wings. The emcee walked past me, stepped on stage, and told a few jokes. Then he began, "Are you ready for your next open miker?" Some in the crowd clapped, a few yelled, but most just waited silently. I thought about turning around and leaving.

The emcee continued, "He's from West Palm Beach. Welcome to the stage Daniel Carr."

I leaned away from the stage and continued to think about bolting and then thought, "Fuck it."

I stepped into the spotlight. I couldn't see anyone because of the spotlight. I heard light applause. I shook the emcee's hand, took the microphone from the stand, moved the stand, and started my three-minute routine. My memory after stepping into the spotlight is fuzzy. I do remember laughter, and I remember walking off the stage. I remember applause. The rest of the night was a blur except when I left and started walking to my car. I saw two guys and a girl walking on the other side of the street. I looked at them. They looked at me. One of the guys pointed at me and yelled, "Hey, dude, you're funny!"

Like a starving Ohio River catfish, I was hooked. Within ninety days of that open mic, I got a paid gig (fifty dollars cash) as an emcee. I performed a few times a month, each time trying new material. Some worked, some didn't, but I gained more and more confidence. That confidence came in handy when I learned in the spring of 2003 that Universal Music and Studios planned to outsource all our jobs to a company in Charlotte, North Carolina. I didn't want to move to Charlotte, so I started looking for another job.

I remembered meeting some executives from a wine and spirits company in Miami once while working for the construction company. Brimming with the confidence of being a comedian and having convinced Universal to hire me, I called Southern Wine & Spirits and asked if they needed someone with my skills. They hired me within ninety days of that first call. Again, my confidence soared like a kite.

I told my colleagues at Southern Wine that I performed comedy, and they should come to see me some time. Many of them did one night when I performed in a contest at the Miami Improv. I won the contest, but not without some controversy.

I almost lost that contest to a young African American comedian who was very funny, except that he stole all his material from Richard Pryor and when I write *stole*, I mean verbatim. He told Richard's bit about wondering how deer ever get to drink water because they are too scared to drink. It's a great physical bit, and this young comedian copied it very well.

Even before knowing how the judges would score our bits, I told one of the judges that the funny youngster's material was all Richard's. Although the audience loved him and loved me too, for that matter, the judges disqualified him. I never saw him at another club again, and sometimes I wonder if that was because of me. I certainly hope not, but if nothing else, he learned not to steal from masters. For winning that contest, I got the chance to emcee shows for a headliner at the Miami

Improv. That chance rolled around on Halloween weekend in 2003.

When I think of that weekend, I think of Miss Lenora Cupp, not because she interrupted my Richard Pryor imitations, but because every time I think of that weekend, I think of Patrice O'Neal and every time I think of him, I think of Miss Cupp.

In October 2003, the green room at the Coconut Grove Miami Improv seemed small, but that was probably because Patrice, a giant of a stand-up comedian, occupied most of it. As if ready to fly, his arms stretched the loveseat from tip to tip. I sat in one of two uncomfortable chairs.

"He's about done," Patrice said to me, the evening's host. "You should get out there. He always ends on this bit."

James started to step off the stage as I stepped up. We shook hands and half-hugged.

"Ladies and gentlemen, give it up for James Jones. Wow! Duct tape and a lead pipe as negotiation tools. Remind me not to fuck with him. I can't imagine that would go well. I'm not sure *quaz* is a word, James. I'm gonna have to challenge that. Where's the dictionary? Fuck the dictionary; it's a new word, bitch. It ain't in that old-ass dictionary. Don't make me get the duct tape and lead pipe! Okay, okay. Triple word it is, you Scrabble-playin' motherfucker."

A few laughs. That's good.

"Alright, that was interesting, but it's about to get really interesting now. Are you ready for your headliner?"

Polite applause, like a pro golfer might hear after sinking a routine putt, rippled in the room.

"You're gonna have to do a lot better than that for this guy! Are you ready for your headliner?" I shouted into the mic.

The crowd clapped and yelled. *There we go.*

"You've seen him on *The Colin Quinn Show.* You've seen him on *Chappelle's Show.* Ladies and gentlemen, give a big Miami round of applause to Mr. Patrice O'Neal!"

The crowd applauded, and some whistled.

"Thank you. Thank you," Patrice said to the electric crowd.

I walked offstage and headed to the back of the club.

Patrice killed that night. The crowd laughed virtually nonstop. Clinks and clatters of plates, forks, and glasses accompanied the roller coaster of laughs and hollers. I emceed five shows for him that week—two on Thursday, two on Saturday, and one on Sunday. The club was closed on Friday for Halloween. Regardless, five shows in four days was an exhausting schedule for a guy who had a full-time nine-to-five, which was me.

While James Jones performed his twenty minutes during the second show, I sat in the green room as Patrice regaled me with his road stories and pet theories, including one about the airlines telling passengers to use the brace position in case of a crash being meant to ensure that passengers die. Most comedians of his stature would not like an emcee in the green room with them, much less engage in conversation. Patrice didn't mind; in fact, he seemed to invite it. By the way, James Jones is not the other comedian's real name, as I cannot remember it, so I made one up. I remember his jokes but not his name.

Standing on that Miami stage during the next show, I told jokes I had written, rehearsed, rewritten, and re-rehearsed too many times to count.

"By round of applause, who can read and write?

"*Yaaaay*, read and write. What about cursive? Who can read and write cursive? *Yaaay*, cursive!

"What about braille? No one, oh wait, one guy back there. He can't clap, though. He's reading the menu."

The audience nervously laughed, and some groaned.

"You know, I don't think they should teach cursive anymore. Seriously, if they don't have enough money for education, they can cut the cursive budget. Why? Why can they cut cursive? Because I learned to write cursive in the third grade in Mrs. Hansing's class, the third grade, I learned to write cursive in the third grade, and every form I've ever filled out since then says, *Please Print*! What the hell are you teaching me this cursive for? You never let me use it."

Good laughter, this is going well, I thought.

"Is it just me, or does it seem that everyone is on trial right now? Martha Stewart's on trial, everybody's on trial. But I gotta be honest, I don't trust the justice system. I don't. I don't trust it because we get off to a bad start every time. Every witness takes the stand, and we make them put their hand on the bible. Do you swear to tell the truth, the whole truth, and nothing but the truth, so help you, God?

"In the history of America, every single person has answered that question, yes, yes, I do. And then, they lie their ass off. And why do they lie their ass off...because they are trying to avoid prison. I'd lie too. Hell, I'd tell 'em my mom did it. That's how much I'd lie.

"But I have a fix. We get rid of, 'Do you swear to tell the truth, the whole truth, and nothing but the truth, so help you, God.' Get rid of that. Throw it out. Instead, we go back to the third grade, when we learned that cursive, and we ask them this. Do you cross your heart and hope to die and stick a needle in your eye?

"You see this, you see this, Martha? This is a sewing needle. You know what a sewing needle is, don't you, Martha? Did you do it? Did you insider trade?"

I mimic poking her in the eye with a needle.

"Owww, shit. Yes, yes, I did it. Goddammit.

"The trial's over in two minutes. And—*and* the beauty of the system is that we'll know who all of the liars are because they'll all be wearing eye patches. And the really stupid ones will have dark glasses and a dog and be learning braille from that cat in the back!"

The crowd laughed and yelled.

They're fired up now. I've done my job.

"Alright, ladies and gentlemen, are you ready to get this show started?"

I introduced James and headed to the green room, where we could hear the other comedians' sets.

"Hey, Dan, I was listenin' to your shit. You want some advice?" Patrice, sprawled out on the couch, asked.

"Hell yeah, I'm pretty new to this."

"Look, first, you're a funny motherfucker for a dude with a job, you know what I mean? Like you got a real job makin' decisions. You said you're in the wine and spirits business, right? I don't think you have a real job unless you're makin' decisions, you know what I mean? So, you do that shit all day and then come here and do this shit at night. I mean, you're kinda crazy, so I give you that. But anyway, that bit at the end. It's funny, and you can do that joke forever, but you can tell it better."

Crinkling my forehead, I replied, "Yeah?"

"It's funny, but you need to work on the timing. You're goin' too fast. You know what I mean? Slow it down a bit.

"Let silence be your friend.

"Use that silence, my man.

"When you say, 'And the really stupid ones will have dark glasses and a dog and be learning braille from that cat back there,' let that shit breathe 'cause it's funny, and they're laughing, but let that die down a bit. Maybe take a drink, let it breathe, and then, almost as if you just thought of it right then….

"'And be learning braille from that cat in the back.'

"It's a fuckin' roller coaster, man. When people laugh, they exhale, but you gotta let 'em inhale too. Fill those lungs so they can do it again. Hell, I won't say shit for twenty seconds, sometimes. Twenty seconds seems like forever when you're up there, but it ain't. You know what I mean?"

Later that night, during his last set, Patrice paused for an unusually long time, more than twenty seconds, before spotting me near the back of the room. He raised his glass of cranberry juice (no alcohol for him), looked at me, and smiled.

The remaining shows that week were much the same. I warmed the crowd, James scared them with talk about lead pipes and duct tape, and Patrice killed them with 9/11 jokes about cereal silos collapsing in the Midwest and a Rice Krispie moment of silence.

During the last show on Sunday night, the crowd was a bit sparse, so I sat closer to the stage and studied Patrice. He noticed me, stopped his act, and looked directly at me.

"Dan, what are you still doing here? I can close this out. You gotta work tomorrow."

I smiled. "It's okay. I wanna enjoy the show."

Patrice laughed and went back to his bits. I admired his thoughtfulness.

Patrice O'Neal is why I think of Miss Lenora Cupp because although he spoke more words to me those nights in a Miami green room than I remember her saying to me for an entire semester, she did her part, too. I don't remember seeing her after my first and last high school speech class, but I wish that I had, so I could have thanked her for pushing not just me but everyone in the class.

Sixteen years or so after pretending to be a piece of frying bacon, I finally summoned the courage to walk onto a stage and do what I was dying to do in that first class with Lenora Cupp: make strangers laugh, and not for hitting my head on the chalkboard and not being able to utter a single word. I still remember her staring at me as I suffered in silence, and I still remember her reassuring grin. And while I do remember seeing Patrice amble down a Coconut Grove street after our shows, what I remember most is him telling me to embrace the silence.

After that final show on Sunday night, I saw Patrice walking toward his hotel as I rounded the corner in the black Beemer my wine-and-spirits job helped me afford. I stopped and rolled down the window. "Hey Patrice, you need a ride?"

"Nah, I'm good."

"Are you sure?" I asked.

"Yeah, I'm sure. Hey, don't forget, though, you're a funny motherfucker for a dude with a job."

I laughed, waved, rolled up the window, and watched Patrice before I headed north toward Aventura. Driving up I-95, I turned off the radio and bathed in the silence.

Sam's First Communion. L - R Uncle Tom, Grandpa George, Amy, Great-Uncle Bud, Grandma Mil, Grandpa Al, Grandma Bessie, Sam, Uncle Dave, Mom, Andy, Forrest Arvin.

Mom making hamburgers in the kitchen in the "House on Audubon" while I sit nearby. "Are they ready yet?"

Dad opening a Christmas present while wearing one of his wild sport coats.

*Christmas with the Evans side of the family in our Section-8
apartment. L-R Uncle Charlie, Aunt Mary, Grandpa Al, Mom, Grandma
Bessie, Uncle Bill. This was Grandpa Al's last Christmas.*

My plastic drugstore football. I put my name and address on it just like Grandpa Al taught me.

Dad admiring the Tommy Hilfiger corduroys I gifted him. This was Dad's last Christmas.

Me and Don Mattingly after I won the "Hot Shot" free throw contest. I was still shocked that I won.

Aunt Kate (left) and Mom sitting in the surf. Mom's first time seeing the ocean.

Me and Mom after I convinced her to walk into the Atlantic Ocean with me.

Mom and Aunt Kate.

L-R Sam, Andy, Mom, Amy, Me.

"You kids are my and Dad's happiness.
We wanted children and we think we have four of the greatest.
You will do well, Dan, I know that."

Dolores Eileen Melchior
"The Silk Finisher"

PART III

THE DRIVE

• • •

The orange needle glowed as it hovered near 120 miles per hour. Ninety minutes earlier, at 2:00 a.m., I had walked into the concrete parking garage of my Aventura condominium overlooking Dumfoundling Bay. The ocean and Intracoastal breezes were as constant as gravity and ripped through the garage's first floor. I felt my first ocean breeze at age twenty. I realized that until that moment, I'd never really felt a breeze in my life. More than sunshine, pretty women and opportunity, the breeze captivated me like nothing else Florida had to offer, and Florida had so much more to offer than Evansville.

At 3:30 a.m., the Florida Turnpike is mostly void of cars. Aventura to Evansville is just over one thousand miles. A couple of years prior, I'd made the same trip in exactly thirteen hours. I made only three stops, all for gas and bathroom breaks. I didn't plan to break my thirteen-hour record on this trip, but I did want to get home fast. Leaving at 2:00 a.m. allowed me to drive well over one hundred miles per hour because cops didn't usually patrol that late or that early, depending on one's perspective. I'd gone to bed at 9:00 p.m., so 2:00 a.m. was early. Usually, for me, a night owl, it was late.

I'd packed a few sodas and salty and sweet snacks. I could eat real food when I got to Evansville. I gazed at the speedometer and the odometer, knowing I had a long way to go and plenty of time to reflect. The orange needle floated in its place.

As I watched white lane markers merge into one long white strip, I knew this visit would be unlike any other. Six months earlier, on March 31, 2004, I found out Mom had lung cancer. That same day I also performed a comedy show fundraiser for MS150 at the Miami Improv. I performed that show on autopilot, not unlike the current drive.

According to my sister Amy, either cancer had invaded Mom's brain or dementia had set in. Mom no longer knew how to use a telephone or make a bed, and she certainly didn't remember how to cook vegetable soup, steak and onions, or chicken and dumplings. Sixty-plus years making beds, and suddenly she didn't know how. I needed to see this for myself.

As the sun began to appear in the passenger window, the brightness of the orange needle faded, and my speed slowed as more and more cars and eighteen-wheel trucks joined the race. I flashed my beams at those who lingered in the left lane. I didn't bother to look at the other drivers as I passed them. I gazed only at the road, the speedometer, and the radar detector. I had to look at the radar detector because Howlin'

Wolf, Muddy Waters, Robert Johnson, Leadbelly, Jimi Hendrix, The Rolling Stones, and Nirvana drowned the sound of the alerts.

The stoplights on Highway 41 that give Evansville its nickname, Stoplight City, actually begin in Henderson, Kentucky, just across the Ohio River. I slowly rolled toward a red light and looked around, noticing a Corvette sitting atop a lofty platform. "Where the Corvette Sits High in the Sky" reverberated in my head. As a kid, I heard that jingle too many times to count. The few times we drove through Henderson, Dad always pointed to the Corvette sitting high in the sky.

Waiting at the light, I gathered up brown sugar and cinnamon Pop-Tart wrappers, Hot Tamale boxes and Gardetto's snack mix bags. I prided myself on not eating fast food on the road, but my logic in replacing it with junk food was shoddy at best, idiotic at worst. I stuffed the garbage into the soft-side cooler among the empty Diet Coke bottles.

The Pop-Tart wrappers reminded me of the house on Audubon. I thought about Mom toasting them and spreading butter, margarine actually, on them. I thought about my economics lessons at the University of Southern Indiana and the choice between guns and butter. In my household, the choice was margarine or butter, and the choice came down to the cheaper one.

I called Amy from my cell phone to let her know that I was close to Evansville. She planned to be at Mom's when I got there, as Mom no longer understood how to use a phone or answer the door. I wondered if Mom would recognize me.

My BMW rumbled as I rolled to a stop behind Mom's apartment. The white table I made when I was twelve still held a pot of marigolds, the same color as the rusty nails holding it together. Seeing Amy's car in the parking lot, I didn't bother knocking. I just opened the back door. Amy stood in the kitchen. We hugged.

Amy led me into the small living room. The room had a single wide window facing Washington Avenue with a divan underneath it. The window didn't provide much sunshine this time of year because of the large trees out front.

Mom rested, laid back with her right leg on the floor. She gazed at the TV much as I had gazed at the roads leading to Evansville.

"Hi, Mom," I said.

She looked at me, and her face lit up. She tried to sit up but couldn't.

"Hi, hon."

She remembered me. I smiled.

I knelt next to the couch and hugged her. She felt much smaller than the healthy five foot, one hundred pounds where she had spent most of her life.

"Are you hungry?" she asked.

Quick to always offer food and drink, Mom might have been the most hospitable person I'd ever known.

"Yeah, I could eat something."

She stared at me, not knowing what to do or what to say next.

"That's Rachael Ray," she said, pointing to the TV.

"Yeah, I know. I like Rachael Ray. She has a good show."

Amy looked at me and smiled.

"There's Grippo's," Amy said, referring to Grippo's BBQ potato chips, my favorite and perhaps the world's most incredible potato chip.

Amy and I walked into the kitchen as Mom continued watching Rachael Ray.

"She just goes in and out. She can't really hold a thought or carry on a conversation. She just kind of says random things," Amy whispered.

"That's okay," I replied.

We walked back into the living room. I sat in a chair near Mom.

"Hi, hon," she said. "Are you hungry?"

"I'm gonna eat some Grippo's. It's almost dinner time."

"That's Rachael Ray."

"Yeah, I know. I like her. She has a good show."

We sat and watched TV as Mom pointed out Rachael Ray again and again.

As I ate Grippo's, I realized that I'd never taste her vegetable soup, steak and onions, or chicken and dumplings again.

One day, during my visit, Uncle Dave, Aunt Peg, Uncle Tom, and his wife, Glascelle, came over to visit

Mom. Amy, Andy, and Sam came over too. We all sat in the living room and chatted. Mom had the strength to sit up, so I sat next to her on the couch.

Like all of our family gatherings over many years, we exchanged many stories, most of them funny. We talked about the house on Audubon, the house on Waggoner and all the fleas that came with it. One story I told that day is perhaps the grossest and one that Amy hates the most.

Mom kept all our houses so clean that we rarely, if ever, saw any bugs or roaches. That changed when we moved to Covert Village. We shared a kitchen wall with our next-door neighbors, whose father was blind like Uncle Bill. Mom felt sorry for the family but did not accept the filthy way they lived. When you live in a building where your neighbors' door is less than two feet from yours, you often sneak a peek into their house when they come and go or bring in groceries. One look into our neighbor's house told Mom all she needed to know. The place looked like a garbage dump.

"How does a house get so dirty so fast?" she asked.

Dad laughed it off, but Mom cringed every time she thought about it.

Her cringing turned to shouts and foul language when she saw a few roaches in our kitchen.

"Goddammit," she yelled as she killed the roaches with a rolled-up newspaper. "These have to be from the neighbors' house." Dad stopped laughing about it. He knew Mom wouldn't put up with roaches in the house.

Mom and Dad had dealt with palmetto bugs—flying cockroaches—in South Carolina, and Mom swore she'd never move anywhere that had so many "racists and flying cockroaches."

The day after discovering those roaches, Dad went to see Leon, Covert Village's maintenance man. Leon said he would come over and spray, but there wasn't anything he could do about the neighbors. He couldn't tell them to keep a cleaner home.

For more than a year, we put up with our filthy neighbors and Leon having to come in and spray every month or so. Mom didn't like the idea of spraying chemicals in the house. She figured if you keep it clean enough, there won't be anything for the roaches to eat, so they will go somewhere else, and then you won't have to spray. Mom believed cleanliness solved many of life's problems.

Eventually, our neighbors moved, so Leon had to complete an inspection. Dad convinced him to let him tag along, and I convinced them both to let me tag along. Like father, like son.

Leon put in a key and turned the lock. As he opened the door, outhouse smells immediately wafted into our faces. We all turned away before looking back into the apartment. Trash bags and litter decorated the living room. The foul stench grew stronger. Leon approached the closed door of the downstairs half-bath, which was situated along the shared wall. He slowly turned the knob and opened the door. Upon doing so, he fell backward, forcing Dad to catch him.

"Holy shit!" Dad shouted.

The toilet had overflowed entirely with just that, shit. It didn't seem as if it had ever been flushed. Cockroaches, whose family members invaded our kitchen, covered the toilet. Dad shouldn't have told Mom the story. I think she nearly vomited that day.

I told that story as we sat in the living room. Mom mostly stared ahead, not saying much of anything. Every so often that day, she would chime in and say something other than "that's Rachael Ray."

I told another story that day about playing gin rummy with Dad. I like to play gin rummy—real two-player gin rummy with points, schneiders, and Hollywood versions—and Dad would sometimes agree to play with me. As he got older and too lazy to get his glasses, he would extend his arm as far as possible and crane his neck to see his cards. When telling this story, I exaggerated his moves to the extreme, looking almost like a contortionist.

"He'd stretch his arm halfway across the table and tilt his head back so far, I'd tell him, hell Dad, you might as well just show me your cards; you've got 'em right in my face," I said, laughing.

"*Don't make fun of your dad!*" Mom shouted from her spot next to me as she stared straight ahead at nothing.

I turned my head and looked at her. I remembered her yelling, "*What?*" when she lost her job cleaning houses.

"Mom, I've told that story a million times. You always laugh. I'm sorry. I thought you liked it."

Mom didn't respond to my apology. She simply gazed into the ether.

I didn't tell any other stories about Dad that day.

As the stories wound down, and Amy let us all know it was time for her to put Mom to bed, we decided to keep the stories going at Sam's house, less than a mile from Mom's.

As Sam and I gathered lawn chairs for sitting and anything that could burn for his portable firepit, everyone else went home for a bit before coming over to Sam and Becky's. Sam and I started drinking beer as we scavenged a few good pieces of firewood and plenty of sticks, branches, and twigs. We figured if we got the pit hot enough and built an orange bed of coals, anything would burn.

Within an hour of leaving Mom's, Uncle Dave and Peg, Amy, Andy, Uncle Tom and Glascelle, and Grandpa George all came to Sam's house. I suspect Grandpa George hadn't come to Mom's house earlier because he didn't want to see her in a dying state. Mom and Grandpa George didn't always have the best relationship, but in the end, he came to care for her as much as she had cared for him. After all, she, not Dad, was the one who invited him over for dinner for many years after Grandma Mil died. They also spent years riding in the Rick-A-Jay van, just like me and Mom.

Rick-A-Jay, three words, three generations. Grapes of Wrath.

As me and Sam tended the fire and the glowing embers, hot enough to ignite anything, Mom's children and her in-laws sat around telling stories, laughing, and drinking beer. I told a few more stories about Mom and Dad, including the one about Dad chasing a car. Mom probably would've laughed at that—even she enjoyed telling that one.

"We were living in Indian Woods after we lost the house on Waggoner. Your Dad managed those apartments in exchange for cheaper rent. We were headed to the store early Sunday morning. We liked to get there right at seven when they opened. As we drove out of the apartments, there were a few pieces of trash and a garbage bag outside the dumpster. Your dad hated that. He felt that if he was in charge, the place was going to look nice. So, we got out of the car to pick up the trash, but your dad forgot to put the car in park."

At this point in the story, Mom begins to smile. Sometimes she had trouble holding her laughter.

"As we walked toward the trash, I turned around and saw the car rolling down the street. I yelled, 'Dan, the car!' Your dad turned around, yelled, 'goddammit,' and took off running. I swear, hon, I never knew your dad could run that fast."

And with that, she howled, laughing.

"Luckily, he caught the car, got in it, and stopped it before it hit anything. His legs were sore for a week. He hadn't run like that since the army."

For almost a month after the near-runaway-car incident, Mom and Dad would look at each other and start laughing. They didn't say a word; they simply laughed.

As the stories wound down and the fire died, everyone called it a night except for Sam and me. The in-laws who gathered that night while she was still alive would never gather in her life again.

Sam had plenty more beer to drink and, if we looked hard enough in the yard, more wood to burn. We reignited the fire, continued to gather wood, and told our own stories, the stories only we knew—the stories of our drunken exploits and close calls, like how on my walk back from USI one night, I nearly drowned in a pond. While we laughed at that story, I couldn't help but think of Mom's cousin whose son, Charlie, died in the plane crash and whose other son drowned. I started to understand why Mom was worried. Crazy, improbable things happen to people every day, and Mom experienced more than her share.

Not wanting to disturb Becky and the kids, we avoided going into the house by peeing in the backyard. Around 2:00 a.m., the wood ran out, so we started looking in the garage. We pulled out cardboard boxes, scrap pieces of wood, broom handles, and folders of paper documenting who knows what. Basically, we gathered anything that would burn. Orange embers, the color of the speedometer's needle, or the coal fire in the boiler at Rainbow Cleaners, hypnotized us as we gazed into the fire. With nothing left to burn, unless we started ripping siding off the garage, which we briefly considered, we watched the orange embers fade and flicker like the fireflies on Audubon Drive. And then, just like that, the last of the orange embers faded to black, nothing but grey and blackish ash left in the firepit. I felt the cold on my back as I walked away.

Driving less than one mile home, I reeked of smoke. Entering Mom's house, I pondered taking a shower but didn't want to wake her at four in the morning. Normally, I would have thrown my clothes on the washer, but this apartment had a shared laundry room, so I didn't know where to throw them. Before collapsing on the couch, still smelling like a campfire, I opened Mom's bedroom door and peeked in. She lay in the same position Amy put her in every night. On her side, in the fetal position, slumbering under a floral comforter.

VISITING HOURS

• • • • •

My remaining days with Mom resembled the beginning of the week. I woke up on the couch in Mom's apartment. Amy came over and helped Mom get ready. We sat around watching TV and talking, mostly about Rachael Ray.

"That's Rachael Ray."

"Yeah, I know. I like Rachael Ray. She has a good show. She's pretty, too," I added.

Mom did mention food a few times. Her favorite breakfast in those last months became frozen waffles, toasted like she toasted my Pop-Tarts. She liked lots of butter, or really margarine, and syrup on her waffles.

"The more, the better," she implored.

"It ain't gonna hurt you at this point," I said.

Mom was down to less than ninety pounds, so Amy let her eat whatever she wanted. When I was a kid, I remember Mom always ate last, even at family gatherings where she prepared most of the food. She always wanted to make sure everyone had enough. Maybe that's how come she never once in her life had a weight problem. And Mom ate everything. Red meat including sausage and bacon, chicken, turkey, fish, vegetables, fruit, sweets—a lot of sweets. When we were young, Mom fixed a dessert or sweet breakfast at least once a week. Apple pies, cakes and cupcakes, muffins, and fudge. Rice Krispie treats, monkey bread, homemade donuts, and cheesecake, the kind from a box, the kind Dad liked for breakfast.

As Mom and I watched Rachael Ray and other morning programs, I mentioned her vegetable soup, the weekday version that she could make in a jiff, as she liked to say.

"That sounds good," she said.

"You want me to make you some?" I asked.

She didn't respond.

I called Amy at work. She usually stayed with Mom during the day, but since I was home, Amy could go to work for a bit; at least, that's what she said. I really think Amy said she was going to work so that she could give Mom and me some time by ourselves. Amy's as thoughtful as Mom.

"Do you think it's okay if I run to the store to get the makings for vegetable soup? I'm going to make some for Mom. She said it sounded good."

"Yeah, she'll be fine. How long will you be gone?"

"I'll make it quick, twenty minutes or so."

"Cool. Mom will like that," Amy said.

With that, I headed to the grocery store, less than a mile away.

Mom had told me her quick recipe during one of our Florida-to-Indiana phone calls. The tomato-based recipe called for browned stew meat, carrots, peas, corn, and green beans. She used frozen corn and carrots but splurged on canned "early June" peas and cut green beans. Mom had told me to drain the grease after browning the meat but to scrape up the bits and put those in the soup.

"They add so much flavor," she insisted.

Diced tomatoes, beef bouillon, and tomato paste established the base.

I added minced onion, salt, pepper, garlic salt, and oregano.

After bringing the soup to a boil, I lowered the heat, covered it, and let it simmer for an hour. At eleven thirty, the smell of that soup permeated the entire apartment.

"I made some vegetable soup, Mom. You want some?"

"Yeah, I want some," she said, not breaking her gaze at the TV.

I went to the kitchen, ladled some in a bowl, and let it cool. I tasted it, poured the bowl back into the pot, and added a bit more salt, pepper, and a pinch of sugar. I let that simmer for another five minutes and ladled another bowl full. I let that cool, tasted it, and shook my head.

I took the soup into the living room, put it on the table, and helped Mom sit up.

"Are you ready for your soup?"

"What soup?"

"I made vegetable soup."

"You did?"

"Yeah, I did. I tasted it; it's good, just like yours."

I cradled the bowl and fed Mom like she must've fed me when I sat in highchairs.

As I fed her by the spoonful, she kept asking for more. In less than twenty minutes, she ate two bowls.

She laid back down and tried to watch TV, but her eyelids grew heavy. She napped as I cleaned up the kitchen and left the soup simmering. I made plenty so that I could have some for dinner, and Amy or anyone else that came over could have some as well. Hopefully, Mom would want some later too. I planned on leaving in the morning and knew I wouldn't be out late the night before a long drive.

That night, Amy and Sam came over, and we talked as Mom mostly slept.

We talked a bit more, a lot more. Amy told me stories Mom had told her that I'd never heard. Stories about Dad, stories about how things had been harder than we knew. I told stories that I knew from witnessing them myself. We told stories that we wished weren't true. Stories about other women, perhaps those impressed by a shiny pair of cufflinks.

I told Amy and Sam that I would leave in the morning, most likely around four, so I wouldn't see them again on that trip. We hugged, they left, and I got ready for bed, or more accurately, I got ready for the couch. I set my alarm for three.

The alarm on my phone went off at 3:00 a.m. I didn't bother showering. Why shower for a four-teen-hour drive home? Because the water will wake me up? It won't. It will only make me want to go back to laying on the couch. I turned on a small lamp and crept around, not wanting to alarm Mom if she heard a noise. I had cracked the door to Mom's bedroom in case I heard something, or she needed my help in the middle of the night. I looked into her room, and it didn't appear as if she'd moved an inch.

I checked and re-rechecked around the living room and the bathroom for phone chargers, sunglasses, and pens. I looked for anything that I didn't want to leave behind. Unlike a hotel room, if I left something, I didn't have to worry as Amy would mail it to me right away. That said, I didn't want to inconvenience her because of my oversight. I packed my two bags and made sure my work computer and all work files were properly stored.

I unlocked the back door and immediately felt the crisp autumn air. Mom loved fall, and so did I. It's the best time of year. Soups, stews, sweaters, and colors. I looked down at the marigolds. They seemed a bit wilted. I loaded my two bags and walked back into the house. I filled a glass with water, went outside, and gave the marigolds a drink. Creeping deeper into fall, they didn't have long to go, but they could still use a little morning pick-me-up.

I went back into the living room, folded my blanket, and put the pillow on top of it. I checked the rooms again for any items I may have forgotten. I opened the fridge and got a few Diet Cokes. I noticed my soft-sided cooler on the counter. "Shit, I almost forgot the cooler."

I quietly loaded it with the remaining Diet Cokes and a bit of ice. I went back to the car with the cooler and Grippo's in tow. I loaded them into the front seat. Walking back to the house, I looked up at the clear sky. Trees blocked the moon—if it was even out there. I only saw a few twinkling stars, but no constellations I recognized. Just lonely stars.

I leaned against the kitchen counter for a minute or so before walking toward Mom's room. I opened the door. She still hadn't moved.

As I peeked in the door, I thought about not being a better son, for childish behavior when I should have known better, for wanting to leave Indiana to find a faster life than most Midwesterners find comfortable. I thought about all she taught me, how to polish shoes, iron a shirt, cook steak and onions, how to bake Christmas cookies, work harder than everyone else, be nice, ask "How are you?" and mean it. And—*and*—not to tarry.

I walked in and knelt by the bed. Her head rested on the pillow. Her hands, resting together near her face and peeking out of the top of the blanket, looked as strong as ever; her hands, the ones she hated, with blue veins and thick fingers. I reached out, touched, and then rubbed them.

"Mom," I whispered.

"Mom, it's Danny. Wake up, Mom."

She opened her eyes.

"Hey, Mom, it's me. Sorry to wake you up, Mom."

"Hi, hon."

"Mom, I gotta go; I gotta get back to Florida."

"Okay, hon."

Tears streamed down my face. I sniffled loudly before bawling. Mom's face didn't move. She slowly blinked.

"I gotta go, Mom. I'm so sorry, Mom," I mumbled.

She continued to stare at me.

"I'm sorry for everything, Mom. I'm sorry I left. I'm sorry I've been gone so long. I'm sorry I didn't want to go to school. I'm sorry for everything. Everything you know and everything you don't. I'm sorry for it all."

"I know."

Her eyes opened wider.

"I had to go, Mom. I'm sorry. I don't know what to say."

"I'm sorry for being so scared, for being so mean. I'm sorry for everything I've ever done to you, to Dad, to everyone. I was so scared, Mom. I had many bad thoughts."

"I know."

"You did everything for us, Mom, everything. I love you so much. You were so good to me. To all of us."

"I know."

Mom's blue eyes continued to stare and occasionally blink.

"Everything I have is because of you. Everything. I don't deserve it. I left you and Dad."

"I know."

She stared at me. Mom looked tired. I felt exhausted after just a few moments of kneeling, kneeling as if to pray.

"I love you, Mom. I love you so much. We'll be okay, Mom."

"I know."

"I gotta go, Mom, I gotta go."

I stood up, leaned over, and kissed her on the cheek.

"I love you, Mom. I love you," I whispered in her ear as I continued leaning over.

Her head didn't move, but her eyes looked up at me as I rose and stood over her bed. I stared down at her and the floral comforter that swallowed her like a baby bird. I stood over her for several beats. I shook my head. The tears dried up. I leaned in one more time and kissed her again, this time on her forehead.

I told her I understood why she didn't want to fight cancer. Dad lost that fight, and although she was tougher than Dad, she would too. I told her she would see Dad soon. She liked that. I'll leave the rest of our conversation between Mom and me, except for this.

"I love you, Mom."

"I love you too," she said, her eyes staring at the nightstand and the faces in the picture frames.

I walked out of the bedroom, looked around the kitchen, opened the door, walked out, looked up at the sky, unlocked my car, sat in the driver's seat, put in the key, turned the ignition, watched the dashboard light up a fiery orange, listened to the engine rumble, pushed the clutch and put the standard in reverse, slowly backed out of the apartment parking space, turned left on Washington heading east, shifted into second, then third, stopped at a few lights, turned south on Highway 41, mashed on the accelerator, shifted, second, third, fourth, fifth, watched the rpm needle jump on the shifts as the car bounced over the road. I noticed the light at Riverside Drive turn yellow, shifted back to fourth, mashed the accelerator, listened to the engine whine, blew through the intersection, and raced toward the twin bridges. One hundred twenty miles per hour read the orange, fire-in-the-boiler needle.

Alone on the Pennyrile Parkway, I thought about the stories Amy told about Dad telling Mom to stand up straight. Osteoporosis and most likely forty years of standing, pressing, cleaning, shopping, bathing, and all other chores completed standing up had taken their toll.

"I can't help it," she apparently told Dad to no avail.

That story triggered my memory as speed limit signs passed like flashcards.

As I watched TV in the family room of the house on Waggoner, I had heard Mom and Dad talking about a woman he worked with. She had been on television in a commercial for the lumber company. Somehow, Mom heard something about those two. They argued; Dad denied it, and Mom insisted. The summer that Mom and Dad argued is also the summer Dad started wearing a gold chain and laid out in the sun in a pair of gaudy Hawaiian shorts, and the summer he sometimes wore a French-cuffed dress shirt. Those were the days when Dad spent at least an hour or two every night at the Colony Cocktail, the place he used to go with Grandpa George after working all day at Rainbow Cleaners. By the 1970s, Dad and Grandpa George no longer hung out. Hell, they could barely stand each other. Grandpa George had sold him out or sold him a "bill of goods," or so Dad thought when Grandpa George convinced him to join him in the dry-cleaning business after he came back from the army. Dad didn't choose the army, and he didn't choose Rainbow Cleaners. He did, however, choose Mom, but that didn't mean he chose only Mom.

Being the last child at home, I heard more conversations than I cared to hear, but in totality, they let me know that Dad had a wandering eye and a French-cuffed shirt with a flashy but cheap Herb Tarlek-like sport coat which didn't hurt his cause when sitting at the bar in a place like the Colony Cocktail. Like flashcard after flashcard, the story became clearer and clearer as I cruised toward Atlanta. On that trip, I realized why my attempt to give Dad a French-cuffed dress shirt caused Mom to shout so loud, but not quite as loud as she did that day at Indian Woods. Mom had seen enough over the years, far more flashes than I had.

VISITATION

● ● ● ●

Five days before I was scheduled to go home and be with Mom as she died, Amy had called and said Mom wasn't doing well.

"Should I go or wait until after the party?" I'd asked Amy.

What if she doesn't make it? I need to impress these people. I should stay. She would want that. I'll leave Saturday morning. Hang in there, Mom. She'll wait for me. She always does, I thought.

Thursday had passed without a call.

At three o'clock on Friday afternoon, I rushed home to change for Southern Wine & Spirits' annual Christmas party, the genuine highlight of the year for those of us that liked to imbibe. Everyone dressed in suits and catsuits, dresses and gowns, too short, too long, too little, too much. The usual gossip ensued.

"Can you believe she wore that?"

"What was he thinking?"

Christmas in Miami, especially the parties, resembled peacocks on parade, unlike Evansville, where the festivities I remembered revolved around turkeys dressed for eating, not admiring.

Red brake lights flashed as I wove down Ives-Dairy Road toward Aventura. It was December 10, 2004, and I had been working as a shared services director, meaning I made the company more efficient via better finance, human resource, and information technology best practices, a job I did but didn't love, for just over a year. The party offered a chance to celebrate the year with friends and coworkers, free booze, hearty buffets, passed hors d'oeuvres, and an over-the-top raffle I was scheduled to emcee.

In my thirteenth-floor—labeled fourteenth for the superstitious—Aventura condo overlooking Dumfoundling Bay, I put on the black suit I purchased for Mom's inevitable funeral. Versatile and understated, according to the salesman at Bloomingdale's, appropriate for celebrating or mourning. I had also purchased a dark, almost venous blood red, French-cuffed shirt, perfect for Christmas or an Edgar Allan Poe story but horrible for a funeral. For that, I purchased a white shirt and black tie. I planned to wear the same shoes—black Ferragamo, double monk straps—for both occasions.

One suit, one pair of shoes, different shirts and ties, maybe a pocket square. Mom would love the efficiency and versatility, but she would hate the price, especially for the shoes, I thought.

As I began to tie a full Windsor, my cell phone rang.

"Hey, man...she died, man. Mom died," my oldest brother, Sam, garbled.

I stared in the mirror at the half-tied knot and venous red shirt.

"See you tomorrow," are the only words I remember muttering.

Staring at the cool travertine floor, I shuffled a few steps toward the Roman tub I never used, sat on the edge, and rubbed my face. Tears poured as I moaned loud enough that neighbors walking the long hallway would have thought someone died. Someone did die. My mom, she died.

I stood up and looked in the mirror. My face matched my shirt. I wiped the tears and snot away and rubbed my eyes with the palms of my hands. I took off the tie, shook it out and started over, finally a perfect Windsor.

Arriving at the Diplomat hotel in Hollywood, Florida, as palm fronds swayed, I noticed dozens of co-workers filing into the grand entrance. We expected to have at least a few hundred revelers, so we required tickets to prevent party crashers, a South Florida staple. I stood in line as Rachel, our HR director, passed out raffle tickets. She knew I was scheduled to travel home the next morning to see my mom and that I would be out the next week, almost certainly to attend her funeral. I looked at her, frowned, and gently, almost imperceptibly, shook my head. She closed her eyes and inhaled.

I wandered into the banquet hall. Chatter, music, and clinking plates and glasses filled my head. My colleagues and I mingled and commented on the decorations and how nice everyone looked as I swirled and gulped goblets of Cabernet. When sartorial compliments floated my way, I responded with a written and rehearsed, "If you ain't good lookin', dress well."

That line usually drew a laugh. Maybe they were laughing at me, not with me. Or maybe, the catty comments I often overheard didn't start until the booze really flowed, and I wouldn't be spared a jab or two. Either way, I didn't care. A laugh was a laugh.

Word spread that Mom had died, and while most offered condolences, some wondered why I stayed. I wondered the same thing but reminded myself that Mom stood at a commercial dry-cleaning press for ten hours, pressing and pressing and pressing, the day after Dad's funeral.

I hoped the raffle would be my distraction and leaned into the anticipation as I read the winning numbers. To heighten that tension, I asked everyone in the running to raise their hands and keep them up until they knew their number wouldn't be called.

"Okay, here we go. Keep those hands up. Six, nine, three...*four*!"

Gasps, *oh*s, and a few expletives ricocheted as hands dropped.

"Six, nine, three, four...*two*."

More gasps and dropping hands.

"Alright, this is it. The last number. Again, let's recap. This is for an LG sixty-inch plasma TV. Imagine the movies, the Dolphins, the Marlins, the Panthers. This is it. For the win. Six, nine, three, four, two...*ssssssix!*"

A long seagull-toned scream pierced the room before fading.

"It sounds like we have a winner. Either that or someone fell down an elevator shaft."

I didn't know it at the time, but that scream came from Yvonne, my future wife.

After the raffle, many of us, including Yvonne and her husband, walked to Nikki Marina, a swanky waterfront bar, to watch yachts float down the Intracoastal. I noticed how the waves lapped rhythmically at the pilings every time a boat passed.

"Don't tarry, son...don't tarry."

Sitting in a window seat the morning after the Christmas party, I watched baggage handlers load a conveyor that fed luggage, like watermelons, into the belly of the jet. With the suitcases and garment bags as a backdrop, I remembered hearing the news that Mom had lung cancer. That had been ten months prior. Suspiciously, Mom had the same cancer that had killed Dad fourteen years earlier. The evening she called to tell me the biopsy was back and that it was cancer, I had a standup comedy show to perform, so we had a brief conversation. I asked her what she wanted to do.

"I don't know yet. I just know that I'm tired."

I got the feeling she meant life, not just tuckered out from a long day.

"I'll call you tomorrow," I said. "We can talk about it."

"Okay, hon. Have a good show."

As we taxied away from the terminal in Fort Lauderdale, I thought of the parallels between the day of diagnosis and the day of her death. On both days, I had somewhere to be. One a party, the other a show—a show that ended as most shows do:with a party. At least the show was a fundraiser for MS150, so I took comfort in raising money for the disease Richard Pryor had.

Airborne, as we approached cruising altitude, I pulled a few letters from Mom that I had packed for the trip home:

> *September 6, 1987*
>
> *Dear Son,*
>
> *I wanted to have this letter done before now. You beat me to it. You said it was easier to express your feelings on paper, that is true.*
>
> *Dad and I are so very proud of you. We are very lucky parents. Not one of you gave us any trouble. Yes, we wish so much that we could have given you more. But we did what we could.*

What we want more than anything is for you to be happy and have a good life and be a nice person.

I am sure you know also that we want you to feel free to come to us with any problem. We have always told all of you that.

I know for sure that Grandma knows that you loved her.

I also hope that when Dad and I are gone that you, Sam, Amy, and Andy can always be close and have each other.

You kids are my and Dad's happiness. We wanted children and we think we have four of the greatest.

You will do well, Dan, I know that.

I regret one thing, I think I let you down when I didn't take you to church or at least give you some kind of religious training. You may someday want to go to some church. Not that you have to go to church to be a good person, you know that. You are a good person and Dad and I love you very much.

Just remember, be happy and love your brothers and sister. Have a wonderful life. I can't write worth a darn. I also can't express myself too well on paper, but I think you get the idea.

All our love always,
Mom & Dad

Because Mom's letter mentioned Grandma Mil, I thought of my twice-weekly visits to Grandma Mil and Grandpa George while commuting between Rick-A-Jay and USI. She told me stories, gave advice, and laughed at my jokes. One night, after walking too many steps revealed congestive heart failure, doctors recommended triple-bypass surgery. Many in the family went to see her before the operation, but because I saw her so often, I decided to play basketball instead. A mistake on the operating table meant I never saw her again, and she never saw me graduate college. When I did graduate, I didn't feel like celebrating without her, so I didn't buy a cap and gown, nor did we have a party. I simply walked to my car after my last final exam and drove home.

I read another letter from Mom; this one was written twelve years later.

January 9, 1999,

I know what you mean about how fast time goes. When your Dad and I were first married I thought we have our whole life ahead of us. I now wonder where it went. Life is too short. Follow your dreams and be happy.

I read on....

I loved James Dean's saying ["Dream as if you'll live forever; Live as if you'll die tomorrow"]. *I should try to do that. In fact, some of our customers who don't know my name and when I am off for a few days are asking about me. Where is the lady with the sweet smile? So I guess I must be smiling quite often."*

Take care of yourself and follow that dream.

I love you always,
Mom

James Dean and Uncle John, neither of whom I met, but they seemed similar to me: Indiana natives, wanderers, dreamers.... As I put the letters back in my bag and gazed out the window, I realized the flight was ending. As we approached Hartsfield-Jackson, I remembered when I was twenty-two and took my first flight, a trip to Atlanta for training with Crawford & Company, the insurance adjuster job. I cried as Mom and Dad stood by the gate. It was only going to be a four-week trip, but to me, having never traveled, it felt like it would be forever. This flight, though, this one from Fort Lauderdale to Atlanta, went quickly.

Waiting during the layover in Atlanta and sipping a beer, I watched hordes of people walk past and wondered who else was going to a funeral. Everyone looked miserable, so perhaps they all were. An entire airport of mourners. I wrote that down in case I wanted to craft a joke about terminals full of mourners. Terminal and mourning are great for wordplay. Terminal (airport), terminal (fatal), mourning (grief), morning (a new day). I ordered another beer and drank it faster than the one before.

Small and powerful regional jets whisk in and out of Evansville, offering a chance to escape and eventually, inevitably return. Again, in a window seat, as we approached, I noticed all the familiar sites. The horseshoe bend in the Ohio River. The twin bridges that connect Indiana and Kentucky. The old Whirlpool plant where Grandpa Al worked. Highway 41. The Lloyd Expressway. I scribbled a couple of notes, sat back, closed my eyes, and waited to touch down.

A hard hit on the runway jolted me out of my doze. Deplaning on the tarmac, I felt the December cold of the Ohio River Valley.

Since I was born, Mom and Dad and then just Mom lived in eight different places: two houses, the rest apartments, each one cheaper than the one before. The apartment on Washington Avenue was a ground-floor, one-bed, one-bath unit with a small kitchen and living room. Mom gave me a key during my last visit.

I put in the key and opened the back door. It didn't feel like the heat was on, or maybe I was just cold. Silence filled my ears. The kitchen counter, sink, and stove glistened as always. A napkin holder filled with napkins sat alone on the table for two. In her bedroom, the bed was made, and a shammed pillow rested on the floral comforter. Sam, Amy, Andy, Dad, and I looked out of frames from atop the washstand.

In the bathroom, the scent of new bars of soap accentuated clean washcloths and towels hanging precisely from their bars. Amy got it ready, just like Mom.

On the day of her visitation, I opened the living room closet and found Mom's ironing board. Solid and heavier than most, she had outfitted it with two covers. I decided to touch up my dark blue visitation suit, a delicate move because hot stainless steel can ruin wool by creating a permanent sheen. I put a linen towel over the crease as I let steam do the work. I planned to take the black funeral suit to Rick-A-Jay as the stench of last night's party lingered. As I pressed, I thought about buying another ironing board cover when I got back to Miami. I also thought about the time a few years ago when I was visiting Mom, and after a quick disagreement, I had to get physical with her.

"Hey, Mom, where's the ironing board?"

"Do you need me to iron something for you?" she asked.

"Nah, I'll do it."

"Are you sure? I don't mind."

"Yes, I'm sure! Where's the ironing board?"

"It's upstairs, but you better let me get it because it's kind of heavy."

"What?" I said, laughing. "You better get it because it's heavy. You think you're stronger than me? That's what you think. You think you're stronger than me? You're five foot and weigh a hundred pounds. Give me a break."

"Maybe," she said, smiling.

"Okay, let's arm wrestle," I said.

We sat at the kitchen table. Mom put her elbow on the table first, her right hand poised to grab mine. Thick, large blue veins on the back of her hand bulged. Veins in her forearm did the same. I rested my elbow on the table, grabbed her hand, and smiled.

"Okay, on three. One, two, three."

Her veins magnified more as she strained. My forearm, neck, and back tensed as they do when taking off in one of those regional jets. Our arms locked straight for many seconds before I leaned in and forced her hand to the table.

"Damn, Mom. You're strong as hell."

She looked pissed.

"Seriously, you are strong as hell."

I went upstairs and got the ironing board, but I let her iron my shirt, which is probably what she wanted all along: another chance to iron my shirt.

Per Mom's wishes, her visitation and funeral were to be a closed-casket affair. Only immediate family would see Mom for just a few minutes before she disappeared for eternity. Once we arrived, the funeral director escorted us into the parlor. Mom rested at the far end of the room. Chairs and loveseats lined the walls, separated by square tables holding lamps and flowers. White and yellow arrangements surrounded her and blended, mirage-like, with the décor, their fragrance unable to conceal the sterile tang of a funeral salon.

I stepped forward to get one last look at Mom. She wore a whisper-faint celery green, almost white, long-sleeve dress with a shimmery pale vest. She purchased that dress in the spring of 1998 for Cousin Jon's wedding. She wanted long sleeves because she hated the look of her forearms due to the bulging veins that matched those on the back of her hands. Her hands, too big and thick for such a small woman, she often said, cleaned us and our house, bathed us, earned her a life-long living, and made the delicate Christmas cookies we all loved. Her hands should have been a source of pride for her, but instead, they were a mark of shame.

Her alabaster face was as smooth as marble, a feature she attributed to forty years working with steam, the same work that developed her hands. The funeral home had done an excellent job, and Mom would have appreciated their effort and care. She needn't have worried. I couldn't see the veins in her hands.

While we were saying our goodbyes, Cousin Jon, who is a year younger than me and a hustler in the kindest sense of the word, walked in with his wife. Perhaps it was seeing Mom's double-duty dress and then Jon that caused my knees to buckle as I lurched toward him, weeping and moaning, searching for a place to curl up, fetal-like. He hugged and held me up before walking me to the nearest loveseat. He sat with his arm around me as I sobbed.

For most of the seven hours, I stood, greeted, and said hello to relatives I had not seen in ages. I was introduced to Mom's friends I had either forgotten or never known...I asked my siblings, "Who was that again?"

Three of Mom's friends I did remember and knew very well. I smiled as I remembered Ethelda Schmidt, Kay Willis, and Helen Miller regularly walking into our home on Audubon Drive and shouting "Yoo-hoo" rather than knocking or walking us to the school bus before my sandwich got stepped on or driving me to school before being dragged down the hall.

As I stood, seeing fewer and fewer people I knew, I saw a man I certainly didn't know, a true stranger. Looking in through the double doors, he seemed lost. He wore a greyish-blue uniform with gold piping and held a white and blue cap with a gold badge matching the one on his jacket. Taller than average, he stood rigid, almost regal. African American, he had a faint mustache and a short afro.

Is he a fireman? Why is the fire department here? I thought. Are we exceeding capacity? There aren't that many people here.

"Can I help you?" I asked.

"Is this Dolores Melchior's visitation?"

"Yes, it is. She's my mom."

We shook hands.

"I read her obituary in the paper and thought to myself, that's the woman from Rick-A-Jay. I'm the fire chief, and I take my uniform and clothes there."

"You know, I used to work there too. She got me a job there as a delivery driver," I said.

He flashed a broad smile.

"Your mom always smiled and greeted me when I walked in even though she doesn't work the counter. She stands over there all day at her station, pressing clothes, but is still so nice to everyone. I didn't really know her, but I wanted to pay my respects and let you know that she always brightened my day."

I smiled sadly. *That Dots is a hell of a worker.*

HER FUNERAL

● ● ● ●

A can of Diet Coke adorned the toilet tank as I looked in the mirror and decided a Shelby knot would work best for the black tie. I believed all knots needed a dimple, so I tied it a few times before getting it just right. I had another Diet Coke before Amy and her husband, Robert, came to pick me up.

I stood outside St. Mary's, Evansville's oldest standing Catholic Church, as unruly winds stung my face and ears, and the cold grew roots. Originally encased in soothing red brick, she stood monotone, long ago covered in a faux veneer labeled "sham-rock." Her proud 175-foot spire watched over me. Reacquainting with the cold, I waved a few dozen family and friends into the vestibule, wanting to be the last inside.

A quiet warmth enveloped me as I walked toward the altar. Mary, Mother of Jesus, stood above the reredos while someone, a statue of a man I did not recognize, stood above her. Muffled coughs, sniffles, and whispers floated like dust in a sunbeam as I glanced around at figures and stained-glass depictions of stories I didn't remember or never knew.

I remembered what Mom had written to me: "*I regret one thing, I think I let you down when I didn't take you to church or at least give you some kind of religious training.*"

Regardless, I enjoyed their splendor. Like a commissioned work, Mom's coffin belonged.

Sitting in the left-facing pews next to Amy, Andy, and Sam, wondering what was next, I heard the priest. I heard him talk. I heard him sing. I heard him pray. I heard him asking us to pray. I heard him asking us to kneel, and I did, following Andy's lead but always a beat or two behind.

After the service, we slowly ambled down the aisle. I noticed the mourners' shoes.

Those should have been polished. Those are very nice and polished. Stop judging.

As soon as the large doors opened, I buttoned my overcoat and put my hands in the warm pockets. Under a cloudless sky, as the sun ate the cold and St. Mary's three bells rang eleven times, we waited to go to the cemetery where Mom could finally rest next to Dad and near Grandma Mil. Inside the small chapel at Oak Hill Cemetery, standing next to the casket alongside my siblings, I thought about our homes and apartments, always clean, always neat, always warm, and full of homemade treats, soups, or snacks.

"Hi, hon. Are you hungry? I made some vegetable soup."

"There are chocolate chips in the cookie jar."

"I made caramel corn."

"How was school? How was work? How was basketball?"

"Hi, hon, how are you?"

Now, who is going to say that?

Who knows your life story like your mom?

I rested my head on her casket and wept.

THE ODDS

● ● ●

On December 10, 2005, the first anniversary of Mom's death, I got up around 1:00 p.m. after a night of attempting to drown what I knew would be the next day's sorrow. Wearing only shorts, I stood on the balcony of my Aventura condo, looked at the water, soaked in a bit of sunshine, and gazed at seagulls and pelicans floating over Dumfoundling Bay. I thought about Mom's trip to see me in 1997, the only flight of her life and the only time she saw the ocean. I went back in, grabbed a beer from the fridge, and flipped on the TV before walking back onto the balcony. After hearing a commercial or two, I heard a CNN newscaster say, "Actor and comedian Richard Pryor died this morning of a heart attack in Los Angeles. He was sixty-five years old."

Holding my beer, I tripped on the door frame rushing back in. I stayed upright and turned toward the TV. Richard's picture stared directly at me. My knees weakened enough for me to seek my leather recliner. Still holding my beer, I stared at the TV before finishing the Red Stripe in one long swig.

That day I questioned a god who I didn't even believe in before beginning to rationalize that Mom and Richard dying one year to the day might be the clearest sign God has given me. Maybe that's what he does. He kicks you when you're down to show you he can and to remind you, "This ain't so bad; you should see what I make people in Africa deal with."

My thoughts raced and fluttered that way throughout the day. There is a god, but there isn't a god; God is mean, violent, and vindictive. God created lions who murder cubs not their own and then rape the lionesses who bore them.

I carried those thoughts about December 10 for almost a decade, but when I learned that Mom proudly shared R-rated videos of my comedy performances with her friends, including Helen Miller, who were almost certainly offended, my thoughts, like the burns Richard Pryor and Mom shared, began to heal. Richard's burns came from a drug-fueled self-immolation, not an accident as originally reported, while Mom's burns were an unavoidable consequence of working with steam for forty years. Regardless of their source, the burns eventually healed, but they left marks, guideposts, reminders of where they'd been and what they had done. I came to appreciate Mom and Richard Pryor both dying on December 10, one year apart, because in the winter, when the trees have lost their leaves and their scars show, they remind me of where I've been and what I've done.

FLOWERS

● ● ●

I thought about the fire chief who came to pay his respects. I couldn't remember his name, but I remembered him. I remembered what he said, and I remembered what Mom wrote in her letter about her smile and thought, where is the fire chief with the broad smile?

More than sixteen years after he arrived at Mom's visitation, I came to know that man to be George Flowers. After some research and help from Amy, I connected with him on Friday, June 19, 2020.

I asked him if he had gone to Rick-A-Jay.

"When they were located on Fares Avenue?" he asked.

"Fares Avenue. Exactly," I replied.

"I'll tell you what, I remember when my stepfather died, and I went out to take his suit because I would take my clothes out there regular to get cleaned, and they blessed me, they said, 'no charge,' and we all kind of got emotional at that moment. Yeah, if your mother worked there, we were friends."

Mr. Flowers saw in Mom what almost everyone saw in her, a woman with a sweet smile who shared that smile with everyone while she toiled on the edges,

in the corners, mostly unseen, but bound and determined to smooth the wrinkles like those in the trousers
I gifted Dad.

I wish I'd kept the gift box that contained those
trousers, and I wish I'd remember what I gifted Mom, a
pot of marigolds perhaps, and I wish I'd gotten another
chance to eat donuts with Dad.

I wish I could make them both a cheesecake, the
kind from a box.

EPILOGUE: EMBERS

● ● ● ● ● ●

Ziemer Funeral Home continues to operate, reminding residents they have been "Proudly Serving Evansville Since 1927."

In 2021, I spoke to William Thompson on the phone for less than a minute. Mr. Thompson declined to speak on the record.

In 2021, I spoke to Patrick Pirrie on two occasions, each time for almost thirty minutes. Mr. Pirrie declined to speak on the record.

Over several years, I left messages for Carole Sue Gentry. She has not returned my calls.

On November 10, 1983, Leslie Irvin died of lung cancer at Memorial Hospital in Michigan City, Indiana. He had been serving a life sentence at the Indiana State Prison.

In 2005, the state of Indiana executed Donald Ray Wallace.

At age ninety, Grandpa George retired from driving the Rick-A-Jay delivery van. On January 10, 2009, he died at his home of natural causes. He was ninety-five.

On November 29, 2011, Patrice O'Neal died of complications from a stroke. He was forty-one.

On March 15, 2013, I filed a claim for survivor benefits under the Energy Employees Occupational Illness Compensation Program Act (EEOICPA). Following is a statement of the case:

> On March 15, 2013, you filed an EE-2, Claim for Survivor Benefits, claiming your father, Daniel Melchior, Sr. hereinafter referred to as "the employee" developed adenocarcinoma of the lung as a result of his employment at a Department of Energy (DOE) facility. On Form EE-3, Employment History, you claimed the employee worked at the Savannah River Site, at the Savannah River Defense Area, while employed with the U.S. Army from August 1, 1957, to November 1, 1958.
>
> You submitted documentation showing the employee was an active-duty enlisted member of the U.S. Army.
>
> Further development of medical or survivorship criteria was not pursued since military personnel are not eligible for EEOICPA benefits and is not considered "covered employment".

Whether claimants smoked cigarettes was not considered when awarding EEOICPA benefits.

In 2014, Julie Van Orden, age sixty-nine, died of natural causes at the Indiana Women's Prison in Indianapolis.

Ray Ryan's murder remains unsolved.

In 2018, at the age of fifty-two, after multiple attempts over many decades in many cities, I learned to swim.

Mr. Flowers told me that he knew the Mr. Flowers who alerted Grandpa George to the ringing alarms at Rainbow Cleaners but that he was not related to that family. Ironically the Mr. Flowers who Grandpa George knew also had a son named George. The two George Flowers, only a few years apart, were often mistaken for each other.

In 2021, I received a Certificate of Death from the County of Los Angeles. Uncle John had died of "cardio-respiratory arrest as a consequence of a possible subdural hematoma," not suicide.

When he was in his twenties, my brother, Andrew George, told Mom he was gay. I didn't write about Andy coming out because that is his story to tell.

REFERENCES

● ● ● ●

NATIVE HOOSIERS

"Big Scare at Auto Races," *Evansville Courier*, May 17, 1906.

"Crowd at the Automobile Races," *Evansville Courier*, May 17, 1906.

"If We Had Woman Police in Evansville," *Evansville Courier*, May 18, 1906.

"Trooper Comes to Take Bride," *Evansville Journal News*, January 13, 1908.

"Think You Had Flu? Fred Survived It in '18," *Evansville Press*, November 28, 1967.

Obituary of Theodore E. Ziemer, *Evansville Journal*, December 23, 1923.

Death Certificate: Theodore Ziemer.

Reitz Memorial High School, *The Memorialite*, (Evansville, IN: Graduating Class of 1926, 1926), pg. 57 Willard Library Regional and Family History Center.

"Formal Opening of the Beautiful New Ziemer Funeral Home," *Evansville Press*, November 8, 1935.

"Mrs. Leatha Jenne Dies Near Douglas Station," *Princeton Daily Clarion*, May 5, 1937.

"Deaths, Funerals, Jack Jenne," *Princeton Daily Clarion*, April 15, 1944.

Birth Announcements, *Princeton Daily Clarion*, September 16, 1924.

"At Rest, John Lewis Jenne," *Princeton Daily Clarion*, January 29, 1932.

Lieberman, Ben. "Roosevelt Pledges Fight on Social Injustice," *Evansville Courier*, January 21, 1937.

"Threat of Worst Flood Increases," *Evansville Courier*, January 22, 1937.

"Flood Continues Spread in City," *Evansville Courier*, January 23, 1937.

"Dress Plaza Buildings Threatened," *Evansville Courier*, January 24, 1937.

"Martial Law Rules in Evansville," *Evansville Courier*, January 25, 1937.

"Hold Speedboat Races Here Today," *Evansville Courier and Press*, August 6, 1939.

"Today...at the foot of Dress Plaza Evansville's Third Annual Speed Boat Regatta," *Evansville Courier and Press*, August 6, 1939.

"Nine Injured in Car Crash," *Evansville Press*, August 7, 1939.

"Driver Recovering from Car Injury," *Evansville Press*, August 8, 1939.

"Man Injured in Auto Crash Seeks $10,000," *Evansville Courier and Press*, August 20, 1939.

"Suits Ask $5,500 for Auto Accident," *Evansville Press*, August 22, 1939.

"Libel Suit Asking $40,000 Filed Against Attorneys: Rudolph Ziemer Demands Damages of Lorin Kiely, Robert W. Armstrong," *Evansville Courier and Press*, October 4, 1939.

Military Records: Abraham Elmer "Bud" Carr.

"Fines Total $154," *Evansville Press*, January 3, 1946.

"Circuit Court Records," *Evansville Press*, January 21, 1946.

"City Court Records," *Evansville Courier and Press*, January 20, 1948.

"Sodomy Charge Filed on Soldier's Statement," *Evansville Courier and Press*, August 31, 1948.

RAINBOW CLEANERS

Future Market Insights, April 19, 2019.

National Academy of Sciences, February 9, 2010.

"Two Christmas Burglaries Reported," *Evansville Press*, December 26, 1947.

MORE TROUBLE

"7 Years of Service in the Same Location," *Evansville Press*, November 29, 1954.

"One Man Injured, Another Loses Car in River Mishaps," *Evansville Press*, July 25, 1949.

"Area Man Is Beaten, Then Robbed of Auto," *Evansville Press*, October 30, 1951.

"Held After Crash," *Evansville Courier and Press*, May 31, 1953.

"Rudolph Ziemer to Face Charge of Drunken Driving," *Evansville Courier and Press*, June 2, 1953.

"Ziemer Pleads Innocent to Drunk Driving Court," *Evansville Courier and Press*, June 25, 1953.

"Ziemer To Be Arraigned Monday in Morals Case," *Evansville Courier and Press*, July 16, 1952.

"Ziemer Fined $300 for Tipsy Driving," *Evansville Courier and Press*, September 26, 1953.

"Ziemer Arraignment Saturday on Drunken Driving Charge," *Evansville Press*, June 1, 1953.

"Ziemer Trial To Be July 21 in City Court," *Evansville Press*, June 25, 1953.

"Ted Ziemer To Start New Funeral Home," *Evansville Press*, July 2, 1953.

"Delay Arraignment of Rudolph Ziemer—Police Records Scanty on Morals Cases," *Evansville Press*, July 15, 1952.

"Rudy Ziemer Arrested on Drunk Charge," *Evansville Press*, September 18, 1953.

"Carr Will Arrange Brinkley VFW Party," *Evansville Courier and Press*, December 14, 1949.

Divorce Record: Abraham Elmer "Bud" Carr.

Military Record: Abraham Elmer "Bud" Carr.

"Ted Ziemer Will Build Mortuary," *Evansville Courier and Press*, July 25, 1953.

A MARRIAGE, A BIRTHDAY, AND A MAD DOG

"Mrs. Daniel C. Melchior—Recent Bride," *Evansville Press*, May 10, 1954.

Wedding Party Postcard.

Wise, Malcolm. "Owner's Wife Shot to Death, Robbed in Liquor Store on Bellemeade Avenue," *Evansville Courier*, December 3, 1954.

Wise, Malcolm. "Powder Burns Show Woman Shot at Close Range," *Evansville Courier*, December 4, 1954.

Wise, Malcolm. "Police Search for Homicidal Maniac," *Evansville Courier*, December 24, 1954.

Wise, Malcolm. "$3,500 REWARD OFFERED IN TWO KILLINGS," *Evansville Courier*, December 25, 1954.

Towsend, Paul. "Debbie Wonders Why Daddy Doesn't Come," *Evansville Courier*, December 24, 1954.

Lannert, Hallie Sales. "Roberts Is Elected by 7,000 Votes," *Evansville Courier*, November 7, 1951.

Wise, Malcolm. "Farm Wife Bound and Shot to Death by Vicious Intruder in Posey County," *Evansville Courier*, March 22, 1955.

"Posey Murder Probe Mired," *Evansville Courier*, March 24, 1955.

Harpe, Shideler. "Anger Tinges Grief at Murder Victim's Burial," *Evansville Courier*, March 25, 1955.

"Cold Does 5 Million Dollars Damage to Area Crops, Fruit," *The Sunday Courier and Press*, March 27, 1955.

Hudgions, Jack. "Three in Family Slain, 4th Near Death in Brutal Henderson County Massacre," *Evansville Courier*, March 29, 1955.

Hudgions, Jack. "Mystery Pair Sought in Slayings," *Evansville Courier*, March 30, 1955.

Hudgions, Jack. "Mrs. Duncan Regains Consciousness; Police Quiz Armed Uniontown Man," *Evansville Courier*, March 31, 1955.

Hudgions, Jack. "Killer Shot Mrs. Duncan Twice; Police Hint She Fought Gunman," *Evansville Courier*, April 1, 1955.

Hudgions, Jack. "Footprints Indicate Father, Son Possibly Murdered By One Man," *Evansville Courier*, April 2, 1955.

Hudgions, Jack. "To Quiz Ex-Convict in Triple Murder; Sailer Case Develops 'New Lead'," *Evansville Courier*, April 3, 1955.

Hudgions, Jack. "Another Man Is Sought in Duncan Case," *Evansville Courier*, April 4, 1955.

"New Murder Lead Fizzles," *Evansville Courier*, April 5, 1955.

"Churchill Steps Down as Britain's Premier," *Evansville Courier*, April 6, 1955.

"Detectives Enter Probe," *Evansville Courier*, April 9, 1955.

Wise, Malcolm; Hudgions, Jack. "Tight Secrecy Screens Quiz of 'Hottest' Murder Suspect, Evansville Ex-Convict." *The Sunday Courier and Press*, April 10.

Wise, Malcolm. "Murder Suspect Faces Lie Test Today," *Evansville Courier*, April 11, 1955.

"Police Press Probe of Murder Suspect," *Evansville Courier*, April 12, 1955.

"Irvin Regarded As 'Hot' Lead After Lie Test," *Evansville Courier*, April 12, 1955.

"Irvin Grilled in Murders, To Talk to Wever," *Evansville Courier*, April 13, 1955.

Blakeslee, Alton. "Polio Vaccine Successful, Distribution Will Start Immediately," *Evansville Courier*, April 13, 1955.

Wise, Malcolm. "SIX MURDERS SOLVED!" *Evansville Courier*, April 14, 1955.

Wise, Malcolm. "Police Charge Irvin with Kerr Slaying; Implicated in Others," *Evansville Courier*, April 14, 1955.

"Two Slain in Princeton," *Evansville Courier*, November 5, 1955.

Aaron, Joe. "Prosecution to Call 8 Witnesses," *Evansville Courier*, December 10, 1955.

Aaron, Joe. "Truck Driver Identifies Irvin As Being at Scene of Kerr Murder," *Evansville Courier*, December 13, 1955.

Aaron, Joe. "Witness Links Irvin, Gun after First Attempt Fails," *Evansville Courier*, December 17, 1955.

Aaron, Joe. "Leslie Irvin Guilty in Kerr Murder; Jury Recommends Death Penalty," *Evansville Courier*, December 21, 1955.

Aaron, Joe. "Unmoved Irvin Hears Death Penalty Set for June 12," *Evansville Courier*, January 10, 1956.

Aaron, Joe; Hall, Howard. "HANDMADE KEY IRVIN USED TO OPEN DOOR TO FREEDOM FOUND BY POLICE," *Evansville Courier*, January 21, 1956.

Lannert, Hallie Bales. "Police, FBI Narrow Search for Irvin to Southern Illinois—St. Louis Area," *Evansville Courier*, January 22, 1956.

Aaron, Joe. "ESCAPE TRAIL OF IRVIN GROWS COLDER," *Evansville Courier*, January 23, 1956.

"Man Hunted in Las Vegas May Be Irvin," *Evansville Courier*, January 24, 1956.

Aaron, Joe. "IRVIN LETTER HELD WORK OF CRACKPOT," *Evansville Courier*, January 26, 1956.

Aaron, Joe. "Irvin Seen in Florida, Evansville, Wisconsin," *Evansville Courier*, January 27,1956.

Aaron, Joe. "Trail of Checks Puts Irvin in Ozarks," *Evansville Courier*, January 28, 1956.

"Irvin Tied to Truck Theft in Northern Arizona," *Evansville Courier*, January 30, 1956.

"Irvin Seen in Arizona," *Evansville Courier*, January 31, 1956.

Aaron, Joe. "Irvin's Cellmate in Gibson Jail Denies Fugitive Had Outside Aid," *Evansville Courier*, February 3, 1956.

"IRVIN SEIZED IN FRISCO," *Evansville Courier*, February 10, 1956.

"IRVIN WINS COURT SKIRMISH TO DELAY EXTRADITION TO PRISON DEATH HOUSE," *Evansville Courier*, February 11, 1956.

Aaron, Joe. "Irvin Traces Path of Flight for Life," *Evansville Courier*, February 11, 1956.

"Irvin Tells the Sheriff He's Sorry for Trouble He Caused by His Escape," *Evansville Courier*, February 12, 1956.

"Irvin Execution Reset Dec. 1 by High Court," *Evansville Courier*, March 23, 1956.

"No Celebration for Irvin on 32nd Birthday," *Evansville Courier*, April 3, 1956.

"40-Accident Week End," *Evansville Press*, May 28, 1956.

THE BOMB PLANT

Military Records: Daniel Melchior.

"Order to Report for Induction," Selective Service System, October 11, 1956.

Savannah River Site History Highlights.

"Police Hold Man Injured During Chase," *Evansville Press*, April 1, 1959.

"Man Calling on Housewife Is Arrested in Harassment," *Evansville Press*, May 5, 1961.

THE OLD KENTUCKY

"Fire Destroys Local Man's Automobile," *Evansville Press*, May 4, 1962.

Benjamin Bosse High School, *The Spirit of '60*, (Evansville, IN: Graduating Class of 1960, 1960), pg. 50 Willard Library Regional and Family History Center.

FOUND

"Ohio River Crests At 43.6 Mark," *Evansville Courier*, March 15, 1963.

"3 GIs Charged in Ziemer Case; Beating Alleged," *Evansville Press*, March 15, 1963.

Levee Project Commemorative Plaque, Dress Plaza, Evansville, Indiana.

"Niemeier Gets Big Ten's Okay," *Courier and Press*, September 15, 1963.

"Coroner Says Ziemer Died of Drowning," *Evansville Press*, March 17, 1963.

Hopkins, Earl. "Remembering Bunny, Evansville's Beloved Elephant, Two Decades Since She Left the City," *Evansville Courier and Press*, September 27, 2019.

"300 Attend Last Rites for Ziemer," *Evansville Press*, March 20, 1963.

"Weather," *Evansville Press*, March 20, 1963.

Uselton, George. "3-Year-Old Boy Killed," *Evansville Courier*, June 26, 1964.

CHANGE OF VENUE

History of Warrick, Spencer, and Perry Counties, Indiana: From the Earliest Time to the Present; Together with Interesting Biographical Sketches, Reminiscences, Notes, Etc., Goodspeed Bros. and Co., Chicago, 1885.

Postcard: Abraham Lincoln Memorial at Boonville, Indiana, c.1933–1940.

"Trial of 3 GIs Goes to Warrick," *Evansville Press*, February 10, 1964.

Flynn, Robert. "Ziemer Murder Trial Jury Selection Begins," *Evansville Press*, November 9, 1964.

Special to the Courier. "Ziemer-Case Defendants Wait Quietly for Trial," *Evansville Courier*, 1964.

Flynn, Robert. "Defense Plan Taking Shape," *Evansville Press*, November 10, 1964.

"New York Faces New Agitation," *Evansville Courier and Press*, November 8, 1964.

"Rights-Case End Near, Official Hints," *Evansville Courier*, November 9, 1964.

BEST KNOWN QUEER

Flynn, Robert. "Girl Tells of Night Ziemer Died," *Evansville Press*, November 18, 1964.

STATE OF INDIANA VS WILLIAM THOMPSON, ET AL. Warrick County Courthouse, Juror Room. 2019. Audio recording.

Flynn, Robert. "Ziemer Case Trial Starts," *Evansville Press*, November 16, 1964.

Porter, Suzanne. "Judge Disallows Character Blast in Ziemer Trial," *Evansville Courier and Press*, November 17, 1964.

Flynn, Robert. "Jury Is Told Autopsy Showed That Ziemer Died of Drowning," *Evansville Press*, November 17.

Porter, Suzanne. "'Confession' in Ziemer Death Entered in Trial," *Evansville Courier and Press*, November 19, 1964.

STATE OF INDIANA VS WILLIAM THOMPSON, ET AL. Warrick County Courthouse, Juror Room. 2019. Audio recording.

THE VERDICT

"Jury Is Told that Autopsy Showed Ziemer Died of Drowning," *Evansville Press*, November 17, 1964.

"World Sadly Remembers Day It Would Like to Forget," Associated Press, November 23, 1964.

"Evansville Death," *Evansville Courier*, November 24, 1964.

"Judge Discharges Ziemer Case Juror as Defense Rests," *Evansville Press*, November 23, 1964.

Porter, Suzanne. "Three Ex-Paratroopers Cleared in Ziemer Death," *Evansville Courier*, November 24, 1964.

Porter, Suzanne. "Jury Stay Out Hour and Half; Juror Charged," *Evansville Courier*, November 24, 1964.

"Verdict Lifts Shadow from Three Lives; Strain Gives Way to Tears," *Evansville Courier*, November 24.

LAST COMMUNION

Birth Certificate: Daniel Carr Melchior II.

"Wheat Field Harvested in Old Way," *Evansville Press*, June 23, 1966.

"Doctor Fined $6,000 in Illegal-Drug Case," *Evansville Courier*, December 23, 1965.

"US opens case against doctor," *Evansville Press*, February 3, 1976.

FEARS

"Shawneetown Marriages Decline," *Evansville Courier and Press*, November 19, 1961.

Public Records, *Evansville Press*, February 5, 1964.

"Local Motorist Hit by Truck," *Evansville Courier*, November 28, 1967.

"Leader Dog Provides 'A World of Difference,'" *Evansville Press*, January 9, 1972.

"Copters That's All They Were," *Evansville Courier*, October 18, 1973.

THE SIGN

Wallace, Phil. "Five-Year-Old Girl Found Murdered; Man, 35, Arrested," 1974.

A GUN, A BOMB, AND A PLANE

"Oilman Ryan Dies in Bomb Blast," *Evansville Courier*, October 19, 1977.

Daves, Rich. "Stars, Mobsters Knew Him," *Evansville Courier*, October 19, 1977.

"Evansville TV Listings," *Evansville Courier and Press*, December 13, 1977.

"UE Basketball Team Dies in Plane Crash," *Evansville Courier*, December 14, 1977.

"Evansville Family of Four Slain," *Evansville Press*, January 15, 1980.

"Police Capture 'Prime Suspect' in Murder of Young Family of 4," *Evansville Courier*, January 16, 1980.

"Girlfriend Tells Police: Suspect Said He Had 'Done Something Awful,'" *Evansville Press*, January 16, 1980.

"Wallace's Dad Paints Boyhood as Troubled," *Evansville Courier*, January 17, 1980.

"In Celebration of Their Life…," *Evansville Courier*, January 18, 1980.

"Intruder Shoots Ex-Mayor Lloyd," *Evansville Press*, March 19, 1980.

Wyman, Tom. "Lloyd Still in Coma, Fights for Survival," *Evansville Press*, March 20, 1980.

Marynell, Herb. "City Inspector Linked to Shooting Suspect," *Evansville Press*, March 20, 1980.

Heiman, Roberta. "Conflicting Portrait of Suspect Emerges," *Evansville Press*, March 20, 1980.

Flynn, Robert. "Family Hangs On to Hope," *Evansville Press*, March 20, 1980.

Mellowitz, Jim. "Officials Take Threats as Part of Job," *Evansville Press*, March 20, 1980.

"A Mother's Viewpoint," *Evansville Courier*, March 21, 1980.

Hulen, Dave. "Former Mayor Dies of Wounds," *Evansville Courier*, March 22, 1980.

"City Mourning Lloyd's Death," *Evansville Press*, March 22, 1980.

Wathen Patrick. "Van Orden Hated Lloyd, Officer Says," *Evansville Courier*, December 9, 1981.

Wathen Patrick. "Lloyd Shot while Lying Wounded, Says Ballistics Expert," *Evansville Courier*, December 11, 1981.

Wathen Patrick. "Lloyd Was Curious but Became 'Mad' as Gun Was Pulled," *Evansville Courier*, December 15, 1981.

Wathen Patrick. "Julie Van Orden Legally Insane, Psychiatrists Say," *Evansville Courier*, December 16, 1981.

WANTED

Greenhouse, Steven. "In Indiana, Centerpiece for a City Closes Shop," *New York Times*, June 19, 2010.

Pryor, Richard. "Wino & Junkie," *That N*****'s Crazy*. Partee/Stax, Reprise, 1975.

"Comedian Pryor Suffers Major Burns," *Evansville Press*, June 10, 1980.

Auction Notice: Evansville Courier.

FLORIDA

Obituary of Daniel Melchior, *Evansville Press*, July 10, 1990.

Associated Press. "World's Richest List Doesn't Include Trump," *Evansville Press*, July 10, 1990.

PROMOTED

Julian, Alan; DeWitte, Dave. "Disaster Toll Is 16," *Evansville Courier*, February 7, 1992.

"It's Like Nothing I've Ever Seen Before," *Evansville Courier*, February 7, 1992.

"Evansville Called 'Excellent' Place to Practice," *Evansville Courier*, February 7, 1992.

Husk, Kim; Dempsey, Eileen. "City Attempts To Cope with Tragedy," *Evansville Courier*, February 8, 1992.

Obituary of Charles Bergwitz, *Evansville Courier and Press*. February 8, 1992.

DeWitte, Dave. "Company Receives Helping Hand in Wake of Accident," *Evansville Courier and Press*, February 8, 1992.

THE SURF

Morrissey, Siobhan. "Woman Killed in Shooting," The Palm Beach Post, January 10, 1996.

Pallesen, Tim. "Nagging Prompted Gunshot that Killed Wife, Man Confesses," The Palm Beach Post, January 10, 1996.

LENORA AND PATRICE

New Times—Miami, October 2003.

ACKNOWLEDGMENTS

● ● ● ● ● ●

First and foremost, I want to thank Debby Englander for seeing what I saw.

I cannot possibly mention everyone who's had a hand in this, but I will name a few. My cohorts at Johns Hopkins University, especially the Montana+ crew, Amanda, Andrew, Bo, Holly, Insha, Raquel, Samantha and our ringleader, Leah. Thanks to Sarah Stephens and Kate Linderman for helping me with all the research.

To my siblings Sam, Amy, and Andy, I can only say thanks for putting up with me. Thanks Dave and Peg for letting me stay with you every now and again and for all the late-night stories told while we sat among the trees. Aunt Kate and Aunt Joan thanks for the walks through time present and past. And, to Yvonne for too many reasons to count.

Posthumously, I give profound thanks to my parents, my maternal and paternal grandparents, my great-uncle Abraham Elmer (Bud) Carr, the coolest cat in the family, Uncle Bill, and Rudolph Ziemer. This is their story.

ABOUT THE AUTHOR

● ● ● ● ● ●

By Natasha Meyer, Tasharazzi Photography

Dan Melchior, the son of blue-collar parents, grew up in Evansville, Indiana, a town in the "Crossroads of America." After earning a BS and MBA from the University of Southern Indiana, he moved to south Florida where he served as an executive at several multi-national corporations. In 2021, he earned an MA degree from Johns Hopkins University and is currently a university administrator. A wanderer, Dan currently resides in San Diego, California.